THE PRENATAL PERSON

Frank Lake's Maternal-Fetal Distress Syndrome

Stephen M. Maret

University Press of America,® Inc.
Lanham • New York • Oxford

Copyright © 1997 by
University Press of America,® Inc.
4720 Boston Way
Lanham, Maryland 20706

12 Hid's Copse Rd.
Cummor Hill, Oxford OX2 9JJ

Library of Congress Cataloging-in-Publication Data

Maret, Stephen M.
The prenatal personality / by Stephen M. Maret.
p.   cm.
1. Psychic trauma. 2. Personality development. 3. Prenatal
influences--Psychological aspects. 4. Maternal-fetal exchange--
Psychological aspects. 5. Lake, Frank, 1914-. 6. Pastoral counseling.
I. Title.
BF175.5.P75M37 1997   612.8'46--dc21   97-3170 CIP

ISBN 0-7618-0768-3 (cloth: alk. ppr.)

☉™ The paper used in this publication meets the minimum
requirements of American National Standard for information
Sciences—Permanence of Paper for Printed Library Materials,
ANSI Z39.48—1984

To Lezlie, Courtney and Brandon

With gratitude to the great minds and souls who
have shaped and inspired my intellectual and
spiritual journey: Tom Oden, Frank Lake, Jack
Wilson, Bill Ury and David Chamberlain

Contents

Introduction

Definition

Several years prior to his death in 1982, Frank Lake referred to "a new paradigm for psychodynamics with revolutionary implications" (Lake, 1978a, 3). In some of the last words he wrote before he died, Lake re-affirmed his earlier description. In the preface of a manuscript titled "Mutual Caring", he wrote that this "new perspective changes almost everything in counselling" (Lake, 1982c, 1), constituting "a radical departure from all that has gone before" (Lake, 1982c, 5). Further, he noted that the "understanding of psychodynamics can never be the same again. Nor its practice" (Lake, 1982c, 1).

What Frank Lake was describing was his formulation of a "maternal-fetal distress syndrome" (hereafter "M-FDS"). The description and analysis of this "new paradigm" and its "revolutionary implications" are the topics of this book.

At the core of this "new perspective" is the simple, commonly-made observation that the environment of an organism seems to have a hand in somehow shaping and molding that organism. The developmental inter-action between nature and nurture, between the organism itself and the immediate environment produces a particular individual with particular characteristics (Anastasi, 1958). What made this essentially "old perspective" revolutionary for Lake was his application of it to early prenatal life. While some of his predecessors had emphasized the importance of the early postnatal environment (i.e. Freud), perinatal experiences (i.e. Otto Rank) and prenatal influences (i.e. F.J. Mott, Nandor Fodor and M.L. Peerbolte), Lake focused upon the first trimester of intrauterine life. He affirmed that the developmental process, not only in the physiological dimension, but also the psychological, emotional, cognitive, and spiritual dimensions, originates not in early infancy or at birth or even in the second or third trimesters of fetal life. Rather, Lake asserted that "we must begin at conception, through the blastocystic stage, to implantation and the events of the first trimester. It is here, in the first three months or so in the womb, that we have encountered the origins of the main personality disorders and the psychosomatic stress conditions" (Lake, 1981g, ix). Thus, while the developmental process begins at conception, this process is manifested both positively and negatively, both in adaptive and maladaptive learning, both in psychologically healthy response patterns as well as psychopathological ones.

The mechanism underlying Lake's formulation of the M-FDS is the pivotal assertion that "powerfully impressive experiences from the mother and her inner and outer world . . . reach the foetus, defining its relation to the intra-uterine reality in ways that persist into adult life" (Lake, 1981c, 5). Describing two extreme "environments" to illustrate his point, Lake wrote:

> The foetus in the womb is not inert, not insensitive, not so primitive and unsophisticated an organism that it cannot differentiate between . . . the womb of a gloriously happy and fulfilled wife and mother-to-be and . . . the uterus of a desperate, dissipated or dishonored woman whose hatred of life may take her own in suicide or that of the foetus in an attempted abortion which didn't quite come off (Lake, 1981f, 65).

It is the uterine environment of the latter which is most likely to cause "the maternal-fetal *distress* syndrome". This syndrome has been operationally defined by one of Lake's co-researchers:

> The behavioral reactions of a pregnant mother affect her fetus in ways that contribute to its perceptions of itself and of its environment in the womb; and these perceptions persist into adult life (Moss, 1987, 204).

While this definition contains the essence of Lake's M-FDS, it does not encompass the totality of the paradigm. What it does describe is the "point of exchange" between mother and fetus. However, before that point occurs, the mother first experiences events in her environment and mediated by her pre-existing attitudes and emotions, subsequently interacts emotionally and attitudinally with these events. Contingent upon the quality of this interaction, these events are translated into particular neurohormones thereby resulting in the ongoing point of "umbilical exchange". Following this exchange is the re-translation of the received "umbilical affect" by the fetus from neurohormones into a perceived experiential environment and finally, into an "interpretation" of that environment. According to Lake, this constant process begins at implantation and only ends with the severing of the umbilical cord. The effects of the process, however, whether positive or negative, conscious or unconscious, are indelible.

Thus, a description of the M-FDS must encompass not only the exchange of "umbilical affect", but also the causes and effects. Further, Lake sees certain "revolutionary implications" following from this "new paradigm".

Depending upon the pre- and perinatal experiences of an individual, this paradigm allows not only for the understanding of the origin and dynamics of disordered states, but also of "normal" emotive states such as anger, doubt, fear and anxiety. According to Lake, the M-FDS serves as "the hermeneutic or interpretive principle for our understanding of the origins of disorder" (Peters, 1989, 145). This "hermeneutic" has wide application and includes the dynamic explanation of numerous psychopathological disorders, including depression, and most importantly for Lake, the schizoid reactions.

A second "revolutionary implication" relates to the cure of psychopathology. Because of Lake's proposed prenatal origin of much psychopathology, he asserted that therapy is most effective when it facilitates the re-experiencing of primal states and encourages a subsequent understanding of the dynamics that contributed toward the present condition. Further, Lake affirmed an added, specifically Christian dimension to his "primal" therapy; the resources of a communicated theodicy. Lake saw that "the Cross of Christ, offered in depth at the point of primal impact, offers immense prophylactic possibilities" (Peters, 1989, 145).

This overtly theological dimension is not only found in Lake's view of the cure for primal pain, but is also suffused throughout his discussion of the M-FDS. Lake saw biblical and theological content in every facet of his theory. He utilized biblical figures to illustrate certain psychopathologies. He sees parallel descriptions of the pain of the transmarginal states in the work of Soren Kierkegaard, Simone Weil, and St. John of the Cross. He views the innocent suffering of Christ on the Cross as paradigmatic of the innocent suffering of the fetus in the womb. His approach is that of a "clinical theology", undergirded by the central facts of Christian theology.

Organization

Following a full and detailed description of the M-FDS (chapter 1) as a "new paradigm for psychodynamics" (Moss, 1986, 52), the present work will analyze Lake's parallel use of the term "paradigm" as it applies to the syndrome. The first line of analysis (chapter 2) will concern itself with the M-FDS as a scientific paradigm. In this sense Lake uses the term "paradigm" to mean "a generally accepted system of ideas which defines the legitimate problems and methods of a research field" (Moss, 1986, 53). Based on the existing data, do Lake's formulations allow for the M-FDS to be "generally accepted as a system of ideas?" What evidence is there for the existence of prenatal memories, cognition, emotion, indeed, for a prenatal psychology? How does Lake's M-FDS correlate with the available evidence? Is the M-FDS paradigmatic scientifically?

The second line of inquiry (chapter 3) examines what Lake does theologically with the M-FDS. In this sense, "paradigm" is utilized more broadly as "a pattern, something shown side by side with something else, inviting comparison of the correspondences" (Lake, 1980b, 3). Lake's use of the M-FDS as a paradigm of comparison with the theological realm brings up numerous questions. How does Lake use the biblical and theological sources and to what extent does he use them legitimately? Following from this analysis, what "correspondences" can be legitimately compared between the M-FDS and theology? Is the M-FDS paradigmatic theologically?

It is in these two overlapping uses that Frank Lake's M-FDS can be examined, analyzed, and critiqued as paradigms. Based on these, conclusions (chapter 4) can be made of the implications of two lines of inquiry, especially where they converge. If there is biblical, theological, and scientific evidence that suggests that a M-FDS exists, then what are the implications?

Chapter One

The Maternal-Fetal Distress Syndrome

The Definition of the Paradigm

Frank Lake asserted that the essence of the M-FDS could be found in the observation that "powerfully impressive experiences from the mother and her inner and outer world . . . reach the fetus, defining its relation to the intra-uterine reality in ways that persist into adult life" (Lake, 1981c, 5). Defined in this manner, the M-FDS is really a part of a larger "Primal Integration" model (Moss, 1984), which not only encompasses negative ("distress") reactions to certain prenatal experiences, but positive ones as well. Thus, the M-FDS as described by Lake goes beyond merely a description of the "distress" reaction to accommodate the complete mechanisms within which the negative reactions can be understood.

The final formulation of the M-FDS came relatively late in Lake's thinking and can only be found in his later works encompassing the final four years of his life. Writing during this period, Lake stated that most of his professional psychiatric career had been spent working "in a half-light, oblivious to the earliest and severest forms of human pain" (Lake, 1981g, vii). This "half-light" was caused by the assumption that "the nine

months of foetal development in the womb were free of significant incident, a blank without possibility of psychodynamic content" (Lake,
1982b, 57-58). Lake was to eventually conclude the opposite, that fetal
life is "not drifting on a cloud, [but as] eventful as the nine months that
come after birth. The foetus is not unaware of itself, or of the emotional
response of the mother to its presence, but acutely conscious of both and
their interaction" (Lake, 1982b, 58). While Lake was not dismissive of
the potential suffering of the post-natal experience, he affirmed that "the
soul-destroying pain and heart-breaking suffering that comes from the
distress of the foetus in the womb when the mother herself is distressed"
is indeed at the root of the "severest forms of human pain" (Lake, 1981g,
viii). This pain occurs during the first trimester of intra-uterine life. Lake
stated that "these first three months after conception hold more ups and
downs, more ecstasies and devastations than we had ever imagined"
(Lake, 1981g, viii).

The Development of the Paradigm

Lake's final conclusions with regard to the M-FDS resulted from a process of gradual development. The component, if incomplete, parts of the
theory can be readily discerned early on. An evolution of sorts takes
place, particularly with regard to the definition of the critical period of
maternal-embryo/fetal/child interaction. What remained essentially static
throughout this evolution was the central assertion stated above; namely
that a mother's behavior and emotional state and the environment which
this creates for the emerging child, are determinative of that child's later
emotional and behavioral state. Given this constant, there are at least four
"phases" or steps in the process that eventually gave birth to the final
formulation of the M-FDS.

"Womb of the Spirit"

As a classically trained psychiatrist, Lake early on affirmed the importance of early infancy, the "first half of the first year of life" (Lake,
1982c, 42). However, looking back on this early period, Lake later wrote
that he stuck his "neck out 23 years ago in affirming birth and the early
months as powerfully relevant occasions of stress" (Lake, 1981g, ix). In
distancing himself from the Freudian emphasis upon the cruciality of the
Oedipal/phallic developmental stage, Lake wrote the following in the
Introduction of *Clinical Theology*:

I have not done justice here to the extensive elaboration pathology which characterizes classical Freudian writing, not because I do not agree with these findings, for they are in accord with my own experience, but because I believe them to be secondary rather than primary. The neo-Freudian modifications of analytic theory have brought the era of significant trauma to within the first year of life, and it is these to which my attention has been drawn. Indeed, Otto Rank's postulation of birth trauma as the first significant source of personality deviation has been abundantly confirmed in many cases I have studied (Lake, 1964, xvi).

During this first phase, Lake still held the assumption that "the nine months of foetal development in the womb were free of significant incident, a blank without possibility of psychodynamic content" (Lake, 1982b, 57-58). But here we already observe the major components of the later formulation of M-FDS: the primacy of the mother-embryo/fetus/child dyad, the existence of repressed memories from early life, the effect of these experiences on the adult personality and his/her present functioning, the ability to "relive" these experiences, and the existence of transmarginal states. Indeed, at this early point, the later definition of the M-FDS could be slightly modified and still hold true; the behavioral reactions of a mother affect her child in ways that contribute to its perceptions of itself and of its environment and these perceptions persist into adult life.

In the Introduction of a pamphlet on personal identity written in the latter part of the 1960's, Lake wrote that "the very earliest experiences which can lead to disturbed feelings of identity . . . take their origins in the distresses of babyhood" (Lake, 1991b, 43). This is illustrated clearly in a schematic representation found in *Clinical Theology* titled "The Womb of the Spirit" in which he writes that "the analogy of the growth of the baby in the womb is an apt one" (Lake, 1964, chart N.b.). This chart illustrates what Lake calls a "dynamic cycle" as the paradigmatic basis for making an "ontological analysis of the normal Mother-Child relationship" (Lake, 1964, chart N.b.). Lake describes the dynamics of each phase, two input and two output, in terms of a sequential effect upon the emerging infant, with each phase influencing and shaping the next in turn. A cyclical pattern emerges in which each phase either receives input from the outside "world" or imparts output to the outside "world", while simultaneously influencing the form of the next phase. Lake's analogy of fetal life, and indeed, his use of the term "womb of the spirit" prefigures his later theoretical emphases.

The first input phase in the cycle, which Lake called "being", is compared with biological actuality: just as "physical being is the result of nine months response by the fetus to the supplies of the Physical Being from the Mother" so "personal and spiritual being is the result of nine months (more or less) response of the baby to supplies of Personal and Spiritual Being from the mother" (Lake, 1964, chart N.b.). Whereas the placenta and umbilical cord serve as the conduits for nourishment during the period of the "womb of the physical", so there is the "umbilical cord of sight" by which spiritual being passes from the mother to the child during the period of the "womb of the spirit." If all goes well, this relational element allows the baby to "come into being as a person, gaining self-hood and the sense of identity by responding to the light of her [his mother] countenance" (Lake, 1964, chart N.b.), just as consistent physical nourishment during the prenatal period will allow the fetus to be born physically healthy. There is a similar parallel with the constriction of supplies. If the supplies of "physical being from the mother are constricted, the foetus will be distressed; if blocked, it dies" (Lake, 1964, chart N.b.). If "being" supplies are constricted, there is a diminishment of personal and spiritual "being" of the infant leading first to panic and then to dread; if all supplies of "being" are removed", "non-being" results.

The second input phase is what Lake refers to as "well-being", resulting from the ongoing sustenance of being. Here the communication of "well-being" is achieved simultaneously in both its physical and spiritual dimensions. Lake writes that "not only is there the obvious in-flow of physical sustenance in the form of milk when the child is at the breast, there is an equally important flow of sustenance from the mother to the baby on every level of personality" (Lake, 1964, chart N.b.). Lake specifically mentions satisfaction, joy, fullness, and graciousness.

The two output stages, designated by Lake as "status" and "achievement", are directly dependent upon the events of the input phases. Lack of "being" and "well-being" ultimately results in adults who manifest these "lacks" in the form of various neurotic and psychotic maladaptive dysfunctions. The description, etiology, dynamics, care and cure of these various manifestations takes up the bulk of *Clinical Theology*. These characterizations remained valid even after Lake's thinking about the M-FDS was formulated. All that changed was the timing of the etiologic experiences. Writing immediately prior to his death in 1982, and referring back to the nine month period of early infancy, namely the "womb of the spirit", Lake noted:

There is one statement . . . which obviously now demands correction [and it is this]: "The roots of all the major neuroses-- hysterical, phobic, conversion, schizoid, anxiety-depressive and obsessional-- derive from separation anxiety in this phase." Some cases of each do . . . but the evidence . . . indicates that, if we are talking about the main roots of personality disorders . . . , it is [to the first trimester that] we must look and not later (Lake, 1982b, 25).

During this period of Lake's intellectual evolution, he clearly was significantly influenced by several thinkers, including Guntrip (1952; 1957; 1961; 1968) and Fairbairn (1952a; 1952b), particularly in his conceptualization and understanding of the schizoid personality type. Also important were both Sigmund Freud and Melanie Klein (Klein, 1975a, 1975b). Both emphasized the primacy of the events of early childhood for later psychodynamic functioning. But when it came to an investigation beyond this period, Lake contends that the orthodoxy of both rendered the "investigation of life, distress and near-death in the womb . . . a 'no-go' area. The obvious distress of much intrauterine existence has been assumed to have no emotional consequences. By definition, nothing could happen there to interest the analyst" (Lake, 1976b, S3). However, Lake saw both Freudian and Kleinian theory pointing beyond itself to indicate the importance of prenatal life for later psychodynamics. For instance, Lake noted that Freud's death instinct is present, by definition, at conception and thus must be functioning in opposition to the life-wish both pre- and post-natally. Lake saw Freud himself "opening the door" to this thinking when he wrote in *Inhibitions, Symptoms and Anxiety* that "there is much more continuity between intra-uterine life and the earliest infancy than the impressive caesura of the act of birth allows us to believe" (Freud, 1936, 109).

In a similar manner, Lake sees Klein's Object Relations Theory as also "opening the door" slightly. Klein's influence on Lake at this time was quite pronounced. Not only was he in full agreement with Klein regarding the cruciality of the mother-child/infant dyad, but also with Klein's contention that because the child experiences frustration and gratification from the same source, usually the mother, this gives rise to a perception of objects as "part objects." This condition of "splitting" the good and bad "part-objects" results in Klein's "paranoid-schizoid position." It isn't until the latter part of the infant's first year of life that she begins to reconcile the two, and this realization results in the depressive position.

While Lake obviously was influenced by Klein, and would see Kleinian theory pointing beyond itself, he critiques Klein for failing to develop the logical implications of her conceptualizations. Lake cites the following Kleinian comment as emblematic: "I have suggested" she wrote, "that the struggle between life and death instincts enters into the painful experience of birth and adds to the persecutory anxiety aroused by it" (Klein in Lake, 1976b, S4). That Klein didn't proceed then to examine in more depth birth trauma and pre-birth trauma, seemed, to Lake, inconsistent.

Birth

Lake early on parts ways with classic Freudian and Kleinian interpretive schemes relating to the non-importance of birth. But there is no clear delineation between Lake's emphasis upon the first months of post-natal life vs. birth as the crucial period for subsequent functioning. In fact, in *Clinical Theology*, Lake emphasizes the importance of both infancy and birth. However, in the extensive chapters and the summary charts of the various disorders in *Clinical Theology*, he treats birth trauma as a part of the process of infancy. In the etiology of the various neuroses and psychoses, it becomes one factor of many in the possible cause of later psychological maladjustment.

Sometime after the publication of *Clinical Theology*, Lake's thinking subtly changes. He begins to place a much greater emphasis upon peri-natal events than before, and speaks much less of the cruciality of the events of early infancy. While Lake never denies that post-natal experiences are not eventful or even momentous, they tend to be less so than earlier events, often being a recapitulation of previous experiences. Illustrative of his de-emphasis of the relative importance of the "womb of the spirit" period of infancy, he makes a comparison between two choices:

> If I were presented with a hard alternative, that in the case of a woman about to become pregnant, she had to undergo nine months distress during the next year and a half, but could choose whether the bad half came first, to be inextricably shared with the unborn baby, or came second, when her baby was already born, I would unhesitatingly urge her to choose to keep the months of pregnancy undisturbed, and face the task of coping with big trouble after the foetus had left her womb. Then she could cry or rage, grieve or despair, while the baby was sleeping, apart from her tumultuous reactions, protected to a significant extent from them" (Lake, 1981a, 3).

For much of Lake's professional psychiatric career, birth and birth trauma were held to be *the* pivotal and crucial events for later "being" and "well-being." In 1977, referring to the previous 20 years of his professional life, Lake wrote: "I had happily taught and theorized on the basis of birth as the first significant psychodynamic event for 20 years [from the age of 43 to 63]" (Lake, 1977a, 5). This emphasis upon the cruciality of perinatal experiences, which includes "events round about the birth; before, during and after birth" (Lake 1976a, 1), was not widely accepted at the time. There were, however, those who concurred with Lake on the importance of the perinatal.

Primary among them was Otto Rank. His book, *The Trauma of Birth*, published in 1924, clearly described Rank's contention that not only was birth the first experienced anxiety, but that it was the prime source material for all the neuroses and character disorders. It was the "original emotional shock underlying all personality dysfunction." Rank wrote that "we believe that we have discovered in the trauma of birth the primal trauma" (Rank in Lake, 1987, 168). He continued, "we have recognized the neuroses in all their manifold forms as reproductions of, and reactions to, the birth trauma." Even at this early stage, Lake quotes Rank as hinting at the importance of the prenatal:

All symptoms ultimately relate to this primal fixation" and the place of fixation is "in the maternal body" and in peri-natal experiences. . . . We believe that we have succeeded in recognizing all forms and symptoms of neuroses as expressions of a regression from the stage of sexual adjustment to the prenatal primal state, or to the birth situation, which must thereby by overcome (Rank in Lake, 1987, 168).

Donald W. Winnicott (1958; 1972) also exerted an influence on Lake as it relates to this period of emphasis upon perinatal events. Winnicott spoke of an event "etched on the memory" that eventually manifested itself in the stresses of later life. Lake quotes Winnicott approvingly:

There is evidence that personal birth experience is significant and is held as memory material. When birth trauma is significant, every detail of impingement and reaction is, as it were, etched on the patient's memory, in the way to which we have been accustomed when patients relive traumatic experiences of later life (Winnicott in Lake, 1978e, 233).

In Winnicott Lake also begins to find resonance for the importance of "intra-uterine experience pre-natally" as determinative and definitive for post-natal affective development. He quotes Winnicott:

> There is certainly before birth the beginning of emotional development, and it is likely that there is before birth a capacity for false and unhealthy forward movement in emotional development (Lake, 1987, 169).

The work of Ivan Pavlov, particularly his research and formulations of "transmarginal" stress, is also influential on Lake's thinking in this period. In Pavlov's research with dogs, he found that the "paradox of trans-marginal stress" results when emotional pain is pushed beyond the threshold of tolerance, thus producing a paradoxical longing and iden-tification with oblivion and death. Lake discovered that Pavlov's formula-tions were in accordance with the findings of his ongoing research utilizing LSD as an abreactive agent. Many of the research subjects who abreacted to the pre-, peri, and early post-natal periods reported para-doxical experiences entirely consonant with Pavlov's descriptions. Lake wrote:

> So far as I know, no one has hitherto used Pavlov's concept of transmarginal stress as the main interpretive hypothesis by which to unify those phenomena of discontinuous responses conceptually (Lake, 1964, 2).

A fourth major influence at this point was Stanislav Grof, who, as Lake had done, began utilizing LSD as a psycholeptic agent in 1953. Grof's re-search with LSD (Grof, 1975; Grof & Halifax, 1977) commenced at approximately the same time as Lake's and lead to the similar results. Both men found that under the influence of LSD, numerous patients de-scribed feelings and experiences, some of transmarginal stress, relating to their pre- and peri-natal experiences. Some of these experiences were later confirmed both by hospital records as well as by those who had been present at the birth of the patient. Lake's LSD research continued from 1953 to 1970 (Lake, 1981g, 7), but beginning in 1969 he started to utilize Reichian (Reich, 1972) and bio-energetic deep-breathing techniques, which he actually found to work just as well or better than LSD-25.

Grof divided up the perinatal experience into four "basic perinatal matrices" and described the phenomenology of each as occurring in LSD sessions. The first, called "Life in the Womb", prefigured Lake's later em-phasis upon prenatal life. This matrix is composed of the recollections of fetal life and involves the summation of experiences with which the baby faces the impending experience of birth. This summation tends to be either the positive "experiences of an undisturbed intrauterine environment where the basic needs of the embryo/fetus/ baby are met" (Lake, 1981d, C56), or the negative recollections of the "bad womb" situation such as fetal crises, emotional upheavals in the mother and attempted abortions.

The second matrix is called "No Exit" and occurs at the beginning of labor but before the cervix opens. The "good womb" experience, where it has occurred, is inexplicably terminated and the supporter of the fetus for the last nine months becomes the aggressor. There is relentless force to "push out" the constricted fetus which can seem destructive or even murderous. Those that have suffered a "bad womb" experience are having their earlier traumas recapitulated and reconfirmed. Regardless of the experience of the first matrix, the still-closed cervix, combined with the contractions of the uterus, temporarily creates a trapped, hopeless feeling of "no exit".

The third phase involves the actual process of birth. The cervix opens and the fetus and womb begin to elongate. The fetus' head is pushed and molded to fit into the inlet to the pelvis. The reaction to this third matrix is variable. Some are active and some passive; some sense a maternal synergy and others maternal opposition; some are excited about the possibility of a new environment and others want to remain in the womb.

Lastly, Grof described the immediate post-birth experience as variable. There is the ideal of close, physical, and prolonged contact with the mother to "soothe away all the foul tensions that have arisen to perplex them, which they cannot understand" (Lake, 1978b). Along with the sense of confusion and bewilderment, there is the possibility of the sense of abandonment, loneliness, separation anxiety, and in the extreme, a sense of nothingness and dread.

Grof's organization of the perinatal experience along these lines was consonant is several ways with Lake's subsequent delineation of the M-FDS. First, there is the affirmation, along with the perinatal, of the prenatal influence upon subsequent functioning. Second, for Grof as for Lake, early experiences become "patterns or principles of perceptual organization for later experiences" and serve as underlying prototypes for later complex reaction patterns (Lake, 1978b, 230). Third, both stressed that biological stress experiences are at the root of later psychopathology.

The Prenatal Period

While in 1976 Lake could say that "pre-natal events are quite important" (Lake, 1976a, 17), sometime in the period between 1977 and 1978, there was a gradual and discernible shift in Lake's emphasis towards the prenatal period as the most influential for subsequent functioning. Toward the beginning of 1978, Lake wrote that "even in the nine months growing in the womb there may be unimaginable sufferings and catastrophes" (Lake, 1978c, 46). In a Research Report from December 1978, Lake wrote:

> Some of you have followed our research into what looked like the earliest re-callable experiences of human beings, namely, the sensations and emotions accompanying one's birth. . . . Increasingly over recent years we have been invaded by evidence that the foetus in the mother's womb is picking up all sorts of messages about itself (Lake, 1978a, 2).

Lake continues to describe the rudiments of a M-FDS:

> The catecholamines which convey the "messages" to do with emotions round the mother's circulation, gearing all her organs and cells to feeling joy or sorrow, love or loathing, vitality or exhaustion, pass through the placental barrier (which to these substances is no barrier) into the foetal blood stream via the umbilical vein. In this context the foetus does its own emotional homework and responds, either passively accepting the mother's bad feelings as its own, as if true for itself, or by being protestingly overwhelmed by them. It can aggressively fight them back, in resolute opposition to sharing the mother's sickness. Others become "foetal therapists", trying to bolster up a debilitated and debilitating mother from their own feelings of relative strength. Sensitivity to "poisonous" feelings coming from a rejecting mother is very great. . . . To be the focus of mother's love imprints a confidence that "sets you up for life" (Lake, 1978a, 2).

The evidence that Lake cited to give credence to this shift in thinking came from the ongoing workshops in which deep-breathing techniques were being used to abreact early perinatal and increasingly prenatal "memories." Lake likewise found support for his findings in the ortho-dox psychoanalytic dream and association analysis work of Nandor Fodor, M.L. Peerbolte and Francis Mott, particularly Mott's utilization of a term first used centuries earlier-- "umbilical affect" (Moss, 1987, 203). Both Mott and Lake used this term to describe the "feeling state of the fe-tus as brought about by blood reaching him through the umbilical vein"

(Moss, 1987, 203). As Mott envisioned it, the umbilical vein not only conveys nutritive resources and as such could be experienced as a "life-giving flow, bringing... renewal and restoration" but could also "be the bearer of an aggressive thrust of bad feelings into the foetus if the mother herself was distressed and 'feeling bad.'" If the mother felt emotionally unsupported, then "this feeling of deficiency, lack of recognition and the failure of looked-for support, would be just as specifically felt by the fetus. It became distressed by the failure of its immediate environment to provide the expected acceptance and sustenance, not so much at the level of metabolic input . . . but to nourish the earliest beginnings of the person in relationship" (Lake, 1978d, S1).

Thus, Lake's formulations are highly similar to Mott's. Where Mott's research primarily focused on dream analysis, Lake's ideas took shape following the results occurring from over 1200 LSD and deep-breathing assisted re-experiences of peri- and pre-natal events. That the two were so highly corroborated encouraged Lake that his findings were not unique. Where Lake differs from Mott is in his final emphasis upon the first trimester as the MOST determinative phase of development.

Thus, with emphasis upon the prenatal stage, the M-FDS is essentially the affirmation that a maternal-fetal "affect flow" exists and consequently the emotional state of the mother is transmitted by way of the umbilical cord to the fetus. This "affect flow" is determinative of subsequent psychological and emotional functioning and perception.

The First Trimester

The fourth and final phase of Lake's thinking with regard to what constitutes the critical period of maternal-fetal affect flow is also the most controversial. That there was a distinction between his emphasis upon the prenatal period in general and the first semester in particular can be determined from a later paper he wrote:

> We thought initially that the pervasive traumatic influence of maternal distress on the foetus would be spread (if it occurred at all) throughout the nine months of pregnancy. We have now modified our thinking in the wake of the evidence that the first trimester is the locus for most of the catastrophes, for most of the sufferers from the M-FDS (Lake, 1977a, 3).

Referring back to the "womb of the spirit," Lake later wrote that from 1966 to 1977, he had applied the "womb" analogy as it related to the spirit to the first 9 months of post-natal life. And while the described dynamics are still true, the term "womb of the spirit" "could now more accurately be transferred to the earlier developmental stage, within the first half of the nine months of pregnancy-- which are the crucial ones-- though extending throughout until birth" (Lake, 1982b, 127).

In a second research Report written in 1980, Lake implied the evolution of his thinking:

> We find that it is not sufficient to look back, to find the origins of significant trauma, of consequent fixated pain, and therefore of the personality reactions that represent flight from that pain, only so far as the first year of life, or even to the traumas of birth. Things go wrong -or go well- much earlier than that (Lake, 1980b, 1).

Referring to these earlier sources of pain, Lake writes that it is the fetus who is vulnerable to "all that is going on in the mother, particularly in the first trimester, that is in the first three months after conception" (Lake, 1976a, 2-3). Lake later reaffirms this in *Tight Corners in Pastoral Counselling* when he wrote:

> The focus for psychopathology is now, for us, the first trimester of intra-uterine life. These first three months after conception hold more ups and downs, more ecstasies and devastations than we had ever imagined (Lake, 1981g, viii).

Thus, it is on the first trimester as the primary and crucial period of life that Lake finally settles. Although Lake continued to affirm that later pre-natal, peri-natal, and post-natal experiences all power-fully affect the post-natal functioning of the child and later the adult, it is the first trimester of intra-uterine life that is most determinative for all subsequent psychological, cosmological and ontological functioning.

The Research Leading to the Paradigm

Within the evolution of the overall theoretical process that Lake was thinking through there were two specific research phases that gave him the "evidence" to conclude that the first trimester was determinative for later functioning: the LSD research (1954-1969/70) and the primal integration workshops (1975-1982).

LSD Research

In a speech given in September of 1976, Lake described his initial introduction to LSD research:

> My chief sent me down to work with Sandison at Powick in 1954 because we were making no headway with alcoholics at all and he'd heard that LSD helped alcoholics to come to some awareness of what it was that made them go on drinking. So I went down . . . [and on return] I was given full time for two years, no other job [but] to pick out patients, [give them LSD,] and sit with them for four hours, six hours, as long as was necessary (Lake, 1976a, 2-3).

He quickly discovered that when used in the presence of a trustworthy therapist, LSD-25 seemed to serve effectively to de-repress the "forgotten" memories of the patient. As he began to take note of "whatever the patients said as the thick crust of repression crumbled under the impact of the drug and the contents of the unconscious mind emerged into consciousness" (Lake, 1964, xix), he noted several striking similarities among what seemed to be a re-experiencing of repressed infantile memories. First of all, "the situation of the baby at the breast, for better or worse" and "the loss of the countenance of the mother, as a significant source of primal anxiety, occurred with painful frequency" (Lake, 1964, xx). Secondly, he wrote:

> I was not prepared for the frequent abreaction of birth trauma. I was assured by neurologists that the nervous system of the baby was such that it was out of the question that any memory to do with birth could be reliably recorded as fact. I relayed my incredulity to my patients, and, as always happens in such cases, they tended thereafter to suppress what I was evidently unprepared, for so-called scientific reasons, to believe. But then a number of cases emerged in which the reliving of specific birth injuries, of forceps delivery, of the cord round the neck, of the stretched brachial plexus, and various other dramatic episodes were so vivid, so unmistakable in their origin, and afterwards confirmed by the mother or other reliable informants, that my suspicion was shaken (Lake, 1964, xix).

A third commonality from the LSD-assisted abreactions of birth and early infancy was the occurrence of discontinuous reactions to severe stress. With regard to both birth and events in the first year there seemed to be a normal reaction to mounting stress, but then suddenly, "dramatically and dreadfully, the struggle to live, reaching a certain margin of tolerable pain, seemed to switch, automatically, into a struggle to die, of equal intensity with the previous struggle to live" (Lake, 1964, xxi). Lake found that Ivan Pavlov had observed this same paradoxical phenomena in dogs. This "transmarginal stress" (Pavlov, 1928; 1957; 1960) seemed to produce autistic, withdrawn, and classically schizoid children and adults. It was in this discovery that Lake saw the root of schizophrenia and the schizoid personality disorder as occurring in the first 6 months of post-natal life.

Related to this observation was a fourth, that the reaction to early emotional stress tended to set up a pattern of similar reacting that is lifelong. Persons who early on reacted "hysterically" tended to react hysterically as adults. Persons who adopted the typical "depressive" defense patterns early on, tended to utilize them as adults.

These observations served as "evidence" to spur Lake on to what would eventually result in the M-FDS. Towards the end of his research with LSD in 1969, Lake did a follow-up study on 68 patients, 57 of whom responded. Half of these persons claimed to have experienced events of early childhood or birth *as if* they were reliving them (Moss, 1983a; 1883b; 1987). Of the 57, 37 reported that they remembered experiencing being born and 21 that they had relived some aspect of intra-uterine life.

In *Tight Corners in Pastoral Counselling*, Lake reported that there was a period of overlap between the residential workshops and the LSD phases of his research. He writes that "only at the very end of the period in which I was using LSD-25 in the therapy of neuroses and personality disorders, that is, at the end of the sixties, did I invite those who wanted to work at primal depth, using LSD, to come to residential conferences with spouse and friends. I soon found how greatly this group work helped the process, and wished that I had realized that earlier." He continued, "At the same time the value of Reichian and bio-energetic techniques broke upon us, and we discovered that deep breathing alone was a sufficient catalyst for primal recapitulation and assimilation. Nothing more 'chemical' than that was necessary, so we stopped using LSD" (Lake, 1981g, 7).

The Lingdale Workshops

With the discovery of the importance of a facilitative group for primal work noted above, the second phase of Lake's research began. In 1958,

Lake began running "clinical theology" seminars. Each seminar lasted for 3 hours and met 12 times, approximately once every 3 weeks for one year. They gradually evolved into the residential workshops that were inaugurated in 1975 at Lingdale, the head-quarters of the Clinical Theology Association in Nottingham. They were initially 3 days in length, later expanding to as long as 6 days in duration, and were offered on various themes and topics. As these conferences developed and evolved, and as the theory underpinning the M-FDS was beginning to coalesce, Lake introduced an integrative seminar called "Primal Therapy in Christian Pastoral Care" (Moss, 1990, 3). Towards the conclusion of 1978, these seminars evolved to the point that some were centered upon personal growth, some explored prayer and healing, and still others focused on primal therapy. Lake brought all three of these elements together into a workshop titled "Personal Growth and Primal Integration in the Small Group" (Moss, 1990, 3). It was in these seminars, along with the primal integration workshops that followed them, that much of the "evidence" for the M-FDS emerged.

Primal Integration Workshops

The Lingdale workshops were conducted during this period at a residential facility immediately adjacent to Lingdale. Located near the center of Nottingham, but on a quite cul-de-sac surrounded by gardens and enclosed by a fairly high stone wall, Lingdale provided an ideal place for a residential retreat-like seminar. The house was quite large, able to accommodate between 14 and 18 persons, with sufficient space to allow for several "primals" to be occurring simultaneously. During the period between 1979 and 1982, over 500 persons attended these seminars at Lingdale, some lasting as long as 7 days.

The seminars, whether at Lingdale or elsewhere, usually began with some brief introductions and the presentation of an itinerary of the days to follow. During the first 2 days of the seminar, the focus centered on getting the participants emotionally comfortable both with each other and the facilitators. A certain degree of comfort was required in order to feel a "sense of safety" and was facilitated by a supportive sharing process whereby each person spoke "of the aspects of their own personality functioning on which they hoped to work" (Lake, 1981c, 7). This process, not unlike conventional group therapy, included probing not only into their current emotional functioning, but also into the history of their lives. Especially noted and emphasized would be any information and memories associated with the circumstances of their conception, prenatal period and birth.

A second component of the first few days of the seminar was some teaching with regard to the biological and physiological facts of embryology. In order to understand better the prenatal environment at each successive stage, a workshop facilitator would give a 2-hour lecture, usually accompanied by slides and other illustrations of embryonic and fetal life, although not always. While this lecture was primarily designed as presentation of the basic scientific facts of embryology, very often either the lecturer or a participant would begin to "resonate with aspects of the story that were particularly applicable to them" (Moss, 1990, 3:6) and communicate this with the other participants. Following this review of embryology and building upon it, the facilitators, often very informally and as a function of other activities, then began to communicate the various principles and practice of primal integration.

After several days of preparation, very often several of the participants would begin with the "work" of primal integration. At Lingdale this was done in a room large enough for four persons to be "working" at a time, each with 3 or 4 persons immediately around them. The room was usually carpeted and comfortable with dim lighting. Lake described the situation:

> Each subject working has, squatting on mats round them, a facilitator from our experienced house team, a workshop member (whose turn would come later) who had volunteered to write down all their utterances as an accurate record, and a third member tending a tape-recorder (Lake, 1982b, 65).

Each "session" lasted from 2 to 3 hours and would be followed up by a feedback-session with the larger group.

The "session" would begin with the "subject" relaxed in a supine position on the floor being guided in a "conception-to-womb talk-down". The facilitator, usually Lake, would simultaneously speak to all four "primalers". This address would begin with a simple relaxation routine, sometimes by way of guided fantasy but always with the use of deep-breathing. The facilitator would then remind the participants of the facts of early life. Lake states that he would rehearse, "in a neutral, emotionally unbiased voice, the undisputed facts of human development, the anatomy and physiology of the meeting of the sperm with the ovum recently released from the ovary whose lifetime it has shared, to conception and cell division to the morula and its hollowing out to form the blastocyst"

(Lake, 1981c, 9). As this occurred, very often the participant would curl up in the fetal position and become totally oblivious to the other participants, "genuinely creating 'a womb' out of the small group and experience within it an authentic transcript of intra-uterine experience" (Lake, 1981g, 27).

In addition to the reiteration of the "anatomico-physiological facts" the "talkdown" included repeated promptings to recall certain forgotten or ignored data related to the participants' mother and father and the entire environment in which conception and early pre-natal life occurred. Along with this recall, the participants were also encouraged to give voice to the emotional memories.

The "talkdown" would proceed in a chronological manner, beginning with an identification with the ovum *as* part of the mother and the sperm *as* part of the father. This was followed by a recapitulation of the emotions and sensations of sexual intercourse and then conception, followed in turn by the zygotic and blastocystic stages and then implantation. Lake wrote that he would seek to lead participants to "tune in" on the emotional state of the mother and father. He would ask them:

> Reflect on their mother's feelings as she joins the father on the night of the conception. How does she feel about herself? How does she feel about having her first child, or adding to the family, or trying again after one or more miscarriages or fatal birth accidents? How does she feel about the man probably her husband alongside her? Is she full of joyful anticipation at being aroused by him, open to him and being entered by him (Lake, 1982, 67)?

The "talkdown" would temporarily conclude at the sixth week, with the crucial suggested awareness of the umbilical flow returning from the mother. Lake, in a transcript of a talkdown from a workshop at Lingdale dated 10/2/80, concluded with these words:

> And breathe up deeply into your strength, and make any kind of neutral noise as you breathe out. Ah. But reach down into contact with any feelings in the belly. What is it that comes in from mother? because she's in contact with all that world outside, the world of men and women, and all that goes on. (pause) So breathe deeply, and explore what it is that comes through from mother into you, and give a voice to it as you breathe out. A-ah. Take your time, and just be aware in your own space of what it was like for you to be in the womb. . . . Breathe strongly and give yourself plenty of air to get into contact with this child as the end of the cord (Lake, 1980a, 4).

Following this phase of discourse by the facilitator, the participants were left to work through the remainder of the third trimester without the aid of a verbalized facilitation. At this point in the seminar, contingent upon the prenatal experience of each participant, the reactions would vary significantly. Lake wrote:

> Each became so totally different, and were discovering their own pace and intrinsic direction of retrieval and re-living. I, as conductor, would "go off the air", leaving them to explore, for the next couple of hours, the unique features of their own record of the first trimester (Lake, 1982b, 65).

Following this period, Lake writes that "at a point usually clear to the long experience of the facilitator" (Lake, 1982b, 65), he would then begin to rehearse the remainder of the fetal experience, moving through the months of the middle and finally third trimesters, to finally conclude at birth. Depending upon the retrieved memories of birth, the session often ended at this point, was prolonged, or needed to be taken up at a second session. Lake continues that "at all points in the journey, from conception to bonding, the subject is in adult contact with their facilitator and small group. They will go out to the toilet and return, immediately in contact again with the foetal world at the point where they left it" (Lake, 1982b, 66).

At the conclusion of the session, following a brief break, a feedback session would ensue in which a greater exploration of what happened would be encouraged. Assisted by the written and recorded records of each "primal", the participant evaluated the experience in light of their present life. What insights have been made? Lake writes that a typical question put forth might be "How far do they recognize, in the foetal states now fully and clearly relived, the source of life-long attitudes and decisions, fixed perception and rooted character stance and posture" (Lake, 1982b, 68-69).

If a second session was needed, the participant would again return in order to finish out the chronological process of the prenatal or ante-natal experience, or, return to that area or period that needed more "work". The entire seminar would conclude with some preparation for "re-entry", often utilizing psychodrama and focusing on how the insights of their experience related to the "here-and-now". For some of the participants, follow-up weekends at Lingdale with an emphasis toward an ongoing mutual care for each other were attended.

The recorded tapes and written transcripts of the sessions provided much of the evidence for Lakes' formulations of the M-FDS. In addition, Roger Moss, a co-researcher of Lake's during this period, completed a follow-up postal survey of those who had attended the residential workshops at Lingdale between October 1979 and April 1982. The survey, consisting of 52 main sections covering 11 sides of paper, was sent out to 500 of the total of 516. A return rate of 56.2% (N=281) was achieved and these were analyzed in light of the data and evidence already at hand.

These results, as well as the data from the Lingdale sessions, provided the grist for Lake's theoretical mill. Based on this evidence, Lake formulated a theory with specific elements.

The Components of the Paradigm

Following conception and prior to the process of implantation is the short preliminary stage of the "blastocyst." Lake affirmed that this period is "often felt to be a good experience of non-attachment, even of unitive and quite 'transcendent bliss'" (Lake, 1981g, 15). "There may be a sense of continuity with the monistic sense of 'union with the Absolute' experienced by some in the first week after conception, a kind of Blastocystic Bliss" (Lake, 1981d, C41). This stage is immediately succeeded by implantation in the lining of the maternal womb, gradually resulting in umbilical circulation through the umbilical cord and placenta. Lake writes:

> As this begins to function, the foetus is evidently put into direct contact with all that is being transmitted round the mother's own body as an expression of her emotional ups and downs. The foetus feels acutely the feelings which are the product of the mother's life situation, for better or for worse, and her personal reactions to it (Lake, 1981g, 15).

According to Lake, the establishment of umbilical circulation allows every woman to have a profound impact upon an emerging fetus within her. This occurs through the phenomenon that Lake called "umbilical affect". This term is defined as the "feeling state of the fetus as brought about by blood reaching him through the umbilical vein" (Moss, 1986, 203). This maternal-fetal "affect flow" transmits the emotional state of the mother to the fetus by way of the umbilical cord in a manner similar to the transmission of nutrients and various teratogens such as viruses and chemical agents. Lake wrote:

Before birth, the foetus may be seriously damaged if the mother is dependent upon alcohol, nicotine or other drugs. It is also damaged by the less readily identifiable changes that transmit to the baby a mother's rejection of a particular pregnancy and of the life growing within her. Any severe maternal distress, whatever its cause, imprints itself on the foetus (Lake, 1981g, 16).

The effects of this "affect flow" are mediated by the interaction between the mother's emotional state and the fetal response to it. The maternal "affect flow" spans the full range of emotional possibilities. At one polarity, stands the ideal of total joy and acceptance resulting in an "emotive flow" that communicates recognition, affirmation, and acceptance to the fetus. The other extreme represents maternal rejection and distress that results in the "invasion of the fetus in the form of a bitter, black flood" (Lake 1981g, 16). Either way, this "invasion" is usually the result of often very complex and mixed emotions. Lake describes these mixed messages:

> She may have been full of anger internally, while fear, compliance or compassion prevented its ever being shown externally. She may have loved the man by whom she became pregnant, while hating the resultant fetus, or loved the prospect of having a baby, while hating, fearing or feeling deeply disappointed and neglected by its father. The fetus receives all such messages but has difficulty in distinguishing what relates specifically to it and what belongs to the mother's feelings about her own life in general (Lake, 1981g, 21).

Similarly, the fetal response varies from "'taking it all to heart' as a judgment against itself, to be passively endured, or strongly to oppose it, or 'to get right out of it' by splitting off the ego, the experiencing 'I' taking leave of the too-badly hurt foetal body" (Lake, 1981g, 21). Whatever it is, the foetal response to the maternal "affect flow" is contingent upon its own constitutional factors as well as the intensity and duration of the emotive flow (Lake, 1981g, 21-22). "The tendency is to feel identified with all of these invading maternal emotions in turn and to react to each" (Lake, 1981g, 21). It is this response, according to Lake, that is so determinative for subsequent functioning, especially when the fetus is responding to an emotive flow of severe distress. The result, depending upon the specific intrapsychic dynamics, is the appearance of a particular group of symptoms and signs that characterize a particular psychopathology. Thus, "this intra-uterine interaction is the source of images, perceptions, meanings, values and personality defenses to cope with them" (Lake, 1981f, 65).

Lake organized the occurrence of "umbilical affect" and its effects on the fetus into three general manifestations and four consequent graded response patterns. The former is primarily based upon the quality and quantity of the "affect-flow" from mother to fetus, while the latter is based upon the response of the fetus to this "affect-flow". Both the response of a woman to her pregnancy and the reaction of the fetus within her to her response are events that actually exist along a continuum of possible responses ranging from absolute and joyous acceptance to horrendous and cataclysmic rejection. In the most general terms, the three main anchors along this continuum include joyful acceptance of the fetus by his mother, conscious or unconscious ignorance and/or disregard of the fetus by the mother, and finally, conscious or unconscious rejection of the fetus by the mother. The four "graded responses to increasing degrees of pain due to un-met intra-uterine and peri-natal needs" (Lake, 1981d, C68) are also somewhat continuous.

Changes in the mother's environment may occur in the course of the pregnancy that drastically alter the fetal environment. The beginning of the pregnancy may be perceived by the fetus as positive and "ideal", while later changing to a negative perception due to some stressor in the maternal environment. An opposite experience is just as likely, with an initial negative environment, due perhaps to a crisis pregnancy, with a later adjustment and acceptance resulting in a much more positive environment.

The Manifestations of "Umbilical Affect"

Positive

One possible manifestation of maternal affect is what Lake termed "positive". This pattern is characterized by joy and acceptance. The mother, upon discovery of her pregnancy, exults with joy and happiness, giving rise to a "flow of the mother's positive, aware, attention-giving emotional regard to the developing foetus within her. The development of a positive Foetal Skin Feeling, as the ground of 'the excellent self' may be perceptible" (Lake, 1981d, C41). Elsewhere Lake writes that the mother's joy and "recognition of her changed state leads to foetal joy in being recognized, accepted, and indeed, welcomed" (Lake, 1981g, x).

Negative

The second general pattern resulting from the maternal-fetal affect flow is what Lake termed "negative". While this manifestation is disconcerting and distressing to the fetus, it is not so because of any perceived attack. Rather, the fetus "wants to feel its presence recognized" and "this is often denied. There is a puzzled, then distressed sense of being disregarded, unnoticed, of no interest or account in the cosmos" (Lake, 1981d, C41). The fetus is frustrated by his mother's "non-recognition of her own body as she works on furiously before and after she knows she is pregnant. It is deeply disturbed by her lack of recognition of herself as pregnant and the fetus as a growing human being inside her when she does know" (Lake, 1981d, C41). As such, the fetus cannot thrive because its yearning is fixated. There is often fetal distress in the awareness of the mother's emotional need and at times a response of "trying to help", of attempting to somehow palliate, ease or prevent the mother's distress. This gives rise to what Lake called the "fetal therapist."

Strongly Negative

The third and final pattern of manifestation and response from the maternal-fetal affect flow is what Lake called "strongly negative". This pattern is what gives this entire paradigm its designation as the "maternal-fetal distress syndrome". As such, and because of its dire and myriad consequences, its discussion comprises by far the most material in Lake's thought and works.

When the "umbilical affect" is strongly negative, the fetal distress that results comes directly as a result of an "influx of maternal distress" (Lake, 1981d, C41), to her distress in relation to the world:

> It may be due to her marriage, to her husband's withdrawal rather than more intimate supporting when he is asked urgently for more than his personality can easily give. It may be due to the family's economic or social distress in a distressed neighborhood . . . If she is grieving the loss of, or nursing a still dying parent, the sorrow overwhelms her and overwhelms her fetus (Lake, 1981f, 66).

Whatever the cause, "the pain of the world, picked up by the family, is funneled by the mother into the fetus" (Lake, 1981f, 66). Included in this dynamic then, is "both the registering of the intrusion of the mother's condition, of yearning, anxiety, fear, anger, disgust, bitterness, jealousy, etc. into the fetus, and its own emotional response to this distressed and distressing invasion" (Lake, 1981d, C41). Particularly distressing, because they give rise to the "fear of being killed by maternal hatred" (Lake, 1981d, C41), are failed abortions and near miscarriages.

When the fetus is invaded by a "black, bitter flood" of "incompatible . . and alien emotions" (Lake, 1981g, x), this transfusion leads to an assortment of possible reactions. The fetus may attempt to utilize various coping mechanisms or may seek to actively oppose this "invasion". The mode of contravention varies with "constitutional factors, intensities and duration of stress, as well as previous experiences severe enough to cause conditioned responses" (Lake, 1981g, x). Thus, the "strongly negative" pattern of manifestation and response, of the "foetus being 'marinated' in his mother's miseries" (Lake, 1981g, 141) and reacting in a variety of ways, results in a variety of serious disorders.

The Graded Levels of Fetal Response

Corresponding somewhat to the three variations of maternal "umbilical affect" are the four variations of fetal response.

Ideal

The first such response is the "Ideal". This condition exists when, from implantation onwards, "the fetus in the womb is well-supplied in every way," its physical, emotional, and spiritual "shopping list" being satisfied by the "hopes of a well-stocked maternal shop" (Lake, 1981d, C68). There is a sense of "warm and contented happiness, even of a deeply embodied bliss. . . . The umbilical connection with the mother from the placenta is wholly satisfactory" (Lake, 1982b, 13). There is the communication of peacefulness, tenderness, love; the mother is said to "keep a warm womb" (Lake, 1982b, 13). Contingent upon her reaction to her life situation is her ability "to meet the emotional needs of the foetus, and fulfill the archetypal 'blessed mother' image" (Lake, 1981d, C68). Ideally, "all the warmth and tenderness of the love she is receiving from her husband, family and neighbors, . . . fortified, perhaps by a spiritual sense that God the Father's exchanges of love are just like this, and as she opens to him too, all her loves mix and are made available to the foetus within her, though she may as yet have only an inkling that she is pregnant" (Lake, 1982b, 14).

Coping

When the maternal affect flow is less than "ideal" but is still "good-enough" to prevent a loss of trust, the second response level is manifested by the fetus. The "Coping Response" results when there is a "discrepancy between need and proper fulfillment . . . but the main conditions of satisfactory interaction are being more or less met" (Lake, 1981d, C68). There is either a maternal failure to meet perfectly the "essential need for recognition and caring attention" or an "influx of maternal distress" (Lake, 1982b, 21), or both. While the fetus has "lost hope of the 'ideal,'" it attempts to "cope with the deficit or the distress" (Lake, 1982b, 21) by accepting the "ongoing exchange with the source person, out of sheer need" (Lake, 1982b, 21). These interactive conditions, although not perfect, are "good enough" to permit the fetus to cope adequately with the disparity. It is only when the emotional supplies of the "maternal shop" are less than ideal and there is the recognition of this lack or "badness", that what has preceded, if "ideal" in some sense of the term, is now defined as having been "good". Thus "fetal coping is really saying 'However hard it is to hang on to the acceptance of the mixed good/bad, rough/smooth stuff that comes in the navel, the alternative, to refuse the good because the bad is so bad, is to cut oneself off from life itself'" (Lake, 1982b, 22).

The consequences of the "coping level" for later functioning are determined by the severity of the deficit and the consequent reaction. However, since the world is not an "ideal" place where one's needs are always met fully and immediately, the coping level is more predictive of future interaction and thus can serve as a kind of vaccination against future deficits and disappointments. Lake states that "those who in the first trimester were well able to cope with a mixed bag of maternal emotional inputs are better placed for dealing with later troubles than those for whom it was so 'ideal' as to have escaped their notice" (Lake, 1981d, C68). Indeed, this level can serve to "flex the muscles of faith" with the spirit expanding "to include the negative aspects of relationships with increasing and justifiable hope and trust" (Lake, 1981d, C68).

A second possible consequence, this time definitively negative and shared with the third and fourth "levels", results from the economy of the exchange between the fetus and his mother. The "good" and "bad" of the "affect-flow" are accepted "with the corollary that the 'badness' must not be fired back at the placenta/mother via the excretory umbilical arteries, but 'loaded up' in the foetus' own body structures" (Lake, 1982b, 21).

Thus the "badness" is displaced and contained within a body part and may include muscle groupings, or any one of the alimentary, respiratory, or uro-genital tracts. Thus the "ostensible ongoing acceptance of the way of exchange is riddled with ambivalence" (Lake, 1982b, 21).

The third possible result of the coping response may be that of the fetal therapist". This result occurs when a constitutionally strong fetus receives an ambivalent or clearly negative affect flow from a weak, inadequate mother. The fetus accepts the burden, often life-long, of doing everything possible to prevent and palliate the mother's stress and resultant distress. This necessitates a denial of and refusal to meet one's own needs.

Opposition

When the "emotional store" of the mother is judged by the fetus to be "not good enough" for trustful coping, total opposition results. Between the previous level and this third one something shocking has happened; "distress has shattered the erstwhile trust between the ego and its world" (Lake, 1981d, C68). Depending upon the constitutional style and strength of the fetus, the oppositional attitude will vary between being aggressively active to passively non-cooperative. What is sought is the immediate termination of a "significant margin of pain" (Lake, 1981d, C68). There is no longer an ability to cope, as was true with the previous level. "In the face of too severe, too prolonged, unremitting deficiency of maternal recognition of the fetal presence" (Lake, 1982b, 22) "the organism stops being its trusting self, open at the interface" (Lake, 1981d, C68) with the mother. Perhaps the fetus has a sense that the "negative umbilical affect" is like "a great nail of affliction or skewer transfixing the foetus at the navel, with an overwhelming invasion of bitter, black maternal emotions" (Lake, 1982d, 22).

The fetal reaction to this umbilical exchange varies. Sometimes the fetus can use the "down time" of the night, when the affect flows ceases or is reduced to a trickle, to "regather its incredibly renewable faith, hope, and love, to reaffirm what ought to be, and wait like Prometheus for the day when the carrion birds return to attack" (Lake, 1982d, 23). A concomitant reaction may be the willing of the death of the source person, which is often repressed because of its "unacceptability." The pain itself must be repressed and "split-off"; "the catastrophic sensations are dissociated from the memory of the hurtful environment. Stable 'character' is based on maintaining this" (Lake, 1981d, C68). Life goes on, but with the unconscious scar remaining.

As with the earlier level of coping, these repressed memories are displaced symbolically, either onto some body system or part, or onto an representative "image." Thus, the "disposal of invasive maternal distress and deficiency . . ." is achieved by "displacement and containment within the foetal organism" (Lake, 1981e, w11), and serves to "contain the badness" (Lake, 1982b, 23).

In extreme cases of level 3 opposition, and yet not extreme enough for the transmarginal stress of level 4, there is successive retreat from the umbilical badness to the point where the fetus is symbolically consigned to one small part of the body or compelled to "leave" totally. The remaining good of the fetus itself is "imaged as taking refuge in the head, or as retreating to just the centre of it" (Lake, 1982b, 23). When this "good" is compelled to leave the body entirely, it is felt to exist "only outside the body, floating in the space above the head" (Lake, 1982b, 23).

Transmarginal Stress

When and if the "affect flow" from the mother to the fetus reaches the point where the fetus perceives a "sheer impossibility of keeping up the opposition to the invasive evil which seems interminable and relentless" (Lake, 1982b, 30), then the fourth level has been reached. When the absolute margin of tolerable pain has been reached and passed, paradoxical and supra-paradoxical response patterns result in which "the self turns against itself, willing its own destruction and death" (Lake, 1981d, C68). The stance of the fetus switches from being life-affirming to death-affirming. Beyond the margin of tolerable pain, of transmarginal pain, the "foetus longs, not for life, but for death. The plea is not for a relief of the weight, but that it may be crushed out of existence" (Lake, 1982b, 30). "There is a loss of 'being' at the center, replaced by a [paradoxical] desire for 'nonbeing'" (Lake, 1981d, C41).

The Effects of the Paradigm

The existence of a "positive umbilical affect" and "ideal" fetal response because of a prenatal sojourn in the "womb of a gloriously happy and fulfilled wife and mother-to-be" (Lake, 1981f, 65) is somewhat rare. That during fetal life this person was well-supplied in every way, that the birth process went smoothly, that the maternal bonding was immediate and strong, and that the environment of infancy and early childhood was affirming, in all likelihood results in an adult whose psychological and emotional adaptation is, while not perfect, near ideal. They have the psychic tools to cope well with the exigencies that dynamic existence gives rise to. They, as Lake de-scribes them, are those with "more robust natures, nurtured in kinder wombs, [and therefore] can shrug off . . . disappointments, or bear them, finding no antecedent pattern of neglect to latch on to" (Lake, 1981e, 2). They, in turn, visit the benefits of their "history" on their progeny to the "third and fourth generation."

That the great majority of persons do not share this ideal "history" gives rise to two other major categories of adults, the "normal" and the "abnormal". The former includes those who cope with life by "murdering the truth" successfully, those who "go along with it" and by the dynamics of repression succeed in keeping the truth of the early trauma and tragedies of fetal life safely at bay. Lake described this dynamic:

> As soon as the tragedy of human life impinges upon the infant, indeed upon the fetus still within the womb, the truth of what has happened is immediately murdered by repression and turned into a lie which denies that it ever happened (Lake, 1978c, 65).

Lake continues to describe this "average man":

> His is a life lived over the top of the tissue of closely woven lies, a fabric of falsehood. . . . Therefore, the line between the 'normal' person and the 'neurotic' is not that the normal personality can function without the intrinsic falsehood whereas the neurotic person cannot. Quite the contrary. We call a person 'normal' if the self-deception that he uses to repress, deny, displace, and rationalize those basic wounds that are ubiquitous in human beings from babyhood works quite well. He is 'normal' in so far as his defenses against too much painful reality are as successful as (all unbeknown to the person himself) they are meant to be (Lake, 1978c, 118).

When the "success" of these defenses against these "basic wounds" begins to flag and the "murdered truth" begins to emerge into present reality, often in an altered form, then the second group of persons emerges: those who are considered psychologically deficient, neurotic or even psychotic. The "normal" person often hides a cryptic "wounded" person who emerges only due to some present life stressor. The manifestation of this emergence takes the form of presenting complaints, which are recapitulations of and reverberations from the earliest fetal exper-

iences, perhaps, as Lake described, in "the uterus of a desperate, dissipa-
ted or dishonored woman whose hatred of life may take her own in suicide or that of the foetus in an attempted abortion which didn't quite come
off" (Lake, 1981f, 65).

The various maternal-embryo/fetal dynamics of the blastocystic and
implantation stages, of the rest of the first trimester, of prenatal, peri-natal
and post-natal life, gives rise to "wounds" and the consequent reaction to
these wounds which manifest themselves in particular patterns. The
original formation of these particular coping pattern depends upon
several components. The intensities and duration of stress, the "input"
point in the "dynamic cycle" at which the stress comes, the active or
passive reaction of the fetus to this stress, and the constitutional
"diatheses" (Lake, 1986, 8) are all important predictive factors.

Diminution of resources at the "being" phase of input in the dynamic
cycle gives rise to the most severe "personality disorders, the most dis-
ruptive of healthy self-hood and relationships" (Lake, 1986, 8): the
schizoid, hysterical, and anxiety-depressive reactions. These "reactions"
are all mediated by the severity and duration of the diminution and the response of the fetus. A reduction of maternal supplies at the "well-being"
input phases results, depending again upon the severity and duration of
the stress and the response of the fetus, in the maladaptive patterns of
paranoia and anxiety-less depression.

Whatever the stress and whenever it strikes, the "womb-distressed" person, Lake writes, "complains *as if* it remembered the bad times it had
been through. It reacts to the world around it *as if* it were still in the bad
place, still having to 'feel its keenest woe.' It reacts defensively *as if* the
attack were till going on" (Lake, 1981e, 4).

These reactive coping patterns, once used, are then utilized again and
again, setting up particular paradigms of "wound management" that are
recapitulated endlessly into adulthood. Lake writes:

> Similar "neglect-shaped" experiences in infancy and childhood plunge these
> unfortunately damaged creatures into an excessive and seemingly un-
> reasonable degree of distress, adding to their new injury all the catastrophic
> feelings and sensations that belonged to the first one (Lake, 1981e, 4).

Thus Lake writes:

> All the common diagnostic entities of psychiatric practice, hysterical, de-
> pressive, phobic, obsessional, schizoid, paranoid, have their clearly

discernible roots in this first trimester. Each of them constitutes a particular view of the foetal-placental world and what goes on in it . . .it is important to recognize these 'world views,' since they are the same fixated patterns of perception which impose themselves, more mistakenly than accurately, on roughly similar events throughout life (Lake, 1981g, 24).

When there is type of "block" from mother to fetus of "being itself", it is, as Lake described it, "an almost irremediable disaster. It is of all things the most destructive of the life of the organism" (Lake, 1986, 8). Three main psychopathologies or "wound management reaction patterns" result; anxiety-depression, the hysterical personality reaction, and the schizoid personality disorder (in its most serious manifestation called schizophrenia).

The Anxiety-Depression Reaction

An active response, due perhaps to constitutional strength, to a diminution of "being-itself" results in anxiety depression. Lake wrote:

> Depression and anxiety emerge from our deepest experiences of loneliness, of being unrecognized, over-looked, ignored, neglected, forgotten, disregarded, dropped, slighted, unnoticed, scorned, given the go-by (Lake, 1981e, 2).

Even though the fetus, in the threat of "objectlessness", would like to "block, squeeze, push, cut or pluck off the [umbilical] cord" (Lake, 1981d, C42), to do this would be to destroy herself. She quickly learns that her active response of anger and rage threaten to destroy her own environment by risking a rupture with the all-powerful mother and therefore must be dissociated from consciousness and immediately repressed. The anger and rage are controlled by "turning its force against the self" and splitting off the memory to the unconscious. When, to this repression, is added a reactive move, "the compulsive development of a rigidly compliant and mild personality to offset the hidden rage, we are in the presence of the dynamics of anxiety depression" (Lake, 1986, 10). All of this "surging conflict is recorded in the history of early uterine life" (Lake, 1981g, 101) and there is "over-whelming evidence that this sense of our presence being painfully overlooked by the person whose loving recognition [i.e. 'being-in-relatedness'] is more necessary than mere physical existence, occurs within the early weeks and months of life in the womb" (Lake, 1981e, 2).

That this same basic process is replayed again and again through the pre-, peri-, and post-natal stages results in a dam of repressed anger and rage. Immense emotional energy is expended by the ongoing attempt to not remember these painful memories. In addition, the erection of a defense of idealized external behavior (i.e. a reaction pattern) exactly opposite of the rage within serves to ward off from consciousness what is truly within. Rage, distrust, despair and apathy within are converted respectively into compulsive compliance, idealization, optimism and doggedness without. "The panic and dread, emptiness and fear, rage and envy, are all dealt with within the repressive layer, and 'appear' in consciousness only as their opposites, confidence and pride, capability and calm, compliance and generosity. The person is entirely unaware of the contents of his unconscious mind, and is aided and abetted by a variety of mental mechanisms in remaining so" (Lake, 1986, 17). This process is propelled by fear of the consequences of the expression of the rage within. Lake stated that "the murderous rage is so strong that to save others, a man may kill himself" (Lake, 1967, 68).

These are the dynamics of depression. That this is common is suggested by Lake when he relates that 75% of persons suffer from depression at some time. Lake writes:

> There are many depressed people whose inner conflict consists in the tiring tussle between ancient rages within, fanned into smoldering anger by present-day frustrations, and the forces of fear that keep such feelings under control. They never burst into flames in consciousness because of the forceful repressive and suppressive mechanisms that control them so totally that such people will deny that they are angry (Lake, 1981g, 98).

The only cure is to help them become aware of the cauldron within and to attempt to get in touch with its primary and early causes. This is where Lake's use primal therapy comes in.

The Hysterical Reaction

The hysterical and schizoid reactions are really the same reaction pattern, but on opposite sides of the "the abyss" of transmarginal stress (Lake, 1981d, C69). Unlike the active response of the anxiety depression reaction, the hystero-schizoid response, perhaps due to constitutional weakness, is passive in the face of the diminution and loss of "being-itself." Referring to the hystero-schizoid reaction to distress, Lake wrote:

A primal injury to the personality has split its roots into two quite separate systems. One grows up to seek the world outside itself [whereas] the other root grows up into the world of the mind, the inner world of reflection, reason, intellectual and mystical resources (Lake, 1967, 33).

The fetal reaction to distress that grows from the root of externalization is the hysterical pattern, which results from the loss or diminution of "being-itself", with a concomitant rise in apprehension leading finally to panic. This panic, stemming from non-attention, from non-recognition of "being" is defended against by a reaction pattern of compulsive attention-seeking behavior and compulsive attachment. This insures that continued "being" (and "well-being"), not given in the intra-uterine period and thus not stemming from within, continues to come to the hysteric from outside himself. His behavior is designed to manipulate and induce a steady flow of "being", of attention, of recognition. Thus any behavior that results in this "goal" is utilized, including histrionic self-dramatization, seductivity, exhibitionism, oversuggestibility, exaggeration, irrational outbursts and impulsivity. That this behavior compels others to give reluctant attention and acknowledgment is simply a recapitulation of the original dynamic, when the resources of "being" were not freely given, but with-held and constricted. The dependent "being" relationships are superficial because there is never satisfaction of the primal hunger for "being", instead there remains the constant anxiety that the source of "being", ever reluctant, will act capriciously and constrict the supply. This leads to further behavior designed to prevent this from occurring.

Since the primal hunger for "being" remains, the hysteric is always "hungry". He is "hungry" for touch and talk, an emotional sponge (Lake, 1964, chart H.a.). Since "being" has never been internalized, and even though much "input" in the form of "being" and "well-being" seems to take place, the "status" of the hysteric is so spirit-impoverished and ego-centric as to prevent any "output"; all "output" energy is directed toward gaining, holding, and maintaining the superficial "input" from others. "Achievement" is limited to self-glorifying, self-assuring, short-term goals.

The Schizoid Reaction

When the loss, constriction and diminution of "being" occurs to a point of absolute intolerability then the hysterical becomes the schizoid. The hysteric seeks "being" outside himself whereas the schizoid detaches herself from the external world and lives in reflective self-creation. Lake wrote:

> Being essentially self-creating, it [the schizoid] continues to be self-sub-sistent. It feeds upon itself, turned in upon its own mental processes (Lake, 1967, 33).

What separates the hysterical from the schizoid and makes them seem the very antithesis of each other is the intervention of a transmarginal break, wherein there is a paradoxical switch that translates the hysterical wish for life and "being" into the wish for death and "non-being." Similar to the genesis of the hysterical reaction type, the schizoid reaction is passive and commences in response to mounting anxiety in the light of the constriction of recognition, in the light of the diminution of the resources of "being". First there is conscious and then unconscious panic. There is a margin of tolerance that ends "at a point determined by constitution, heredity and recent experience" (Lake, 1967, 34), which when passed, results ultra-maximal stressing and dread. "The heart breaks and there is a falling headlong into the abyss of dread and non-being. The self is annihilated. God is dead. . . . There is an identification, not with human beings, but with non-being" (Lake, 1967, 34). Despair, intolerable dereliction, an overwhelming sense of forsakeness, feelings of futility, hollowness, nothingness, inferiority, depersonalization and uselessness are characteristic of this "death of the spirit." Paradoxical reactions result; previous to the transmarginal stress, the fetus desired to be affirmed, recognized, and loved; after she desires to be left alone and isolated. Pain is now embraced where previously pleasure was pursued. A desire for death replaces a desire for life. Perceptions are disorganized and include hallucinations and delusions. The sense of time is inverted. There is self-scorn, self hatred, and self-destruction. A sense of ontological guilt that "I ought not to exist" is characteristic.

That all this had its root in the first trimester was clearly affirmed by Lake. The origins of affliction, he wrote, that are responsible for "many of the characteristic and severely self-damaging features of schizoid affliction . . . must be firmly placed in the first trimester, within three or so months of conception" (Lake, 1981g, 23). A horribly bad umbilical flood has invaded the fetus, "overrunning all defensive barriers, pene-trating the whole body" (Lake, 1981d, C42). Thus, all of the body becomes loathsome to the person, and the ego splits itself off from what is now considered revolting. The "good" takes refuge in the head, or in extreme cases, in a disembodied "spirit". There is a basic awareness of "to be me is to be bad."

This experience of dread and the "abyss" is split-off from consciousness and deeply repressed. "A great fear and hatred of this weak, hurt, wretched, humiliated, annihilated, disintegrated self and spirit, keeps it most rigorously repressed and defended against as 'not-me'" (Lake, 1964, chart S.a.). Instead of the compulsive attachment of the hysteric, there is compulsive detachment, distrust and introversion. There is a strenuous avoidance of commitment and intimacy coupled with a clinging to autonomy. Emotional flatness, spiritual poverty, and overintellectualization are the result. Contempt for others hides envy and jealousy. Sexual expression is often fetishistic and impersonal.

Since there has been no sense of inculcated "being" and consequently no sense of "well-being" at the input phases, the schizoid sufferer has nothing to expend in the "output" phases. Unlike the hysteric who looks for "being" and "well-being" from others outside himself, the schizoid had no "being" and gains sustenance ("well-being") from ideas. There is no essence of integrated self-hood and thus no self-identity. Consequently, the "status" and "achievement " of the schizoid are not characterized by giving, but by negativity.

While the hystero-schizoid and anxiety depressive reactions result from a loss of "being", the depressive and paranoid reactions are the outcomes of a blockage, constriction or diminution of "well-being". Thus, basic "being" is not the issue and is indeed assumed. What is at risk are the ongoing resources that allow for continued growth and conveyance of an inflow of affirmation, love, kindness resulting in "good spirits, courage and personal vitality" (Lake, 1964, 133).

The Paranoid Reaction

When the fetal reaction to deprivation of sustenance is passive, the paranoid personality reaction results as a defense against the primal loss of "well-being". "Being-itself" is secure and thus the integration of ego is not threatened. Rather, the root experience of the paranoid is the gradual loss of a sustaining supply in relation to his own increasing needs for physical and emotional sustenance. When this occurs in the first trimester, and Lake was insistent that it did, the umbilicus and placenta gradually shut down their flow of supplies. The fetus has the sense of having it's rights violated and of being denied, with the attendant feelings of worthlessness, humiliation, helpless, inferiority. She feels undervalued and has an extremely low sense of self-esteem.

These feelings are eventually split-off, denied and repressed with reaction patterns to maintain the repression taking hold. The main line of defense is usually projection, in which the paranoid unwittingly attributes to others her own denied desires and faults. Even though she projects an air of sufficiency and confidence, sometimes by belittling others, defensiveness, suspiciousness, argumentivity and hypersensitivity to criticism remain. Because her "rights" were previously violated, she is determined to exercise these rights. Since self-esteem ("status") is constantly being established, she is constantly and vigilantly on the lookout for possible detractors. Thus, she never enjoys "status" because it is constantly in flux, always awaiting the next indication that it does indeed exist. Her achievements are trumpeted and failures are explained away as someone else's fault. She is constantly trying to prove her point and prove herself to the world. Thus, the "output" of her "achievement" is always in the service, not of others, but of proving her "status".

The Depressive Reaction

Just as an active response of a constitutionally stronger fetus lead to depression when the sources of "being" are restricted, so an active response to the constriction of "well-being" also results in depression. Whereas the first also includes anxiety because the very "being" of the organism is threatened, the depression or "accidie" resulting from the blockage of "well-being" does not have the dimension of anxiety to it. The fetus reacts to this cutoff of supplies with rage, bitterness, sullenness and resentment. There is "ample experience of unmet need, of rage at the injustice of it" (Lake, 1981g, 101). Behind the secondary process of rage is the primary cause, "the situation of basic needs which the mother could not or did not meet." This rage is restrained, sometimes out of fear and sometimes out of sympathy for the mother who seems not to have any supplies to give.

In the normal mother-fetus relationship the umbilical exchange is mutual (i.e. nutrients from mother exchanged for waste from fetus) is undeniable. However, the exchange of supplies between mother and fetus is most often perceived to be unidirectional. It is the fetus, because of its relative lack of strength, that is usually supplied and/or "invaded" by the mother's "affect flow" and not vice versa.

However, the existence of the umbilicus provides for the mechanism allowing a reversed flow to occur, and indeed, this does occur. Lake states that a reaction at times arises where the "foetus feels a need to give to this poor, weak mother. Well aware that it has little to give because little has been received, none the less there can be a fateful sense that 'it is my role to keep her alive'" (Lake, 1978c, 20). Thus, when a constitutionally strong fetus receives an ambivalent or clearly negative affect flow from a weak, inadequate mother, the "fetal therapist" form of depression results. The fetus accepts the burden of doing everything possible to prevent and palliate the mother's stress and resultant distress. This necessitates a denial of and refusal to meet one's own needs.

This often results in a life-long pattern of a reversed flow of love and caring, from child to parent. At the root of this behavior, even involving adult children with their parents, is the "valiant attempt to get a small modicum of maternal tenderness" (Lake, 1978c, 20). Also recapitulated into adult life is a denial of and refusal to meet one's own needs. In "dynamic cycle" parlance, there is no input, and thus there tends to be no output. Since the "input" sense of "being" is tenuous and the input sense of "well-being" is almost nonexistent, the "output" phases of status and achievement are meager.

The Psychosomatic Reaction

Whereas the "fetal therapist" response pattern results from a dysfunctional reversed flow of fetal-maternal exchange, another common "wound management" coping pattern results from a mixed affect flow from mother to fetus. The "good" of the needed nutrients of "being" and "well-being" are mixed in with the "bad" of the "foetus being 'marinated' in his mother's miseries" (Lake, 1981g, 141). In order to get the "good", the "bad" must also be accepted "with the corollary that the 'badness' must not be fired back at the placenta/mother via the excretory umbilical arteries, but 'loaded up' in the foetus' own body structures" (Lake, 1982b, 21). Thus the invasive "badness" of both the experiences themselves and the repressed memories that follow is dealt with in one of two ways. The first and most common involves the dis-placement and containment within the fetal organism (Lake, 1981e, wll). This is done either by displacement into an emotional state such as depression or paranoia, or by displacement in or on a body part. The second mode of dealing with the "badness" involves a symbolic dis-placement onto some representative "image".

When a displacement occurs onto or into a part of the body, then psychosomatic symptomology results. In Lake's 1969 survey of clients who had experienced an LSD-assisted abreaction of pre- or peri-natal events, 34 out of 57 reported some type of psychosomatic affliction. Lake saw the fact that none of these reported a worse condition as a result of the experience and 16 reported an improvement as an indication of the connection between their present complaints and the early genesis of them.

According to Lake, somatic displacement of early emotional wounds accounts for much of the presenting complaints of "sickness." Depending upon which constituent segment of the body is the "diatheses," and thus which is displaced upon, different somatic "diseases" (Lake, 1981d, C41-42, C59-60; Lake, 1981e, w11; Lake, 1981g, 30-37) or outcomes result.

Displacement onto the head, face, or scalp, which is usually the last refuge of the "good" as it is being invaded by the "bad", results in flitting or persistent headaches, migraines, facial tics, and perhaps Sydenham's chorea and Tourette's syndrome. Specific naso-pharyngeal displacement results in a chronic running nose and a susceptibility to catching colds. Displacement into the mouth effects oral tension, a clenched jaw, and a compulsive biting the skin of the mouth whereas tightness in the throat follows from displacement into the throat. Transfer of the "badness" to the eyes results in conjunctivitis, or either "shame-faced" aversion of eye contact or visual (i.e. "if looks could kill") daggers.

When the "badness" is shifted onto respiratory tract and lungs, the bronchial musculature, usually used to "expel" the bad, now can also paradoxically "contain" it. Coughing, hawking, spitting, along with a general noisy and angry demeanor result. Cystic Fibrosis, wherein there is an attempt to expel the mucus without the fluid to do it, is re-presentative. Likewise, bronchitis, asthma, hay-fever and myriad other allergies result due to an hypersensitivity to various "foreign" environmental substances which can "enter and cause harm" and are thus symbolic of the invasive entering and harming of the "foreign" flood of maternal affect.

Transference of the "badness" to the musculo-skeletal components of the body results in chronic back pain, aching muscles and joints, cramps and stiffness, local swelling of hands, feet, legs, ankles, and arms. Nail-biting, lumbago and arthritis, as well as the more specific possibilities of sero-positive Rheumatoid Arthritis, Sjogren's disease, and carcino-embryonic antigen (CEA) follow displacement into the feet, knees, ankles, wrists, hands, and fingers.

Hypertension and stroke, atopic eczema, anal and genital paroxysmal itching, urticaria and localized dermatitis, are the outcome of displacement onto the heart and skin respectively. Nausea, vomiting, dyspepsia, flatulence, bloating, anorexia nervosa, diarrhea, mucous and ulcerative colitis, colic, peptic ulcers, diverticulitis, hypochondriasis and constipation all derive from alimentary tract displacement. "The feeling of having a bladder or accumulations of badness somewhere underneath the sternum . . . [such that] it feels to be . . . filthy, black, bad, heavy, lumpy, gooey, brown, green, bitter" (Lake, 1981e, w11) is what Lake terms "substernal displacement". Slightly farther down in the body are the bladder, genitals and genito-urinary tract. Displacement here produces the irritable bladder syndrome, frequent and urgent micturition, enuresis, pre-menstrual tension, dysmenorrhea, amenorrhea, vaginitis, sexual frigidity and impotence.

According to Lake, all of these result from displacement of experiences and memories resulting from an invasive negative or strongly negative affect flow from mother to fetus. Lake affirmed that this type of displacement results because of a specific "diatheses," and thus in a specifically psychosomatic outcome. When the "diathesis" is mental or emotional, then the more classic psychiatric categories result.

This is the M-FDS in its basic paradigmatic format. Lake utilizes it in two ways; first as a physiological and psychological model and then as a theological one.

Chapter Two

The Evidence for a Scientific Paradigm

Before the "revolutionary implications" of Lake's assertions can be seriously considered, the underlying validity of the "paradigm" itself must be verified. Is there evidence to corroborate the central assertions of the M-FDS so as to allow it to be generally accepted as a system of ideas giving definition to the problems and methodology of psychodynamics? The methodology required to answer this question first necessitates some kind of central definition of what is being affirmed so that it can be accepted or rejected based upon the evidence. Thus stated, the M-FDS has been defined in the following manner: "the behavioral reactions of a pregnant mother affect her fetus in ways that contribute to its perceptions of itself and of its environment in the womb; and these perceptions persist into adult life" (Moss, 1987, 204). This definition, however, is somewhat inadequate for our purposes because fetal perceptions of the self and the environment are incapable of being ascertained. That adult perceptions of the self and the environment are based somewhat on the fetal experience may be true, but again, it is impossible to ascertain their origin. Thus, for the purposes of this endeavor, the general definition of a maternal-fetal syndrome is as follows: "the fetal environment as mediated by the mother affects fetal movement, sensation, memory, learning, affect, and behavior."

At its most basic level, the M-FDS is simply affirming that the environment of the pre-born baby influences his or her psychological development in both the immediate and long-term senses. That this is assumed to be true of postnatal existence, even of infants, is generally accepted. Wide-ranging research studies have clearly shown the effect of both positive and negative environmental influences on subsequent perception and behavior.

If the same is to be said regarding prenatal experience, as Lake affirms, then the same or similar mechanisms which allow such influences to occur postnatally must be shown to exist prenatally. What allows environmental influence postnatally is the ability of an organism to apprehend the environment, this through the senses and nervous system. Thus, the same applies prenatally. Is the brain and nervous system sufficiently developed to allow for neural transmission? Are the various specialized neural sense receptors capable of visual, tactile, auditory, gustatory, and olfactory sensation? Is the nervous system sophisticated enough to allow for intermodal fluency between the senses, for cognition, memory, learning, habituation, imitation, conditioning, and emotions? Further, can the pre-born not only apprehend the environment, but also signify themselves to the environment through crying, motor movement, and facial expressions? If the above questions can be substantially confirmed by the empirical evidence, then it could be affirmed that the structure and mechnsms which would allow for the M-FDS to exist are indeed present.

The Psychological Environment Prior to Lake

The growing elaboration and sophistication of embryology and fetology has laid the groundwork for a return to substantial speculation about the psychological sophistication of the prenate. Early thinkers in both the East (i.e. Susruta and Caraka) and the West (i.e. Hippocrates, Aristotle, Galen) had commented and theorized substantially on fetal capabilities and had come to a wide variety of conclusions.

Certainly critical to the debate in the modern period has been the theoretical speculations of Sigmund Freud. His impact upon the sub-sequent psychodynamic understanding of fetal life has been profound. Commenting on Freud's influence, deMause writes, "virtually all contemporary psychoanalytic theory denies the possibility of mental life before or during birth. The newborn is believed to be without memory, ego, objects, or mental structure" (deMause, 1982, 247).

But it can be affirmed that whether he intended to or not, Freud "opened the door" (Lake, 1976b, S5) to the psychodynamics of intra-uterine life. For instance, even though Freud wrote in *Inhibitions, Symptoms and Anxiety* that "birth still has no psychic content" and that "birth is not experienced subjectively as a separation from the mother since the foetus, being a completely narcissistic creature, is totally unaware of her existence as an object" (Freud, 1936, 130), in the same work Freud also referred to birth as the "earliest anxiety of all" and the "primal anxiety" (Freud, 1936, 137). Lake even quotes Freud as writing that "there is much more continuity between intra-uterine life and the earliest infancy the impressive caesura of the act of birth allows us to believe" (Lake, 1976b, S5). Phyllis Greenacre describes Freud's position:

> Even though he doubts the importance of the individual birth experience in influencing the quantum of the anxiety response, largely because the birth experience is without psychological meaning; at the same time, nevertheless, he emphasizes the continuity of the intrauterine and the postnatal life. (Greenacre, 1952, 52).

Freud's schizophrenic attitude toward birth is perhaps illustrated by his initial embrace of Otto Rank's book *The Trauma of Birth* as "the most important progress since the discovery of psychoanalysis" (Lake, 1981g, 3). However, he apparently turned against Rank (Taft, 1958) at the behest of Abraham, Jones and some of the others of his inner group who warned that Rank's hypotheses would eclipse Freud's work. Lake writes that these persons "inflamed his [Freud's] fear 'lest the whole of his life's work be dissolved by the importance attached to the trauma of birth'" (Lake, 1981g, 3). Later, in writing to Abraham, Freud alluded that he was "getting further and further away from birth trauma. I believe it will 'fall flat' if one doesn't criticize it too sharply, and then Rank, who I valued for his gifts and the great services he has rendered, will have learned a useful lesson" (Fodor, 1971).

Otto Rank began his study of the possible effect of birth experiences in 1904, finally publishing *The Trauma of Birth* in 1923. This work, which clearly laid the groundwork for an understanding of the effect of pre-natal events on subsequent functioning, elaborated Rank's contention that not only was birth the first experienced anxiety, but that it was the prime source material for all the neurotic and character disorders of adulthood.

It was the "original emotional shock underlying all personality dysfunction." Rank wrote that "we believe that we have discovered in the trauma of birth the primal trauma," and that "we are led to recognize in the birth trauma the ultimate biological basis of the psychical." He continued: "We have recognized the neuroses in all their manifold forms as reproductions of, and reactions to, the birth trauma" (Rank, 1952, xiii).

What makes Rank important for an understanding of prenatal "psychology" are his allusions to the significance of the prenatal: "All symptoms ultimately relate to this "primal fixation" and the place of fixation is "in the maternal body" and in peri-natal experiences" (Rank, 1952).

Building on Rank's work, Donald W. Winnicott, a British pediatrician and psychoanalyst, continued to push the "primal" influence back earlier, alluding more strongly to the importance of pre-natal life. Although, like Rank, his primary emphasis was still on birth as an event "etched on the memory" that manifested itself in the stresses of later life, he also alludes strongly to the possible effect of the prenatal period, extending back as far as conception, upon the developing psyche. He writes:

> There is certainly before birth the beginning of an emotional development, and it is likely that there is before birth a capacity for false and unhealthy forward movement in emotional development (Winnicott in Lake, 1987, 169).

An American contemporary of Winnicott's was Phyllis Greenacre, who, in her book *Trauma, Growth, and Personality* also affirms the potential impact of the prenatal environment, but subsequently seems to back away from the implications. She writes "The fetus moves, kicks, turns around, reacts to some external stimuli by increased motion" (Greenacre, 1952, 54). Indeed, research showing the increase of fetal heart rate and fetal movements to such stimuli as loud noises and maternal nervousness would indicate that these are signs of anxiety, as they would be in the child or adult. While Greenacre retreats from any kind of assertion of a distinctly "fetal anxiety", she did affirm that anxiety-like responses in the fetus give rise to a "predisposition to anxiety" in the child and adult. She summarizes her own ambivalence about birth and pre-birth anxiety when she wrote that "perhaps the struggle of birth is at once too terrifying and too inspiring for us to regard it readily with scientific dispassion" (Greenacre, 1945, 40).

While Freud, Rank, Winnicott, Greenacre and others all made allusions to the possible importance of the prenatal, it is in the work of Nandor Fodor and Francis Mott, that the prenatal is particularly emphasized. It is

Fodor's work *The Search for the Beloved: A Clinical Investigation of the Trauma of Birth and Pre-Natal Conditioning*, published in 1949, that really marks the beginning of the modern "prenatal psychology" movement. As is evident in the subtitle, the first part of the book was de-voted to birth trauma, while the second part is devoted to the "Traumata of the Unborn." Mott's work was primarily based upon the analysis of various case histories, particularly utilizing dreams. He differentiates his work from Rank's: "Otto Rank made the first attempt to biologize psychoanalysis. His approach was philosophical; mine is clinical and independent of his claims" (Fodor, 1949, v).

All of the major components of Lake's M-FDS can be delineated in Fodor's work. Lake saw his research as confirming and building upon Fodor's, and others, such as Mott's and Grof's work. Fodor affirmed, as Lake later did, the importance of birth for later development, the therapeutic effect of re-experiencing birth and prenatal life, the specific problems raised by particular maternal habits and behavior, particularly maternal rejection of the fetus and attempted abortion. Fodor writes:

> The life of the unborn is not necessarily one of unbroken bliss. The un-born child is dependent on his mother's blood-stream for oxygen, for food, and for the elimination of its waste products. There are many maternal afflictions that affect and perhaps weaken the child before birth. Many children seem to start post-natal life with a handicap (Fodor, 1949, 396).

Fodor likewise affirms, as did Lake, that the prenatal period is more crucial than birth for subsequent psychological functioning. He writes:

> The release of the trauma of birth is the introductory phase of the integration of pre-natal trauma. The more vital phase concerns the shocks suffered prior to birth. In order to release these shocks, the mind must take cognizance of their existence and nature (Fodor, 1949, 400).

Finally, Lake's affirmation of the primacy of the first trimester can also be found in Fodor's work. He approvingly cites Sadger:

> I believe first of all that which all my patients assert, that the embryo already feels plainly whether its mother loves it or not, whether she gives it much love, little love, or none at all, in many instances in fact in place of love sheer hate (Sadger, 1941, 336).

Francis Mott is as explicit in his emphasis upon intrauterine life as Fodor is. His fundamental principle was that "every psychological feeling derives from an older physical feeling." For instance, the very basic psychological sense of "I" is originally derived from the physical sensation of contact between the fetal skin and its environment (Ridgeway, 1987, 64). Thus, the bi-directional flow of blood from mother to fetus as mediated by the placenta and the umbilical cord, gives rise to the physical "feelings" of aggression, submission, emptiness, fullness, giving and taking that is the basis for subsequent psychological "feelings". Mott utilized the term "umbilical affect" to designate this exchange, defining it as the "feeling state of the fetus as brought about by blood reaching him through the umbilical vein" (Mott in Moss, 1987, 203). As Mott envisaged it, the umbilical vein not only conveys nutritive resources and as such could be experienced as a "life-giving flow, bringing . . . renewal and restoration" but could also "be the bearer of an aggressive thrust of bad feelings into the foetus if the mother herself was distressed and 'feeling bad.'" If the mother felt emotionally unsupported, then "this feeling of deficiency, lack of recognition and the failure of looked-for support, would be just a specifically felt by the fetus. It became distressed by the failure of its immediate environment to provide the expected acceptance and sustenance, not so much at the level of metabolic input . . . . but to nourish the earliest beginnings of the person in relationship" (Mott in Lake, 1976b, S1).

It was in this general milieu that Lake formulated his own thinking with regard to birth and subsequently, prenatal life. Some of his own work was contemporaneous with others, especially Grof's (described in chapter 1) and Mott's. It is fair to say that the views of Lake and all those who preceded him in this area have never been widely affirmed or accepted.

What follows is substantial and yet nonexhaustive review of some of the present available empirical data that appears to lend support to Lake's M-FDS. As with neonatal and postnatal physiological and psychological processes, those of the prenatal can be organized into several categories, including movement, sensation, learning, memory, affect, dreaming, and the much more elusive and difficult-to-determine categories of personality and consciousness.

Morphological and Psychological Evidence for Lake's M-FDS

Embryonic Development

From the moment of conception through the end of the embryonic period, numerous important aspects of development are unfolding and laying the foundation for all later developmental occurrences. The embryonic period typically concludes at the end of the eighth week and the fetal period begins. This division is somewhat arbitrary because there is no clearly distinct delineation in the activity or development of the emerging child to allow for the division. The same is true with the somewhat arbitrary notions of trimesters, each generally defined as encompassing approximately three months. While Moss states that traditionally the first was a period of development, the second of growth with the third understood to be a period when life outside the womb is possible, this too is somewhat misleading. Growth and development are taking place throughout all three "trimesters" and infants as young as 5 months, clearly within the second trimester, have survived outside the womb (Chamberlain, 1983, 2).

The mere fact that at the conclusion of the embryonic period most of the major systems of the brain and body are present which would be necessary for some kind of rudimentary embryonic "consciousness" is not synonymous with their function. As Chamberlain writes:

> It is difficult to identify the precise function of the 'separate' parts [of the brain] since parts are closely interrelated and under conditions not fully understood take over for each other (Chamberlain, 1983, 4).

Lake's claim that the "interrelated functioning" of the morphological structure during the embryological period allows for a prenatal "psychology" of sorts will be evaluated in the final chapter. However, it is important to note that Lake's emphasis and use of the terminology of "first trimester" in practice tended to correspond with the embryonic period. For instance, Moss writes that "he tended to stop the first trimester 'fantasy journey' at about the stage when umbilical circulation was clearly established. Strictly speaking, this is probably a good deal before the end of the third month" (Moss, 1990, 4:6).

Neurological Development

The morphological development of the embryonic central nervous system is extremely complex. This complexity continues to multiply during the fetal period concomitant with an ever-increasing complexity in fetal behavior (Richmond & Herzog, 1979). Of particularly significant importance is the development of the cerebral cortex, specifically the differentiation of the dendrites and the dendrite spines since "they provide a major portion of membrane surface for integration of synaptic inputs from a variety of sources" (Chamberlain, 1983, 4). Research has identified the maturational period of these dendrites between the 20th and 28th week after fertilization (Purpura, 1975a). Thus, according to Purpura (1979), since the requisite nerve cell circuitry is morphologically present to allow for "consciousness and self-awareness", he dates the beginning of "brain life" to the period immediately following; namely 28-32 weeks. Chamberlain concurs:

> Knowledge of the morphogenesis of these structures by 32 weeks in utero indicates a readiness of the nervous system to transmit signals back and forth through a complex mass of unnumbered cells, signals which miraculously arrive at all the right muscles, glands and organs. How these electro-chemical signals are ultimately transformed into meaningful messages, ideas, decisions, or memories cannot be explained in physical terms alone. Explanations are necessarily metaphorical or metaphysical (Chamberlain, 1983, 4).

Others have identified the presence of viable synapses above and below the corticle plate as early as the 8th week and within the plate itself by the 23rd week (Molliver et al, 1973). EEG measurements indicate neural response in the cortical areas of the brain pertaining to the auditory, visual and tactile systems from stimulation of the peripheral organs to be functioning no later than 32 weeks (Vaughn, 1975).

With the advance of technology, babies born as early as 28 weeks have survived outside the womb, presenting opportunities for "external" observation of the 28th through the 40th weeks of gestation. Studies that have examined the systematic development of fetal growth have found that there tends to be great similarity of development between babies regardless of whether they are in or outside the womb (Gesell, 1945). Further, there seems to be a regular advance in detectable development every 4 weeks in terms of "strength of responses, the degree of muscle tone and endurance, more regular waking and sleeping patterns and a more definite cry" (Chamberlain, 1983, 5). EEG results have confirmed this similarity. There is an on-going pattern throughout the fetal period of increasing organization, ever-steadier activity, the development of more regular sleep-wake cycles, and greater synchrony within and between hemispheres.

Movement

One of the first indications of a functioning nervous system is the response of movement, which seems to begin at around 8 weeks (Liley, 1991). The movements of 8-20 week-old fetuses obtained by hysterectomies have been described as slow and "wormlike" (Goodlin, 1979). Tactile stimulation seems to elicit more rapid and forceful movement than occurred spontaneously. An early study by Preyer (1885) is described by Goodlin:

> In 1885, Preyer recorded movements of the extrauterine human fetuses, apparently from therapeutic abortions. He concluded that spontaneous fetal movements could occur before they are felt by the gravida, that fetal movements continued for a considerable time even when the fetus was without oxygen supply, that fetal movements were affected by temperature, that they could be elicited by stimulus (such as touching with a feather), and that these fetal movements were apparently independent of the mother's condition" (Goodlin, 1979, 3).

While some studies have found "rolling movements" as early as 6 weeks (Goodlin, 1979), others have found that up until the middle of the 7th week, embryos appear incapable of movement (Hooker, 1952; Humphrey, 1978). The first reflex movement, contralateral (moving away) head flexion, appears at 7.5 weeks with a second, ipsilateral (moving toward) head flexion coupled with mouth opening appearing a week later). Hooker writes that numerous studies, beginning around 1920, looking at movement in 7-8 week old embryos did find some movement among some embryos of this age but ran into several problems, among them the "progressive anoxic condition of the embryo, maternal anesthesia, and a group of physical factors" (Hooker, 1952, 57). He began his studies in 1932 and attempted to deal with these problems in the following manner:

> This team worked with over 140 human embryos and fetuses of various ages obtained by cesarean delivery in cases where therapeutic abortion was deemed necessary by a committee of obstetricians. Within two minutes of

delivery they were placed in an isotonic fluid bath at body temperature and stroked gently with a fine hair to test for reactions (Chamberlain, 1983, 5).

While "spontaneously executed activity" (Hooker, 1952) is apparent at 8.5 weeks, others have found that by this time, not only is the fetus moving his head, trunk, and arms, but "he has already fashioned these movements into a primitive body language-- expressing his likes and dislikes with well-placed jerks and kicks" (Verny, 1981, 37). Using ultrasound technology, some have observed that as early as the end of the first trimester, regular exercise patterns have been observed including rolling, turning, leg kicks, flexing, and waving of arms" (Van Dongen & Goudie, 1980). Others have observed that fetal movement becomes sufficiently pronounced in the 10th or 11th week to allow for a change in the position of the fetal body (Goodlin, 1979). The fetus will change positions constantly in reaction to the intra-uterine environment. Propelling himself by means of his arms and legs is the mechanism by which he changes "ends" in the uterus while the mechanism by which he switches "sides" in the uterus is a little more complex. According to Liley, the fetus employs a "longitudinal spiral roll [which] at the midpoint of his turn has a 180-degree twist in his spine" (Liley, 1991, 193). He continues by describing the method of turning:

> He [the fetus] first extends his head and rotates it, next his shoulders rotate and finally his lumbar spine and legs-- in fact, he is using his long spinal reflexes. Insofar as this is the obvious way to turn over, there would be nothing remarkable about it except that according to textbooks of neonatal and infant locomotor function the baby does not roll over using his long spinal reflexes until 14-20 weeks of extra-uterine life. However, we have unequivocal films of the fetus using this mechanism at least as early as 26 weeks gestation, and it is apparent that the reason we do not see this behavior in the neonate is not that he lacks the neural coordination but that a trick which is simple in a state of neutral buoyancy becomes difficult under the newfound tyranny of gravity (Liley, 1991, 194).

By 15 weeks, 16 distinct movement patterns in pre-term infants that resemble those of post-term infants are clearly distinguishable (de Vries et al, 1982). Some studies of third trimester babies shows that they rarely go more than 10 minutes without some "gross motor activity including breathing spurts during REM sleep" (Roberts et al, 1980, 482).

As to whether movement itself can be considered significant psychologically to the embryo or fetus, various studies have certainly shown that such movement is very psychologically important for pregnant mothers. Perceived attachment to the developing fetus is greatly enhanced following the first sign of movement (Grace, 1989; Heidrich & Cranley, 1989). Further, numerous studies (Comparetti, 1981; 1986; Comparetti & Gidoni, 1967; 1976; Ianniruberto & Tajani, 1981; Valentin & Marsal, 1986; Van Woerden et al, 1989) have correlated fetal movement and lack of movement to other fetal variables. Accordingly, researchers have stated that "alternation of movement and immobility in the fetus is in itself an expression of an existing organization" (Gidoni et al, 1988, 349). Further, movement in utero has been correlated with later neonatal behavior (Ishikawa & Minamide, 1984).

The Tactile Sense

As noted above, movement is often in response to tactile stimulation, or the sense of "touch". This sense is really a combination of three different sensory capabilities; those of pressure, temperature and pain. All three develop simultaneously so that by the 32nd week, "tactile responsivity can be demonstrated for all parts of the fetal body" (Chamberlain, 1983, 5).

The position of the fetus in utero is often in response to the tactile environment within the womb. According to Liley, many changes in the environment provoke movement, including Braxton-Hicks contractions, maternal movements, and external palpation. The fetus will repeatedly and purposefully move to avoid a knuckle on the prominences or the "sustained pressure of a microphone or phonendoscope" (Liley, 1991, 194).

By the second month, the embryo will kick and jerk if poked at, and by the fourth month the stroking of the eyelids will result in squinting instead of a violent jerking movement; indeed stroking the lips results in sucking behavior (Verny, 1981). Tickling the scalp of the fetus at the surgical induction of labor will result in movement. Liley writes that "stroking the palm of the prolapsed arm elicits a grasp reflex, and to plantar stimulation the footling breech obliges with an upgoing toe" (Liley, 1991, 195). By the fifth or sixth month, the fetus is "as sensitive to touch as any one-year old" (Verny, 1981, 37).

In addition, the fetus will respond with "violent movement" to a needle puncture. Goodlin reports that during the performance of "hundred of amniocenteses" normal, healthy, near-term infants would invariably respond to "needle sticks" with movement and drastic fetal heart-rate changes. For some of these fetuses, he reported that prior to performing the amniocentesis, he recorded the fetal heart-rate up to five minutes. He writes "if we obviously stuck the fetus with the needle during the amniocentesis, we invariably found the FHR (fetal heart-rate) abruptly changed" (Goodlin, 1979, 193). This change was usually in the direction of acceleration, but on occasion, deceleration occurred, or as other researchers have discovered, "a sudden crash" to a silent pattern of non-movement. In one study (Neldam and Peterson, 1980), six of seven of these "silent" fetuses did not move for two minutes. Goodlin reports that during amniocenteses where there was no feel of puncture by the fetus, there was no observable change in FHR, suggesting to him that the fetal responses to the needle were those of pain.

Interestingly, many have denied the sensation of pain in the fetus based upon an incomplete understanding of the process of myelinization of the neurons in the central nervous system. DeMause (1987) has pointed out that this has occurred because of an uncritical acceptance of a faulty study by J.R. Langeworthy in 1933 titled "Development of Behavior Patterns and Myelinization of the Nervous System in the Human Fetus and Infant." This study made the assertion that "incomplete myelinization of sensory tracts" resulted in the inability of the fetus to receive neural messages from it's specialized sense receptors.

As has clearly been shown in numerous subsequent studies (i.e. Anand & Hickey, 1987; 1988), this is untrue. According to Larrouche (1966), the cranial nerve roots are myelinated very early, preceded only by myelinization in the spinal cord at about the 22nd week after conception. Almost concomitant with cranial myelinization is that in the medulla and pons, followed quickly by the cerebellum and the cerebral hemispheres (Larrouche, 1962). While full myelinization, which occurs only after birth, does increase the rapidity of conduction, it is not essential for sensory functioning. Well-organized neural activity and sense receptivity, including pain, occurs long before the nerve fibers are completely myelinated (Bekoff & Fox, 1972). As Windle has written:

> In a general way the functional development and acquisition of myelin by certain fiber tracts are related. Nevertheless much well-organized activity of animal fetuses is present before there is any myelin. There are no myelin sheathe on fibers of the peripheral nerves, spinal cord, or brain of cat fetuses prior to the last third of prenatal life, but many coordinated movements can be elicited reflexively before the middle of gestation (Windle, 1979, 71).

Using multiple fetal x-ray films, Liley described the process of birth and particularly contraction as one of "frantic" flailing fetal movement, with the arms and legs being thrown about and what appeared to be an active resistance to each contraction. He observed that this behavior is characteristic of the reaction of a post-birth human being to severe pain:

> If one attempts to reproduce in the neonate by manual contraction a mere fraction of the cranial deformation that may occur in the course of a single contraction the baby protests violently. And yet, all that has been written by poets and lyricists about cries of newborn babies would suggest that newborn babies cried for fun or *joie de vivre*-- which they never do afterwards-- and in all the discussions that have ever taken place on pain relief in childbirth only maternal pain has been considered (Liley, 1991, 196).

Further, studies have found that in the early stages of labor, healthy in utero fetuses will often respond with FHR changes or movement of some kind in response to various noises and sounds produced outside the intra-uterine environment. But as the labor continues, this reaction will cease. While some have described this as an instance of fetal habituation, others state that it is rather a response to the distraction of the overwhelming fetal pain associated with labor (Goodlin, 1979). Liley writes that the first sleep of neonates after birth is "more profound than any subsequent sleep" based on the strength of the stimuli needed to awake them, thus perhaps testifying to the ordeal that labor has indeed represented.

Normally, the fetus will not experience temperature less than his mother's because he lacks a truly "external" surface. In fact, the placenta acts as a heat exchanger which keeps the fetal temperature a constant .5 to 1.5 degrees Celsius above the mother's. Should she run a temperature, so will the fetus within her. However, experimental studies have shown that the fetus will respond to temperature changes. Goodlin reports that the fetus will respond to cold saline flushed into the amniotic space at 18-20 weeks with fetal heart rate changes and movement. He concludes that these responses reflect intact temperature receptors in the skin. The fetus does not, however, have the sensation of "wetness" due to her constant and total immersion in the amniotic fluid.

Crying

Audible fetal crying is rare because it requires the presence of air in the fetal trachea. Called *vagitus uterinus*, it most often occurs after an air amniogram. Goodlin writes:

> There is no way to prove the point, but presumably the normal fetus is frequently "crying in utero", but only the presence of air within the uterus makes it obvious. . . . It therefore seems reasonable to assume that fetuses are often as uncomfortable (enough to cry) "in utero" as "extra-utero" (Goodlin, 1979, 193).

Chamberlain notes that various researchers have recorded the cries of abortuses from 21-24 weeks weighing 650-930 grams (Chamberlain, 1988). One study discovered that early clamping of the umbilical cord resulted in much greater crying than late-clamping, "suggesting that babies were experiencing something that they did not like" (Greenberg et al, 1967, 64). In addition, spectrographic studies of the cry response after birth indicate meaningful expression of various pain states, including hunger, pain, loneliness or discomfort which are clearly distinguishable from each and correlatable to the neonatal state (Chamberlain, 1988).

The Vestibular Sense

Of the "senses" of the body, the vestibular apparatus appears first, at around 9.5 weeks (Chamberlain, 1988), with morphological maturity at 14 weeks (Goodlin, 1979). It is unknown how early the sense of balance is functioning, but Hooker has reported 25 weeks as the earliest "definite human vestibular response" (Hooker, 1952, 70). As early as 1927, Galebsky had shown that by birth the semicircular canals are functional to the extent that the neonate experiences any type of sudden movement, including rotatory, vertical and horizontal.

The Gustatory Sense

The "sense" of taste also appears quite early in the fetal period, with microscopic analysis of fetal tongues finding that taste "buds" are present at 8 weeks, morphologically mature by 12 weeks (Goodlin, 1979), with all the necessary components such as the pores and hair cells present by 14 weeks. Thus, researchers have concluded that the gustatory sense is functional by 15 weeks (Bradley & Stern, 1967). Since amniotic fluid begins entering the mouth at 9.5 weeks and the fetus begins swallowing at 12 weeks (Chamberlain, 1987b), it is likely that the fetus is tasting the glucose, fructose, citric, lactic, uric, fatty and pyruvic acids, amino-acids, phospholipids, creatinine, urea, polypeptides, proteins, salts, and other chemical agents in the amniotic fluid for up to 28 weeks prior to birth (Misretta & Bradley, 1977). Thus taste preferences at birth are related to the fetal experience with various tastes during the intra-uterine period.

The fetus drinks amniotic fluid regularly, reaching a rate of 15-40 ml. per hour during the third trimester. Research modifying the taste of amniotic fluid produces dramatic results. An early study done by de Snoo in 1937, found that the injection of saccharin increased the rate of fetal swallowing in 34-38 week fetuses. Liley confirms this, stating that the rate usually doubled. However, some conversely drank less. An almost total cessation of fetal drinking occurs with the injection of Lipidol, a "iodinated poppy seed oil which tastes foul to an adult or child and which causes a neonate to grimace and cry" (Liley, 1991, 196). The fetus digests the constituent components of the amniotic fluid and this caloric intake may reach 40 calories a day (Liley, 1991).

Swallowing, tongue and lip movements all originate between the 10th and 12th weeks followed by a gag reflex apparent in the 18th week. Sucking and puckering are present in the 22nd, with the possibility of audible crying occurring between the 21st and 23rd week. Fetal hiccups occur and are fairly common. Indeed, they can be induced by "irrigating the amniotic cavity with cold solutions" (Ridgeway, 1987, 74).

Not only is the fetus an experienced swallower by the time birth occurs, but in many cases it also has extensive sucking experience. Obstetric sonography and radiography has produced images of thumb-sucking as early as 9 weeks. The sucking of fingers and toes, which is a common occurrence in the fetal period, seems to be an early manifestation of the "rooting" reflex seen among neonates (Liley, 1991).

The Olfactory Sense

While no evidence exists which allows one to conclusively state that human fetuses smell, this is not all that surprising given the absence of air within the uterus. Without the airborne particles needed to stimulate the specialized receptors within the olfactory epithelium, smell is impossible. However, some animal studies have found evidence of olfactory function in utero (Petersen et al, 1983) and have connected odors with aversion conditioning (Smotherman, 1982).

Research done with neonates immediately following birth, however, clearly demonstrates that the sense of smell is present and functional at birth (Schaal, 1988). Research has shown behavior indicating "acceptance and satisfaction" to the odors of bananas, strawberries and vanilla while indicating "rejection" to the odors of rotten eggs and fish (Steiner, 1977; 1979). In a similar study, babies from 1-6 days old turned away from the smell of ammonia on either the left or right indicating the ability to spatially orient the source of the smell and react accordingly (Rieser et al, 1976).

Other researchers have demonstrated learning behavior related to the sense of smell. Studies have shown habituation and dishabituation to various smells (licorice, garlic, vinegar and alcohol) by neonates with the clear ability to distinguish between pairs of smells (Engen & Lipsitt, 1965; Engen et al, 1963). Newborns between 2 and 7 days can also distinguish between their mother's used breast pad and an unused one, and within several days distinguish between their mother's used pad and another woman's (Macfarlane, 1975). Breast-fed neonates also learn very quickly to discriminate their mother's underarm odor from that of other women (Cernoch & Porter, 1985).

The Auditory Sense

The morphological structures which would allow hearing to occur are present and functional in the fetus from 20 weeks on (Eisenberg, 1969). Due to the presence of fluid in both the middle and external ear, there has been some debate among researchers as to sound levels actually reaching the fetus. Research does indicate that hearing does indeed take place through bone conduction (Jensen & Flottorp, 1982), and thus is mostly at the higher-frequency levels (Tomatis, 1987). Regarding fetal hearing, Liley writes:

[The] averaging of foetal electroencephalographic records with repeated stimuli shows sound-evoked cortical potentials and demonstrates as does experience with deaf mothers that the foetus is responding directly. . . . Higher frequencies suffer less loss than low frequencies in transmission though tissues and fluid. Therefore, it is probable that with sound, unlike light, intrauterine spectra are similar to extrauterine. Further, it is worth noting that, unlike most foetal organs which start off in miniature, the structures of the inner ear are very nearly of adult size from initial development. This magnitude of course is necessary because cochlear spectral response obeys simple physical laws dependent on cochlear dimensions. If, for instance, the cochlear grew in proportion to the rest of the body, babies and children would hear in a different frequency range from adults and the communication gap between generations would be even wider than it is already (Liley, 1991, 199).

Other research has shown that from the 24th week on, fetal listening is quite constant (Wedenberg & Johansson, 1970). One study examining fetal movement of the eyes, arms, legs and head in response to sound found that responses first occurred between the 24th and 25th weeks, with consistent response following the 28th week (Birnholz & Benacerraf, 1983).

That this is true is not surprising given the noise level inside the uterus. Utilizing an intrauterine photocatheter, noise as loud as 85 decibels reaches the fetus (Liley, 1991), mostly from the mother's bodily internal activity. Less noisy, but still around 55 decibels are the intermittent sounds of voices, including the mother's and father's, and the more regular sounds of the flow of blood in synchrony with the mother's heartbeat. Research done by Salk (1970; 1973) and others (Chamberlain, 1987; Vitz, 1972) has shown that this early fetal hearing is "remembered" after birth. With reference to the constant sound of the mother's heartbeat in utero, Liley writes:

Does this long exposure explain why a baby is comforted by holding him to your chest or is lulled to sleep by the old wives' alarm clock, or the magnetic tape of a heartbeat? Does this experience explain why the tick of a grandfather clock in a quiet study or library can be a reassurance rather than a distraction, why people asked to set a metronome to a rate which "satisfies" them will usually chose a rate in the 50-90 beat per minute range -- and twins show a strong concordance in independent choice (Liley, 1991, 199-200)?

Using recordings of heartbeats at an "ideal" 72 per minute, Salk played these for a group of newborns while a similar "control" group heard no recordings. Even though both groups recorded the same amount of food intake, the experimental group gained more weight and gained it quicker. The difference in time spent crying was also significant with the control group spending 60% vs. 38% for the experimental group in time spent crying (Salk, 1973).

Any sudden noise in a room will cause a startle response in a fetus lined up under an image intensifier (Liley, 1991, 199). Further, when fetuses are tonally stimulated, their heart rates changes immediately and they begin to move (Bernard & Sontag, 1947; Lecanuet et al, 1986). Indeed, the simple observation of fetal reactions to tones of sound are quite predictive of deafness (Granier-Deferre et al, 1985). As the decibel level of sound increases, so does the activity and heart rate of the fetus (Bartoshuk, 1962). Using the fetal heart rate as a measure of response, 40 decibels in amplitude and 300 milliseconds in duration seems to be the parameters of auditory sensation (Eisenberg, 1965). Thus, many of the normal sounds of life are within the auditory scope of sensation and some studies seem to indicate a "remembering" of familiar noises, particularly their mother's voice (Ockleford et al, 1988).

Research has also shown that four and five month-old fetuses will respond differently to various types of music (Olds, 1986), quieting down to Mozart and Vivaldi and exhibiting "violent kicking and movement" to the music of Beethoven and Brahams and rock music of every type (Clements, 1977). Olds relates the account of a pregnant woman who attended a rock concert and came home with a broken rib due to the violent kicking of her fetus in response to the music (Olds, 1986). From about 25 weeks on, infants will "jump" in synchrony with the beat of an orchestral performance (Liley, 1991).

Using sophisticated technology (acoustic spectrograms and sonocineradiographic tracings), researchers (Truby, 1975; Truby & Lind, 1965) have found that fetuses in utero were, through hearing of some sort, receiving and "remembering" various maternal speech features. Interestingly, Truby found similar correspondences of the infant cry related to the speech rhythms and intonations of the mother in extremely premature neonates (900 grams). The fact that newborns of mute mothers do not cry at all, or if so, cried in a very peculiar manner, lead Truby to speculate that the reception of incoming maternal speech is necessary for the production of speech. Further, confirming other studies related to fetal crying, Truby noted that fetuses seemed to be practicing the neuro-muscular gestures of crying and vocalization.

Much research has also focused upon the ability of newborns to apprehend various sounds. Using brainstem electric response audiometry (BERA) it has been shown that normal neonates hear as well as adults (Schulman-Galambos & Galambos, 1979). While newborns seem to be especially responsive to sound frequencies within which the human voice falls, namely in the 500-900 Hertz range, they seem to prefer higher rather than lower frequency noises (Chamberlain, 1987). Newborns can distinguish the directions of sound sources (Wertheimer, 1961) and they consistently respond to various noises when awake and asleep as measured by brain-wave patterns (Goodman et al, 1964; Weitzman et al, 1965). They react to recorded infant cries by crying themselves (Simner, 1971; Sagi & Hoffman, 1976), but to their own recorded cry by ceasing to cry, perhaps indicating a recognition of their own familiar voice (Martin, 1981).

The Visual Sense

Vision is the most complex of the specialized senses and in some ways has proven to be the most difficult to determine as it relates to fetal visual acuity. Chamberlain notes that even up until the middle 1960's, pediatric textbooks were reporting that newborns were virtually blind (Chamberlain, 1987). Allik and Valsinger (1980) note humorously that infants seemed to develop new visual capabilities with each improvement in the ingenuity and methodology of the researchers. Although the womb is quite dark, light can and does pass through to the fetus (Weaver & Reppert, 1989). Research has shown that from the 16th week on, the photoreceptors in the fetal eye are sensitive to light (Prechtl & Nijhuis, 1983). Flashing light applied to the maternal abdominal wall produces fluctuations in the fetal heart rate (Smythe, 1965) and will cause a startle response often followed by a turning-away of the head (Verny, 1981).

Research done with premature infants has shown that the papillary reflex is present and functions variably given the intensity of light present. The same response that occurs in utero to flashing light occurs in these premature infants, including changes in heart rate and the rate of respiration, the eye-blink reflex and the startle response often accompanied by "the eye-neck reflex involving a backward thrust of the head" (Chamberlain, 1987, 38). The ability to both horizontally and vertically track movement has also been demonstrated in preterm babies between 31-32 weeks (Dubowtiz et al, 1980).

As with the auditory sense, much research has been done on the visual abilities of newborn infants. The first few months of post-natal life bring about great maturation in vision, but even at birth vision, movement and object perception are coordinated, cross-modal and meaningful (von Hofsten, 1983). At birth the neonate has a visual acuity of between 20/500 and 20/150 (Dayton et al, 1964), but he can still make out most of the features of his mothers face if she is 6-12 inches away and can spot the outline of a finger as far as 9 feet away (Verny, 1981). Infant acuity is more or less adultlike by 8 months (Norcia & Tyler, 1985). At birth neonates will track attractive moving targets with their eyes (Aslin, 1981; Dayton et al, 1964; Wolff & White, 1965). Likewise, enough rods and cones are present at birth to permit the perception of various colors and hues (Werner & Lipsitt, 1981; Dobson, 1976). Differential electro-encephalograph responses indicate neo-natal responses to different wave-lengths in the color spectrum (Chamberlain, 1987). Likewise, research has shown that infants as early as 1-2 weeks old indicate a rudimentary depth perception (Ball & Tronick, 1971; Bower, 1974; Bower et al, 1970a, 1970b).

Research done with neonates as young as 10 hours old also indicates various preferences in their visualization. They prefer patterns to plainly colored surfaces (Fantz, 1961; 1963; 1964; 1965) as well as showing preferences for curved vs. straight lines, chromatic vs. achromatic stimuli, three-dimensional vs. two dimensional objects, complex vs. simple patterns, and faces vs. non-faces (Cohen, 1979).

Thus, to summarize the fetal period regarding the senses, deMause writes this regarding the 3rd to the 6th month:

> The fetus . . . now floats peacefully, now kicks vigorously, turns somersaults, hiccoughs, sighs, urinates, swallows and breathes amniotic fluid and urine, sucks its thumb, fingers, toes, grabs its umbilicus, gets excited at sudden noises, calms down when the mother talks quietly, and gets rocked back to sleep as she walks about (deMause, 1982, 253).

By birth the summary of behavior is a little more elaborate, but not substantially. From the first minute after birth the newborn has the ability to suck, swallow, get rid of wastes, look, hear, taste, smell, turn the head, and signal for help (Caplan, 1973). As Chamberlain summarizes, "all sensory systems are functioning; many have been functioning for some time" (Chamberlain, 1983, 6).

Intermodal Fluency

As with so many of the other areas of fetology, the integrative capa-bilities of the fetus and the neonate between sense modalities have been grossly underestimated. Much of the research already cited assumes a certain level of intermodal fluency and coordination between the senses and motor movement. For instance, the fact that the auditory and visual systems work together with motor control when a neonate looks at the source of sound is evidence of these capabilities (Bower, 1974). The same can be said of the fetus, with motor movement coordinated with the tactile, visual, auditory, gustatory, and olfactory sense modes.

Research on premature and full-term newborns specifically illustrates the capabilities that exist at birth, thus allowing for the assumption that these capacities existed in some approximate form prior to birth.

Many of the findings of the research studies cited above require motor and sense coordination. For instance, the ability to both horizontally and vertically track movement with the coordination of the visual and motor spheres in preterm babies between 31-32 weeks (Dubowtiz et al, 1980) indicates this ability so that at birth, vision, movement and object perception are "co-ordinated, cross-modal and meaningful" (von Hofsten, 1983, 241-242).

Sander's research between newborns and their fathers, utilizing slow motion film, showed that motor synchrony with the visual sense mode took place to allow for anticipation of movement. As fathers moved their heads to look down at the neonate, the baby's head and eyes began to look up. This occurred repeatedly, as did the synchrony of the father's and infant's hands. When the father's right hand moved up, the neonates left hand moved up and grabbed the father's finger (Sander, 1981).

Using frame-by-frame microanalysis of the body movements of new-borns as they relate to adult speech patterns shows that infant movement became synchronized with adult speech, whether live or recorded, whether English or Chinese. Newborns did not react in the same way either to the broadcast of pure tones in a simulation of the rate of human speech or to a babble of disconnected vowel sounds (Condon, 1977; Condon & Sander, 1974). All 16 newborns in the study acted similarly, continuing to move through speeches of up to 125 words in length. Given the sophistication of this behavior, Condon has concluded that at birth the neonate has "an ability to steadily track auditory speech variations with almost as great an ability as that of an adult" (Condon, 1977, 167).

In an experiment using smooth and nubby pacifiers, researchers illustrated the transfer of information from one modality (tactile) to another (visual). A pacifier of the smooth or nubby variety was placed in the mouth of blindfolded newborns who were later able to identify by sight the type of pacifier which had been in their mouths (Meltzoff & Borton, 1979). Other research (Papousek, 1967; 1969; Papousek & Papousek, 1977) on newborn operant learning has connected head move-ment with the delivery of a squirt of milk if a bell sounded, thus linking the interoceptive, gustatory and auditory modalities. These researchers have concluded that learning and other such "conceptualizations" by their very nature are cross-modal and have stated that "in natural situations, stimulations effecting the newborn are almost by principle 'plurimodal', not only visual and auditory, but also tactual, thermal, olfactory, vestibular, and kinesthetic" (Papousek & Papousek, 1982, 369-370). Thus the qualities of "perception, learning, and memory are implied . . . [which infer] such integrative processes . . . [as] sensory awareness, information processing, the organization of adaptive, behavioral responses, cognition, affect and memory--an integration basic to all interactions with the environment" (Papousek & Papousek, 1987).

Specifically, Liley writes regarding the concept of sensory space:

> The subject has received some much-needed simplification by the evidence that the various sensory modalities all feed and share a common space, and that this space in fact is the effective motor space. . . . When does such a concept of space begin? Refined experiments on the neonate suggests that his sensory space is a little ball, that although he may receive visual and auditory signals from more distant sources he is not much interested in anything outside the sphere which extends just beyond his toes-- a restriction which very neatly corresponds to his recently vacated home (Liley, 1991, 200).

Beyond the evidence for the existence of the morphological "hardware" for movement and sense perception is the evidence that these capabilities allow for the "higher-level" processes of learning, habituation, conditioning, memory, affect, dreaming, cognition, and self-expression. And indeed, the existence of these capabilities in the fetal period allows for the inference of a still "higher-level" organization of them into what might tentatively be called "consciousness", or even a "psychology".

Learning

Having presented evidence that a variety of stimuli can be sensed by the fetus and can in turn be responded to, we have the rudiments of what might be termed learning. Since learning requires a rehearsal of what has been learned, we must also assume the rudiments of memory. Thus we could define learning as "a change in behavior that accrues over time as a result of experience" (Chamberlain, 1987, 23). Chamberlain continues and states that "learning and memory are linked, behavior on later occasions being influenced by what happened in the past".

Much research has focused upon the learning capabilities of neonates (Brackbill & Koltsova, 1967; Lipsitt, 1969; Lipsitt & Kaye, 1977; Lipsitt & Werner, 1981; Trowell, 1982). The newborn is described as having exceptional abilities for "differential responding, discrimination learning, and conditioning, often achieved in a matter of minutes" (Siqueland & Lipsitt, 1966, 357-58) after birth. These capabilities, by extension, can be inferred in some measure to prenates (Kolata, 1984), at least late-term fetuses. A typical example of very early learning is described by Liley:

> Babies who have had as few as 10 heel punctures for blood samples in the first 72 hours after birth, for weeks or months afterwards will promptly cry if you thoughtlessly grasp their foot (Liley, 1991, 201).

But, as Lipsitt has warned, learning and other abilities do not necessarily follow an ever-increasing straight line of accumulative skill. Rather, some abilities actually diminish rather than increase with time and he puts forth the thesis that it is "time for someone to present the thesis that the newborn human creature is about as competent a learning organism as he can become" (Lipsett, 1969, 228). The same can be said for the fetus at any given developmental stage, and indeed, some research has shown that prenatal intervention "enrichment" programs enhances the post-natal maturation process (Logan, 1987; 1988; 1991; van de Carr et al, 1988; van de Carr & Lehrer, 1986; 1988). Studies examining pre-natal "bonding" done through increased verbal communication from the mother to the fetus, found the positive effects of greater alertness and control at birth, earlier talking, independence and better concentration post-natally (Bowen, 1983; 1988; Jernerg, 1988; Lundington-Hoe & Galant, 1985; Thurman, 1988). Other research has indicated the positive effect of extra stimulation and attention on preterms even up to one year later (Bender, 1988; Field, 1985; Kramer & Pierpoint, 1976; Ray & Martinez, 1984; Rice, 1977; Trowel, 1982) and on full-term infants up to five years (Kennell & Klaus, 1983; Mustaph, 1988; Ringler et al, 1978; Scarr-Salapatek & Williams, 1973), including improved disposition, language ability and intelligence.

When considering fetal "learning" a distinction perhaps can and should be made between the observation in utero of "normal" fetal learning that might take place and attempts to condition the fetus and thus introduce "non-normal" learning into the intrauterine environment (Hepper, 1989). Perhaps the first study that attempted to demonstrate fetal "conditioning" or habituation was that of Peiper in 1925. His somewhat crude methodology involved emitting the sound of a car horn several feet from a mother's abdomen during a late-term pregnancy. He noted that this resulted in marked movement by the fetus which upon repetition gradually diminished. He concluded that the fetus thus habituated to the noise.

The study of habituation, defined as "a decrease in response due to the repeated presentation of a specific stimulation" (Thompson & Spenser, 1966) in newborns (Hinde, 1970; Kessen et al, 1970; Peek & Hertz, 1973) has found neonatal habituation in response to auditory (Bartoshuk, 1962), olfactory (Engen & Lipsitt, 1965; Engen et al, 1963), and visual (Friedman et al, 1970) stimuli. Studies utilizing habituation as an measure of fetal learning have proven to be the easiest to do because of their lack of any invasive procedures and thus the majority of "fetal learning" research involves habituation. Habituation of fetal heart rate (Goodlin & Lowe, 1974; Granier-Deferre et al, 1985) and body movements (Leader et al, 1982a; 1982b; Madison, 1986; Sontag & Wallace, 1934) in response to vibration and auditory tones has been clearly demonstrated in fetuses as early as 23 weeks after fertilization and seems to appear first in females (Leader et al, 1984). Another study found true fetal habituation in fetuses aged 28-37 weeks (Madison et al, 1986).

Since true habituation implies abilities for learning such as "a certain level of sensory competence, associative and memory capabilities" (Hepper, 1989, 291) then it stands that those fetuses deficient in these qualities should have deficits in habituation. Research on post-natal subjects suffering from schizophrenia (Gruzelier & Venebles, 1972), Down syndrome (Dustman & Callner, 1979) and hyperactivity (Hutt & Hutt, 1964) has shown this to be the case. Various studies have shown that future cognitive abilities and skills are predictable from habituation abilities during both the fetal period (Madison et al, 1986) and early infancy (Bornstein & Sigman, 1954). Other studies have shown this same predictability using prematurely born neonates (Rose & Wallace, 1985) and newborns whose mothers had received high doses of anesthetic during delivery (Bowes et al, 1970). Habituation deficits have also been shown in fetuses' suffering from brain disorders such as microencephalia and anencephalia (Leader et al, 1982).

An alternate methodology seeking to demonstrate fetal learning capabilities has used classical conditioning. Ray, in an early study from 1932, paired vibration as a conditioned stimulus with a loud bang as an unconditioned stimulus. While no data were reported by Ray as to the success of his experiment, the study was repeated by Spelt in 1948, who reported that after 15-20 pairings of the CS (conditioned stimulus) and

UCS (unconditioned stimulus), the CS alone elicited a response among 16 fetuses in the last two months of pregnancy.

More recently, similar studies have found comparable results. In a series of studies (Feijoo 1975; 1981), fetuses ages 30-37 weeks were classically conditioned with the repeated pairing of music as the UCS with the mother's relaxation as a CS. After 24 pairings, fetuses stopped all movement upon hearing the music alone. Feijoo found that this "learning" was retained following birth for fetuses that had been conditioned between 22 and 36 weeks. These newborns stopped crying, opened their eyes and showed fewer clonic movements upon hearing the same music as early as 6 minutes after birth.

Studies examining the ability to classically condition preterms and neonates are numerous. In 1928, an early study of aversive conditioning was done by Aldrich. After twelve pairings of a bell with pricking the sole of a neonate's foot with a pin, the bell alone produced a reflexive response. A more recent study (Polikanina, 1961) on 2-week old preterms pairing the smell of ammonia with a tone produced the same result. Perhaps taking their cue from Pavlov, numerous studies conditioning neonates related to heart rate, pupillary dilation and constriction, eye blinks and sucking as well as various studies examining fetal conditioning have been done by Russian researchers from the early 1920's (Brackbill & Koltsova, 1967).

A third category of "learning" studies has examined more naturally occurring events in the fetal environment. For instance, several studies have examined a variety of fetal responses in connection with voices, particularly the mother's voice. Using 3-day old newborns as subjects, various researchers have shown that neonates will alter their sucking response (either increasing or decreasing it) in order to hear their mother's voice (DeCasper & Fefer, 1980) but will not do the same to hear their father's voice (DeCasper & Prescott, 1984). Presumably, the constant prenatal auditory contact with the mother's voice vs. the father's voice gives rise to these preferences.

Seeking to test the memory of auditory learning from the prenatal period vs. mere familiarity with the mother's voice, researchers had pregnant women read a story repeatedly to their fetuses. Newborns were found to alternate their sucking responses to this same story read by another women but did not respond to a novel story read by the same woman (DeCasper & Spense, 1978). Thus, the conclusion was that "the foetus has learned and remembered something about the acoustic cues that specified the story read to them in the womb, and conclusively demonstrates prenatal learning of acoustic cues in the womb" (Hepper, 1989, 290).

One other study (Hepper, 1988) found that the newborn children of mothers who watched a particular soap opera during their pregnancy tended to stop crying and became alert when the theme song of the program was played. Infants of women who had not watched the same program showed no response to the music.

Numerous other studies have focused on the abilities of newborns to learn. For instance research has illustrated neonatal abilities to imitate behavior (Field et al, 1982; Meltzoff & Moore, 1977; 1983), to change sucking behavior in response to negative and positive pressure on the gums (Sameroff, 1972) in response to regular or blunt nipples (Brown, 1972), and in response to plain and sweet fluids (Kobre & Lipsitt, 1972). While these studies are quite simple, newborns have shown quick learning ability even in the mastery of complex and confusing sets of contingencies and even continue to learn when these contingencies are reversed (Siqueland & Lipsitt, 1966). Associated with these learning tasks, newborns have been found to have good memory associations, including procedural memory (Rovee-Collier, 1985; Tulving, 1985), semantic memory (Brody et al, 1984; Ungerer et al, 1978), episodic memory (Slater et al, 1982; Werner & Siqueland, 1978) and emotional or affect memory.

Emotion

Whether fetal or neonatal emotion exists in the same or similar manner of adults is impossible to determine due to its relatively inherent subjectivity. Research with both prenates and newborns, however, has shown clear evidence for at least the external behavior normally associated with internal emotion. For instance, crying, of both the intra-uterine and extra-uterine varieties, has been connected to the internal states of pain, anger and "rage".

As stated earlier, audible fetal crying is rare because it requires the presence of air in the fetal trachea. However, Ryder, after a comprehensive review of the literature from 1800-1941, reported 123 cases by 114 different observers (Ryder, 1943). More recent corroboration has presented three instances when fetal crying occurred in response to rupture of a membrane, manual displacement of the head or the attachment of electrodes for internal monitoring (Thiery et al, 1973). Audible crying has been reported from infants weighing as little as 650 grams (Peiper,

1963) and Humphrey (1978) cites instances of aborted fetuses from age 21 weeks audibly crying.

It has been argued that fetal crying is not indicative of any emotional state, but is undifferentiated. The same has been asserted with regard to neonatal crying. However, research has shown that crying of pre-term and full-term infants is very differentiated, even from each other (Friedman et al, 1982). Utilizing spectrography to produce "cry-prints", researchers have clearly distinguished various cries as communicating different emotional states (Lester & Boukydis, 1985; Truby & Lind, 1965) including between birth, pain and hunger (Wasz et al, 1968). Spectrographic distinctions have been found in the cries of infants who are had been prenatally and perinatally chronically stressed (Zeskind & Lester, 1978), who have chromosomal aberrations (Vuorenkoski et al, 1966), hyperbilirubinemia (Wasz-Hockert et al, 1971), and fetal mal-nutrition (Juntunen et al, 1978; Lester, 1976).

Other studies have also illustrated the range of communicatory cries possible with newborns. Using sonography and audio tape recordings be-fore, during and after circumcision, one study (Porter et al, 1986) demonstrated that certain distinctions in "cries" were definitely correlated to degrees of pain as measured by the relative degree of the invasiveness of the surgical procedure. Definite differences in pitch, temporal patterning and harmonic structure were discernible with various degrees of pain.

Another study (Izard & Read, 1986) with older infants aged 2-10 months was also able to sonographically distinguish various degrees of pleasure and displeasure. In this study, two month old infants showed emotional expression across the entire continuum of possible affect states, from extreme pleasure to extreme displeasure. Still another study (Papousek et al, 1986) demonstrated easily discernible audible sounds of pleasure in child-parent interactions in infants from 2-4 months of age.

Another category of the external indication of internal affect states in-cludes various facial expressions, particularly smiling. The earliest smiles occur during the REM stages of sleep (Reppert et al, 1987; 1988; Reppert & Schwartz, 1983) perhaps indicating "expressions of private pleasure in dreams" (Roffwarg et al, 1966, 610). What makes REM sleep so significant is the correlation of this stage with dreaming activity. The above study found that various measurable alterations in specific physiological systems (i.e. gross motor movement) was identical for adults as for full-term and premature neonates, leading to the conclusion that even premature infants and fetuses dream. Whether this activity involves the full visual imagery and the other characteristics of adult dreaming is impossible to determine, but the REMs of neonates and adults are alike in every measurable way. The big difference has to do with the amount of time spent in REM vs. non-REM sleep. Older adults spend less than 1 hour (13% of sleep time) in REM; adolescents 20%; full-term newborns 50%; 36-38 week preemies 58%; 33-35 week preemies 67%; and virtually 100% for 30 week-old premature infants. Interesting, this study noted many expressions of emotion on the faces of the various infants during REM sleep: grimaces, smiles, whimpers and even the nuances of affective expression such as perplexity, disdain, skepticism, and amusement.

Smiling has often been observed at birth (Leboyer, 1975; Star, 1986), but until recently it was thought to be a "physiological artifact" (i.e. caused by gas). However, research has identified neonatal smiling in response to specific tasks and also a wide variation in the frequency of smiling (Wolff, 1978).

Other facial expressions indicative of affect states have been clearly identified in newborns, including expressions that seem to indicate sadness, fear, disgust, happiness, surprise, anger, interest, and distress (Emde, 1980). Using videotapes of neonates in the first week of life, Eisenberg and Marmarou (1981) revealed of full range of clear-cut expressions of emotion. Another study (Johnson et al, 1982) examined neonatal affect states as perceived by their parents. Ninety-five percent reported seeing joy and interest, 78% saw anger, 68% surprise, 65% distress, 40% sadness, 40% disgust, and 35% fear in their babies during the first week of life. The introduction of new information resulting in the quick appropriate change of affect suggests the dependence of emotion upon cognitive beliefs and cognitive processes (Kagan, 1978).

The Fetal Environment and Its Effects

Key to any verification of Lake's M-FDS as a possible paradigm must be the explanation of how the maternal-fetal "affect flow" functions. Lake noted early on that the reaction to early emotional stress tended to set up a pattern of similar reacting that is life-long. Persons who early on reacted "hysterically" tended to react hysterically as adults. Persons who adopted the typical "depressive" defense patterns early on, tended to utilize them as adults.

How does the emotional life of the mother effect the developing fetus? Lake's understanding that "powerfully impressive experiences from the mother and her inner and outer world . . . reach the foetus, defining its relation to the intra-uterine reality in ways that persist into adult life" (Lake, 1981c, 5) is analogous to Francis Mott's. Mott conceptualized a bi-directional flow of blood from mother to fetus as mediated by the placenta through the umbilical cord, which gives rise to various physical "feelings" that are the basis for subsequent psychological "feelings". Lake picked up on Mott's term "umbilical affect" to designate this exchange, defining it as the "feeling state of the fetus as brought about by blood reaching him through the umbilical vein" (Moss, 1987, 203). As both Lake and Mott define this exchange, the umbilical vein not only conveys nutritive resources and as such could be experienced as a "life-giving flow, bringing . . . renewal and restoration" but could also "be the bearer of an aggressive thrust of bad feelings into the foetus if the mother herself was distressed and 'feeling bad.'" If the mother felt emotionally un-supported , then "this feeling of deficiency, lack of recognition and the failure of looked-for support, would be just as specifically felt by the fetus. It became distressed by the failure of its immediate environment to provide the expected acceptance and sustenance, not so much at the level of metabolic input . . . but to nourish the earliest beginnings of the person in relationship" (Lake, 1976b, S1).

Certainly the biological morphology for this exchange exists very early on, from about the fifth week after fertilization until birth. With the development of the placenta and umbilical cord (Mulders et al, 1986, 283-293), the embryo/fetus exchanges carbon dioxide, urea, hormones and waste products for oxygen, vitamins, antibodies and other nutrients. But the morphological structures which allow this "natural" exchange to occur also allow for the passage through the placental barrier of various teratogens, particularly pharmacological agents and almost all viruses. Much research has been done on the deleterious effects of various teratogens and other prenatal "conditions".

The idea that the pregnant mother's emotional state during pregnancy might have a positive or deleterious effect on the developing baby within her is certainly not new (Van den Bergh, 1990). In an early study from 1941, Sontag found that pregnant women who were anxious, angry and/or afraid tended to have babies with higher heart rates, greater digestive problems, lower birth weight, and more hyperactivity. Numerous studies (Carlson & La Barba, 1979; Istvan, 1986; Van den Bergh, 1983) since have confirmed these findings, reinforcing Sontag's original results. For instance, emotionally disturbed women tend to have infants who are irritable (Dodge, 1972), poor sleepers (Ferreira, 1960), more prone to gastrointestinal difficulties (Glavin, 1984; Turner, 1956), have higher activity rates (Sontag, 1966), cry more (Farber et al, 1981), are perceived by their parents as having a difficult temperament (Vaughn et al, 1987), and score lower on mental and motor skills tests (Davids et al, 1963).

Several studies have connected anxiety (Crandon, 1979; Grassi & Caracciolo, 1983) and/or various psychiatric diagnoses (Peterson et al, 1988; Rider et al, 1975) in pregnant women with a much higher incidence of various birth complications.

For instance, Batchelor, Dean, Gray & Wenck (1991) examined 37 children with severe emotional/behavioral disorders vs. 119 children with severe emotional handicaps vs. 211 "normal" children. Using 26 items from the MPS (Maternal-Perinatal Scale; Dean & Gray, 1985), this study found that the item with the highest correlation as a "predictive factor" of post-natal emotional and behavioral disorders was cigarette smoking, followed closely by maternal stress throughout pregnancy. Using an odds ratio developed by Mantel (1963), this study found, for instance, that maternal smoking throughout the pregnancy resulted in a odds ratio of 4.34 (i.e. mothers who smoked during pregnancy are 4.34 times more likely to have a child who eventually ends up being diagnosed as behaviorally or emotionally disordered. The score for stress throughout pregnancy was 4.22 and was higher than other factors such as low birth weight (3.37), preterm delivery (2.75), edema throughout the pregnancy (2.04), too little weight gain (1.74), hypoxia (1.18), mother over 35 years old (1.14) and maternal ingestion of alcohol (.63).

This study reinforced other studies that have connected maternal stress with general behavior problems (Cocchi et al, 1984; De Sousa, 1974), attention deficit disorder (Varley, 1984), childhood autism (Finnegan & Quarrington, 1979; Foulatier, 1987; Gillberg & Gillberg, 1983; Mason-Brothers et al, 1987), psychosis (Torry et al, 1975), schizophrenia (Medick et al, 1987; Ritzman, 1989; Rutt & Offord, 1971), and psychiatric disorders in general (Huttunen & Niskanen, 1978).

Various studies have also correlated the likelihood of spontaneous abortions and birth complications with the level of fear, anxiety, and guilt in pregnant women (Golanska & Bacz, 1988) as well as disturbances in attitudes toward the child within them (Goshen-Gottstein, 1969; Laukaran & Van den Berg, 1980).

Research has also shown a connection between various psychological factors and preterm delivery (Blau et al, 1963; Gunter, 1963). For instance, premature delivery is more likely to occur in women who have negative attitudes toward the pregnancy, were emotionally immature, had unresolved conflicts toward their mothers, a history of traumatic experience with a previous pregnancy, a high level of anxiety, feelings of inadequacy in female roles (De Muylder, 1986), difficulty in accepting the pregnancy, poor "communication" with their fetus (Riley, 1988), lack of a spouse (Newton, 1988), husbands who offered little or no support, and an initial negative reaction to their first menses (De Muylder & Wesel, 1988). Another study (Iatrakis et al, 1988) found a significantly higher incidence of vomiting and nausea in the first 12 weeks of pregnancy in those women who had poor communication with their husbands and who had stress and doubts about the pregnancy.

Indeed, the sum total of research seems to indicate that potentially any emotional stress to the mother can lead to complications of various types (Laibow, 1988; Michel & Fritz-Niggli, 1978; Spielberger & Jacobs, 1979), not only after birth but even before birth. For instance, mothers under severe emotional distress are more likely to have hyperactive fetuses (Ferreira, 1965; McDonald, 1968; Montagu, 1962; Wolkind, 1981) and mothers who are anxious (Copher & Huber, 1967) or emotionally upset (Eskes, 1985) are likely to have fetus's suffering from tachycardia. One study illustrated the effects on 28 fetuses aged 18-36 weeks in response to their mother's reactions to an earthquake (Iannuruberto & Tajani, 1981). Using ultrasonography, the researchers were able to observe the intense hyperkinesia in all of the fetuses lasting from 2 to 8 hours. Other studies (Benson et al, 1987; Van den Bergh, 1988; 1990) have also connected fetal behavior to maternal emotional state.

What allows the affect state of the mother to effect the child she is carrying are the neuroendocrinological interactions of the endocrine system and the nervous system, particularly a group of hormones called catecholamines (Lagercrantz & Slotkin, 1986; Moyer et al, 1978; Simkin, 1986), including epinephrine, norepinephrine and dopamine. Beginning in the 1925, W.B. Cannon found that fear and anxiety could be biochemically induced in animals. His method was simple; he withdrew the blood and thus the catecholamines of already fearful and frightened animals and injected them into calm and relaxed animals. Within seconds and in the absence of any fear or anxiety producing stimuli, these animals began to act fearful and anxious. Cannon discovered that the catecholamines acted like "a circulating fire alarm system," provoking all the physiological responses to fear and anxiety, particularly those of the sympathetic division of the autonomic nervous system.

This identical process allows the developing embryo and fetus to be affected by the mother's affective processes. When the gravida is anxious or fearful, various hormones, including adrenaline, flood into the blood stream and easily cross the placental barrier, thus provoking, biochemically, the physiological reaction to anxiety and fear in the fetus (Kruse, 1978; Peters, 1988). The mechanism that allows this process to work begins with the mother's brain, which is sensing and perceiving the environment. External circumstances, actions and thoughts are perceived in the cerebral cortex and subsequently affectively reacted to in the hypothalamus. The hypothalamus, in turn, directs the endocrine system and the autonomic nervous system to produce affect-appropriate physiological changes. For instance, sudden fear in a pregnant women quickly results in the hypothalamus directing the sympathetic division of the autonomic nervous system to make the heart beat faster, the palms to sweat, the blood pressure to rise, the pupils to dilate and the muscles to tense. The hypothalamus also directs the endocrine system to flood the woman's body with hormones, which as noted above, pass through the placenta to the fetus.

What is so important about this process is the effect it can have on the developing embryo and fetus. The various hormones released by the endocrine system, while variously reversible in adults, can be more-or-less irreversible at certain critical periods in development during the embryonic and fetal stages. What seems to be produced is a psycho-physiological predisposition to respond that some researchers have traced into adulthood. While there is not yet a precise under-standing as to how the psychological and physiological dimensions interact to cause long-term psychophysiological behavior changes, it is clear that something is going on. Recent evidence seems to indicate that the hypothalamus, as the "emotional regulator" of the body is key in this transaction.

Sontag, in an early study titled "War and the Maternal-Fetal Relationship" (1944), observed that the babies of women whose husbands were serving in the armed services and thus daily threatened with death tended to be crankier and have a greater array of physical problems. He theorized that the intra-uterine environment of constantly worrying mothers would have a deleterious effect on a whole generation of infants. Sontag coined the term "somatopsychics" to describe the way "basic physiological processes affect the personality structure, perception, and performance of an individual." This term infers the mirror process of "psychosomatics", which refers to the way in which psychological processes effect physiological ones (Verny, 1981). Thus, the developing fetal morphological apparatus is influenced by the intra-uterine environment in such a way as to predispose certain psychological processes following birth.

Several studies (Stott, 1973; Stott & Latchford, 1976) have found what seem to be discriminations of stressors by the maternal-fetal unit. Stott found that no negative effects, either physical or emotional, seemed to be present in the children of mothers who had suffered fairly intense, but brief stressors (i.e. witnessing a violent dog fight, suffering a scare at work, having an older child run away for a day). The argument that the brief exposure of the fetus to the "bath of neuro-hormones" necessarily limits the possibility of negative effect and this was true. But Stott and others have also found that intense, long-term stress did not always result in post-natal deficiencies. In 1983, Reading found that the impact of anxiety and stress is often moderated by other factors, such as attitudes toward the pregnancy, psychosocial support and appraisal of the threat of the stressor. Further, when prolonged stress did not directly threaten the mother (i.e. illness of a close relative) there seemed to be no ill effects, while stressors that did effect the potential well-being of the mother seemed to produce problems. Stott found that 10 out of 14 women suffering from personally threatening stressors which were long-term delivered babies with some physical or emotional problem. Two characteristics were significant in the problem-causing stressors: "they tended to be continuous or liable to erupt at any time and they were incapable of resolution" (Verny, 1981, 46).

There seemed to be a pronounced effect when the source of the stress was a close family member, usually the husband. Stott found that a bad marriage or relationship was among the greatest causes of stress. Studying over 1300 children and their families, he estimated that a women trapped by a stormy marriage with an abusive or unsupportive husband runs a 237% greater risk of bearing a emotionally or physically handicapped child as opposed to a woman from a secure, nurturing stable marital environment. Further, Stott found that unhappy marriages tended to produce babies who were on average 5 times more fearful and "jumpy" than offspring from happy marriages (Stott, 1977). Verny writes that "these youngsters continued to be plagued by problems well into childhood. At four and five, Dr. Stott found them to be undersized, timid, and emotionally dependent on their mothers to an inordinate degree" (Verny, 1981, 50).

Several other studies have found different results regarding even short-term fetal behavioral response in reaction to induced maternal emotions.

One study (Van den Bergh et al, 1989) found no significant fetal response when their mothers watched a film on delivery, perhaps considered mildly stressing. Two other studies (Rossi, 1987; Rossi et al, 1989) found significant fetal movement in response to their mother's anticipation of an amniocentesis vs. a group of controls. A fourth study (Benson et al, 1987) found that fetuses of anxious mothers, but not depressed or hostile mothers showed elevated heart rates.

Verny, in commenting on Stott's study, writes:

> The only way to make sense of the difference [between the two groups subjected to long-term stress] is in terms of perception. In one case, the children were able to sense that while very real, their mother's distress was not threatening to her or them; in the other case, they sense, accurately, that her distress was a threat (Verny, 1981, 50).

Thus, some kind of fetal perceptual apparatus is assumed to enable the ability to distinguish between threatening and non-threatening neuro-hormones. One possible mechanism that might explain this is through a concomitant ongoing exchange between mother and fetus that communicates the positive vs. negative feelings of the mother herself to the child.

Numerous studies have examined the role of maternal attitudes (Ainslie et al, 1982; Condon, 1985; Eggersten & Benedetti, 1984; Reading et al, 1984), particularly attachment (Gaffney, 1986; Mercer et al, 1988; Sjogren & Uddenberg, 1988; Stainton, 1985; Wu & Eichmann, 1988) toward the fetus growing within them. One study (Lukesch, 1975) examined 2000 pregnant women and found that the single greatest factor in neonatal outcome was the attitude of the mother toward her child while the second most important variable was the quality of a woman's relationship with her spouse. The subjects in this study all had the same quality and quantity of prenatal care, were equally educated, and were of the same social and economic class. Lukesch and others (Condon, 1987) have found that the infants of mothers who were accepting of their pregnancies and who looked forward to the arrival of the baby were much more likely to give birth to an emotionally and physically healthy child than mothers who had negative attitudes towards the pregnancy and were "rejecting." Another study (Rottman, 1974) on 141 pregnant women duplicated Lukesche's results. Using various psychological tests, Rottman divided the pregnant women into 4 groups. Results with the two extremes were clear, with "Ideal" mothers (who consciously and unconsciously wanted their unborn children) having the easiest pregnancies, the most trouble-free births, and the most physically and emotionally healthy infants. "Catastrophic" mothers (who consciously and unconsciously were rejecting of their unborn children) "had the most devastating medical problems during pregnancy, and bore the highest rate of premature, low-weight, and emotionally disturbed infants" (Verny, 1981, 48).

Two other groups of mothers emerged, called "Ambivalent" (consciously wanting while unconsciously rejecting) and "Cool" (consciously rejecting while unconsciously wanting) mothers. The former gave birth to an unusually large number of neonates who suffered from behavioral and gastrointestinal problems, while the latter gave birth to babies who tended to be apathetic and lethargic. Verny hypothesizes that regardless of the various stresses that these women went through, the acceptance or lack of acceptance by the mother is somehow perceived by the fetus and that among those fetuses who felt accepted, a measure of maternal "support" and "acceptance" was evident enough which somehow enabled them to better cope with the stresses that emerged.

Chapter Three

The Evidence for a Theological Paradigm

Frank Lake referred to the M-FDS as "a new paradigm for psychodynamics with revolutionary implications" (Lake, 1980b, 3). One of the "revolutionary implications" of Lake's theoretical structure relates to his paradigmatic correlation of the M-FDS with certain theological considerations. Lake, in his series of epigrammatic charts titled "Studies in Constricted Confusion" writes:

> The harshness of the affliction which an innocent foetus has often to endure, early in life in the womb, as outlined in this paradigm of human origins, calls for a much more exacting theological paradigm of reconciliation and reparation . . . So, the deepening of the psychological paradigm to include the exigencies of the pre- and peri-natal journey, its dire circumstances, the daily impasse of having to depend on a source that is remembered as perpetually disappointing, requires a theodicy to cover it (Lake, 1981d, T1).

As has previously been noted, Lake's use of the term "paradigm" above and elsewhere assumes two somewhat overlapping denotations. The first, examined in the previous chapter, defines the term as "a generally accepted system of ideas which defines the legitimate problems and methods of a research field" (Moss, 1986, 53). The second, more general sense, utilizes "paradigm" to mean "a pattern, something shown side by side with something else, inviting comparison of the correspondences" (Lake, 1980b, 3). Lake sees numerous correspondences between the psychological and physiological dimensions of the M-FDS and certain religious and theological issues.

But it is at one particular point that Lake sees a profound correspondence; namely that the innocent suffering of Christ on the Cross is paradigmatic of the "innocent" suffering of the fetus in the womb. Lake writes:

> If they [the correspondences] appeal to the observer as close enough to be significant, he will tend to use the new paradigm whenever he looks at problematic areas of living, on the off chance that the data will fall into place in relation to the newly offered pattern (Lake, 1980b, 3).

That the data did fall into place for Lake excited him immensely regarding the potential clinical and therapeutic ramifications of a "communicated theodicy." He envisioned "the Cross, of Christ, offered in depth at the point of primal impact . . . , [as offering] immense prophylactic possibilities" (Peters, 1989, 145).

In Lake's issue-long article "The Theology of Pastoral Counselling" published in *Contact* in 1980, he cites three general defining theological variables for his work: the thoroughly theological grounding for everything he does, the communication of a cross-based theodicy, and finally, the development of a theodicy which can even incorporate fetal suffering (Lake, 1980c, 1). Thus, each of these will be considered in turn as they relate to the M-FDS as a paradigm.

From the very beginning Lake was concerned to build the structure of his psychology and psychiatry on the foundation of a rigorous theology. His stated intention was "to show that Theology is the uncrowned queen of the Clinical Sciences [and] this has been our *raison d'etre* for twenty-two years" (Lake, 1980c, 1). Earlier he had written:

> I rely for myself and my work on the Incarnation of the Son of God, the Crucifixion and Resurrection of Christ, and the giving of the Holy Spirit within the continuing life of the universal Church, in the Word it proclaims, the sacraments it celebrates, and the fellowship which anchors it in every human society in every age. This divine-human fellowship and destiny I take to be central to the meaning of human history. . . . I acknowledge that my philosophy is agnostic about the ultimate meaning of human life apart from Christ. I do not see Him merely as an example of truths I discover elsewhere.

He is my criterion of truth, and the principle datum of all I know about man's freedom, and deliverance, and destiny (Lake, 1964, xv-xvi).

Although essentially "conservative Christian", Lake's theological perspective was quite eclectic. While his background could be classified as representative of evangelical Anglicanism, he read and quoted a large variety of theological perspectives, from Pope John Paul II to the medieval Christian mystics, from those who represented the Charismatic renewal to classical Buddhism. While Lake would have claimed the authority of Scripture as the final arbiter of ideas and doctrine, he nonetheless felt free to liberally use whatever he saw as illustrative of his ideas. This was especially true with regard to the theological dimension of the M-FDS.

In his final work before his death, titled "Mutual Caring", Lake sought to flesh out theologically in greater detail some of the theological components of the M-FDS. Using the three possible manifestations of "umbilical affect" (positive, negative, and strongly negative) and the four graded levels of fetal response (ideal, coping, opposition and transmarginal stress), Lake added various salient theological considerations to each.

The Model

The point of departure for Lake is that any understanding of what it means to be a "normal" human being requires a standard example of "normality" with which to compare every other example. Thus, for Lake Christ is the one unspoiled "normal", and yet not average, specimen and he alone provides us with both a pattern for our humanity, and, since we will live forever, a pattern for our divinity. The life of Christ, beginning with the miraculous Holy Spirit-induced conception and continuing in the womb of Mary and in relationship to her, serves as the paradigmatic norm for all human health. Christ is the only model which correlates the biblical and theological material "with the sum of our knowledge of human personality growth and development and the disorders that affect them" (Lake, 1986, 2).

The correlation that Lake refers to is the M-FDS and how Christ's life reflects his own fetal experience. That the all important "umbilical affect" of the first trimester from Mary is "positive" and that the fetal response from Christ as an embryo is "ideal" is crucially important for Lake.

Four possible scenarios exist with regard to the maternal-fetal exchange. When the umbilical affect is "positive", the fetal response is "ideal", whereas the response is "coping" to a less-than-positive, even "negative" flow from the mother. For Lake, the pregnant Mary and the fetal Jesus are paradigmatic of these first two "scenarios". Lake's "paradigms" of the third and fourth "scenarios" ("negative" and "opposition"; "strongly negative" and "transmarginal stress") are for him found primarily in the theological works of St. John of the Cross, Simone Weil, and Soren Kierkegaard.

Umbilical Exchange: Positive and Ideal

When "the fetus in the womb is well-supplied in every way," it's physical, emotional, and spiritual "shopping list" being satisfied by the "hopes of a well-stocked maternal shop" (Lake, 1981d, C68), there being a sense of "warm and contented happiness . . . and a deeply embodied bliss" (Lake, 1982b, 13), the "ideal" umbilical exchange between mother and child exists. That this ideality is rare is not to say that it is impossible. Lake describes the "one 'Ideal' among the troubled many":

> All the warmth and tenderness of the love she is receiving from her husband, family and neighbors, on the basis, one would assume, of a foetal life and childhood of a similar quality when her basic character formation was beginning within her mother, fortified, perhaps, by a spiritual sense that God the Father's exchanges of love are just like this, and as she opens to him too, all her loves mix; all this is made available to the foetus within her (Lake, 1982b, 14).

According to Lake, this description delineates the exchange between Mary and Jesus, at least during the first trimester. According to Lake, Mary's role is of "crucial importance, under God, to the developing personality of her Son, Jesus Christ our Lord" (Lake, 1982c, 125). Lake writes:

> What we now know of the foetal awareness of what is going on in the emotional and spiritual life of the mother, well within the first trimester, indicates that Christ, as the foetal person within her [Mary], would be an intimate sharer of the extraordinary vicissitudes taking place in the life of his mother (Lake 1982b, 126).

It all begins, according to Lake, with the importance of the Annunciation by the Angel, as a "quite necessary act of pre-pregnancy counseling, in order that, in spite of the most distressing circumstances, the Blessed Virgin could remain at peace, and the foetal Son of God within her be sustained in undisturbed faith in God's good ordering of all things. To be pregnant under such circumstances could have led, under strict Jewish law, to her being condemned and stoned to death, had Joseph taken a hard line-- which he did not --or being 'put away privately' to bring a fatherless child into the world" (Lake 1982b, 125). Following the announcement by the angel Gabriel, Mary immediately asks a question regarding the possibility of conception, as she had no husband. Lake writes that the response of Gabriel "lifted the whole dialogue out of the realm of ordinary human emotions and normal biological possibilities. Her objection was set aside by God's promised action. . . . The transformation of all emotional hesitations took place with Mary's leap of faith and commitment" (Lake 1982b, 128-129). Thus, "Christ Jesus, the Son of God, the Second Person of the Blessed Trinity was 'conceived by the Holy Spirit'. The self-regulating process continued with the implantation of the perfect sphere into the womb of Mary" (Lake 1982b, 129).

Elsewhere Lake writes:

There is, from the viewpoint of the first-trimester development and its crucial importance, far exceeding that of subsequent months, an exact appropriateness in the movements and provisions which the Blessed Mother Mary makes for herself and the developing foetus within her (Lake, 1982b, 16).

Mary does not confront Joseph with the truth nor does she stay in Nazareth. Rather, she immediately seeks out her cousin Elizabeth. Lake continues:

Elizabeth, too, is having a child by divine appointment, long past child-bearing years, who is to be the herald of a far greater Coming One. So Mary "rose up in haste", and hurried down to the hill-country of Judea to spend three months with Elizabeth. The greeting of the agile John, leaping in Elizabeth's womb as Mary enters, confirmed the arrangement. So the two holy and wise women are left in peace and to their prayers, totally open to God, who had more to do with what was growing in their wombs than any menfolk (Lake 1982b, 16).

During this period spent with Elizabeth, described as a "tranquil" and "ideal 'first trimester'" (Lake 1982b, 16), Lake describes what he imagines to be Mary's attitude toward her pregnancy, partly based on the content of the Magnificat:

> She knows who she is, because of who God's word and plan have made her. The womb of a woman who becomes pregnant is often an organ she abhors and would like to disown. Not so Mary; her womb is the holy of holies in her body, a specially favored place in a highly favored woman (Lake, 1982c, 131).

For Lake, the influence of the first trimester on subsequent functioning of every type is critical. Indeed, this is one reason he makes such a point of Mary's visit to and the time spent with her cousin Elizabeth. Christ, who was to be the perfect "normal" example for all humankind, needed an ideal first trimester and God sovereignly provided it. Lake describes this period as ideal for Mary because of the "mutual help at the deepest possible level" (Lake, 1982b, 16) which came from Elizabeth, but also as "ideal for Jesus, who, by this arrangement, was ensured the most perfect possible time of sharing with his 'lovely and beautiful' mother, the Beloved to whom his foetal yearning reached out and by whom he was fully satisfied" (Lake, 1982b, 16). Thus, Mary, and more significantly, Jesus, are prepared to face the "very tricky situation back in Nazareth with Joseph."

Umbilical Exchange: Negative and Coping

When the maternal affect flow is less than ideally positive and the fetal response is consequently less than ideal, then, according to Lake's rendering, the affect flow is said to be "negative." The "negative" affect flow, while not advantageous to the fetus, is certainly preferable to the "strongly negative" affect flow so characteristic, at least in Lake's scheme of things, to the genesis of psychoses. The fetal response to a negative affect flow is also mediated by several factors, including the duration and extent of the exchange, the constitution of the fetus, and the previous "history" of the maternal-fetal exchange. When the umbilical affect is "negative" but is still "good-enough" to prevent a profound loss of trust, then a second response level is manifested by the fetus, that of coping.

The "Coping Response" results when there is a "discrepancy between need and proper fulfillment . . . but the main conditions of satisfactory interaction are being more or less met" (Lake, 1981d, C68). There is either a maternal failure to meet perfectly the "essential need for recognition and caring attention" or an "influx of maternal distress" (Lake, 1982b, 21) or both. The latter describes Mary's situation as she heads to Nazareth to deal with Joseph. What she faced was a "particularly distressing social situation," a "severe trial of faith", and a situation which "could hardly have been worse" (Lake, 1982c, 134). In addition to Joseph's initial intention to divorce her, Mary also faced at least the possibility of death by stoning, the punishment for engaging as an unmarried woman in what usually occasioned pregnancy.

Lake describes two ways of understanding Mary's emotional state at this point:

> Either we can picture the Blessed Virgin Mary as so superior to ordinary human emotions that the discovery of her condition, the incredulous suspicions of Joseph, his decision to divorce her, his hesitation, the suspense, the eventual marriage, then the talk of the neighbors when a baby was seen to be on the way at the same time as the wedding, either all these ordinarily distressing events made absolutely no impression on her exalted spirit, or we can think of her as a human person like her Son, subject to the feelings which, in spite of a willing spirit, show that the flesh is weak." (Lake, 1982c, 132).

That Mary would have been emotionally distressed is clear to Lake. That this distress would have been transmitted umbilically to the fetal Jesus is just as clear. This period of time, however long it was, was one "when only her [Mary's] supreme faith would protect the divine foetus within her from being deluged by her distress, her very realistic anxiety and anguish" (Lake, 1982c, 135). Thus, Jesus experiences the "coping" reaction to "negative" umbilical affect. Lake writes:

> Unless some quite unnatural and unknown placental barrier mechanism were specially provided in Christ's case, to cut him off from the emotional flow that is normal between the mother and the foetus, in joy and distress, in peace and anxiety, then Christ's **humanity was rooted in sharing, as we do, in the psychosomatic, emotional reactions and spiritual resolution (or lack of it) of our mothers** [emphasis Lake's] (Lake, 1982c, 135).

That this apparent inflow of negative umbilical affect is of relatively short duration and follows Jesus' ideal first trimester, limits the scope of the long-term consequences. Lake continues:

Three months of [ideally] loving interchange . . . would have established a powerfully competent foetal personality by the time the Blessed Virgin turned to face the home-coming to Nazareth (Lake, 1982c, 136).

At the same time, Lake points out that it makes sense that the "suffering servant" described by Isaiah should, as the writer to the Hebrews makes clear, "suffer in every way as we have" (Hebrews 2:17-18; 4:15-16). That Jesus shared in Mary's suffering in this particular way is a foreshadowing of his Cross, in which he shares in the suffering of every person who ever lived. Lake addresses this shared suffering by asking a question and then answering it:

What were the special qualifications of the Blessed Virgin Mary for the task of enwombing the Savior of the World? Surely the same qualifications and character resources her son would need, those of the faithful Suffering Servant. . . . It would be a most strange exception to this rule of the trial of faith, if the Blessed Mother of our Lord were denied this royal road to sharing the character of God the Father, which was to be her Son's royal road (Lake, 1982c, 134-135).

That the fetal Jesus suffered does not mean that he suffered indelible psychic trauma. One of the typical responses Lake described on the part of the "coping" fetus to "negative umbilical affect" was that of the so-called "fetal therapist", first mentioned in chapter one. Lake describes this stance when he writes:

We have listened to and recorded dozens of instances where the relationship of mother and foetus is basically good and mutually supportive, when the foetus has responded to temporary trouble and crisis in the mother's world by a clear sense of being eager and able **to support her** [Lake's emphasis]. Its own sense of security is, by this stage, quite well-enough established to enable it to form the intention of supporting the mother, wanting her to be free of any charge on her attention on its account. There is no reason to believe that, by the beginning of the fourth month-- and even much earlier, this would have been the case with Jesus (Lake, 1982b, 17).

Where would the resources come from which would enable the fetus, "out of his own stores" (Lake, 1982c, 138), to extend support to his mother? Lake mentions that just as the fetus shares in the negative experiences of the maternal environment, so also it can share in the positive. Not only does the fetus have the somatic, emotional and psychological "stores of experienced love" to extend to the mother, but is well able to cope with severe periods of anxiety. The foetus also the spiritual stores and fruit that the mother has channeled to herself through the Holy Spirit. Lake writes:

> If the mother is the channel to herself of love, joy, peace, patience, kindness, goodness, faithfulness, gentleness and self-control --wherever she derives these spiritual resources-- from the order of creation or the order of redemption . . . they are both channeled into the foetus. So sustained, the foetus already understands enough to cope with some incomprehensible interruptions of the mother's tranquillity. It has been given loving trust for long enough to bear, without wavering in trust, times when the mother's attention is being taken up by outside troubles. The detriment is not serious (Lake, 1982c, 137).

Indeed, the typical adult pattern of the "fetal therapist" is one who loves "as they have been loved, with no need of further reward. Having freely received, they freely give" (Lake, 1982c, 138). This result assumes that a mother being helped does not take advantage of the "natural helpfulness" and "cash in on it."

Another potential benefit results from the "coping" response, something akin to an emotional vaccination. Since the world is not an "ideal" place where one's needs are always met fully and immediately, the coping response is more predictive of future interaction in a sinful world full of potential deficits and disappointments. Indeed, this level can serve to "flex the muscles of faith" with the spirit expanding "to include the negative aspects of relationships with increasing and justifiable hope and trust" (Lake, 1981d, C68).

Umbilical Exchange: Negative and Opposition

When the foetus is unable to handle its situation by coping "in the face of too severe, too prolonged, unremitting deficiency of maternal recognition or because the sense of 'negative umbilical affect' is like a great nail of affliction or skewer transfixing the foetus at the navel, with an overwhelming invasion of bitter, black maternal emotions" (Lake, 1982b, 22) then "opposition" exists. The qualitative difference between "coping" and "opposition" is that "distress has shattered the erstwhile trust between the ego and its world" (Lake, 1981d, C68), and what is sought is the immediate termination of a "significant margin of pain" (Lake, 1981d, C68).

The fetal reaction to this umbilical exchange varies. Sometimes the fetus can use the "down time" of the night, when the affect flows ceases or is reduced to a trickle, to "regather its incredibly renewable faith, hope, and love, to reaffirm what ought to be, and wait like Prometheus for the day when the carrion birds return to attack" (Lake, 1982b, 23). A second response may be the willing of the death of the source person, which is often repressed because of its "unacceptability." The pain itself must be repressed and "split-off", but the tell-tale scar, although unconscious, remains.

This "tell-tale scar" manifests itself in various pathological patterns, the most common being depression. In a lecture in 1967 Lake commented on the external religious manifestations of the various types of repression:

> The personality structures enshrined in the average church-goer and in the more respectable clergy tend to be either depressive or obsessional. In terms of personality orientation, such people are rooted in an attitude that clings to the past, or some aspect of it, as basically good. This is in sharp contrast to the hystero-schizoid dynamics which . . . are in blind flight from the memory of total badness (Lake, 1967, 33).

Thus, according to Lake, the external manifestation of the conservative church parishioner often reflected an internal personality which gains assurance from clinging to the past, hence his or her conservatism.

This embrace of the "status quo" and the subsequent need to idealize the church reflects the internal need to deny the "bad"; to deny the "negative" umbilical affect flow from the intra-uterine period. But Lake affirmed that this denial, this "murder of the truth" really hides that "unattractive hinterland of depression . . . [which] is marred by repressed rage and hate, lust and envy, anxiety, distrust, doubt, and even, at times, despair" (Lake, 1967, 33). All of these must be denied and repressed, although they eventually manifest themselves as depression.

The theological dimension of depression often includes a fixated image of "god" as a "stern condemnatory parent who approves only of those who keep the law, who accepts the sinner only when full reparation has been made, and who demands a constant flow of good works" (Lake, 1967, 33). This person, this "work-weary man or woman" must be brought to the place of rest, mainly through the unconditional acceptance of Christ as embodied by the counselor. The internalized repressed anger and "murderous rage" against "god" must be expressed. Lake writes:

The murderous rage is so strong that to save others, a man may kill himself. The Cross of Christ is begging the depressed religious man to trust him [Christ] sufficiently to offer the murderous rage to him not just mentally, but physically, to direct the evil on to him whose work is to take away our evil, at the cost of his own death (Lake, 1967, 33).

In response to the objection that anger, that "murderous rage" ought not to be expressed but rather repented of, Lake responded:

Most "religion" based on "what I ought to do" parts company with Christian, Christ-based living. The only "ought" left to the Christian is that of relating first of all to Jesus, of going straight away, without delay of a preliminary wash-and-brush-up, to the Christ and his cross. This is, to me, the "repentance" and *metanoia,* or change of mind, we most urgently need, namely to change from our habitual tendency to deal with our "badness" by telling ourselves what we ought to do about it, in order to please God at once, by taking the whole bellyful of our "badness" direct to the "scapegoat" God the Father has himself appointed, and off-load the lot obediently onto the Son (Lake, 1975b).

Another manifestation of the negative umbilical affect flow coupled with opposition by the "innocent" fetus is the hysterical reaction. While the depressive person is so because of a denial of an internal anger and rage based upon events in the past, the core of the hysterical person "is the mental pain of separation . . . from the presence and countenance" of the mother or some kind of substituted "personal source of being" (Lake, 1964, 380). Thus, the hysterical mode of repression is to "murder the truth" of the early intrauterine or extra-uterine experience of the loss of "being" and instead embark on a life-long pursuit of a dependable source of "being."

Umbilical Exchange: Strongly Negative and Transmarginal Stress

When the "umbilical affect" is strongly negative, the fetal distress that results comes directly as a result of an "influx of maternal distress" (Lake, 1981d, C41) in reaction to various environmental factors. Commenting on any pregnant woman Lake writes that:

It may be due to her marriage, to her husband's withdrawal rather than more intimate supporting when he is asked urgently for more than his personality can easily give. It may be due to the family's economic or social distress in a distressed neighborhood. If she is grieving the loss of, or nursing a still dying parent, the sorrow overwhelms her and her fetus (Lake, 1981f, 66).

Whatever the cause, "the pain of the world, picked up by the family, is funneled by the mother into the fetus" (Lake, 1981f, 66) resulting in the invasion of a "black, bitter flood" of "incompatible . . . and alien emotions" (Lake, 1981g, x) not unlike being "'marinated' in the mother's miseries" (Lake, 1981, 141). This "invasion" is twofold:

> It is both the registering of the intrusion of the mother's condition, of yearning, anxiety, fear, anger, disgust, bitterness, jealousy, etc. into the fetus, and its own emotional response to this distressed and distressing invasion. Particularly distressing, because they give rise to the "fear of being killed by maternal hatred," are failed abortions and near miscarriages (Lake, 1981d, C41).

When and if the "affect flow" from the mother to the fetus reaches the point where the fetus perceives a "sheer impossibility of keeping up the opposition to the invasive evil which seems interminable and relentless" (Lake, 1982b, 30), then "transmarginal stress" has occurred. When the absolute margin of tolerable pain has been reached and passed, paradoxical and supra-paradoxical response patterns result in which "the self turns against itself, willing its own destruction and death" (Lake, 1981d, C68). The stance of the fetus switches from being life-affirming to death-affirming. Beyond the margin of tolerable pain, of transmarginal pain, the "foetus longs, not for life, but for death. The plea is not for a relief of the weight, but that it may be crushed out of existence" (Lake, 1982b, 30). "There is a loss of 'being' at the center, replaced by a [paradoxical] desire for 'nonbeing'" (Lake, 1981d, C41).

The theological weight that Lake brings to bear on both the "negative" and "strongly negative" invasive maternal flood and on both the "opposition" and "transmarginal" fetal reactions are substantially the same. While there is a qualitative distinction between the two, it primarily results due to the quantitative degree, amount, and duration of the invasive maternal flood. Thus, the theological dimension is relatively similar for both maternal and both fetal "states."

St. John of the Cross

Frank Lake sees in St. John of the Cross not only an insightful, "reliable provider of accurate maps and models" (Lake, 1981d, T8) of the human condition, but also a biography of fetal distress. After affirming that John was himself a "humanly distressed personality," Lake wrote:

> An unprejudged reading of what St. John of the Cross wrote about the psychosomatic concomitants of the Dark Night of the Spirit show them to be related to his own particularly severely stressed and, indeed, schizoid personality. In his poem "I die because I do not die" he shows the clearest possible familiarity with what we have called the Level 4 of Transmarginal Stress (Lake, 1981d, T9).

Lake quotes John's poem as "evidence" of his particular suffering:

> This life I live in such a way/Is nothing but life's deprivation,/One prolonged annihilation/Till at last I live with Thee./Hear, my God, hear what I say,/I do not want this life of mine;/I die because I do not die.

> Even the fish drawn out of water/Does not lack alleviation;/Death comes at last, the termination/Of the death-throes that it suffers./What death is there to equal this./This sad, despairing life I live?/The more I live the more I die.

> Lift me from this death, release me,/Give me living life, my God,/Not keep me in so strong a bond/To cripple and impede me;/For look, I long, I grieve to see Thee,/My sickness fills me so completely/That I die because I do not die.

Lake allowed that the reason for John's familiarity with the dynamics of the schizoid position was his experience of "life in the womb". He writes that "the life-situation of the mother of the Saint when she was carrying him was singularly distressing" (Lake, 1981d, T10). Lake goes on to cite in detail the facts of John's mother's situation. Poor and destitute, reduced to begging and facing the gradual death of her husband, Catalina conceives John. Describing her situation, Lake writes:

> To the sadness of [her husband's] impending death would be added the anxiety of even severer poverty impending with the loss of the bread-winner. The stage of life, set by these tragic events, provided the inevitable emotional coloring to the pregnancy which gave, to the church and the world, St. John of the Cross (Lake, 1981d, T10).

Thus Lake sees in John's work an "alternative nomenclature" (Lake, 1964, 558) describing the dynamics of the "negative" and "strongly negative" flood of maternal emotions coupled with the "opposition" and

finally "transmarginal" break of the fetus. Lake describes what he imagines Catalina's state of mind and thus state of womb to be:

> No imaginative construction of Juan's mother's state of mind and feelings
> of her likely utterances and sensations, on discovering, some weeks after
> conception, that she was again 'with child', can make light of the tragic con-
> sequences for her of becoming pregnant at that time, under those circum-
> stances of constriction and confusion . . . .
> "Not now!, Not now! That this should happen to me now is total disaster."
> Some words such as these, which a number of mothers have told me rose to
> their lips, out of the shock of recognition of pregnancy in situations such as
> this, have radically transformed the cosmos for the foetuses who have later
> become my patients. With a clarity of "memory" which is, to them, un-
> shakable, they have re-lived the sudden devastating impact, on them in the
> womb, well within the first trimester, of the mother's appalled recognition of
> her pregnant state and its consequences for her life.
> The tragic irony is that the impact on the foetus, of the mother's usually
> only temporary sense that its coming into existence in her womb at this time
> is a disaster, is permanent. She would above all things, want to have avoided
> this final imprinting of her baby with this verdict. But the evidence is strong
> that the mother's feelings about herself become, for the one in the womb, the
> whole basis of its own sense of being and worth and wantedness. The result
> can be a life-long pervasive sense of worthlessness, of being a disaster, "a
> bad thing" (Lake, 1981d, T10).

In John's adult writings, Lake cites two sections from "The Dark Night"
as resonating with his prenatal experience of ultramaximal pain. The
passive dark night of the spirit is described as "horrible and awful to the
spirit" (St. John of the Cross, 1949, 371):

> Sense and spirit, as if beneath some immense and dark load, are in such great
> pain and agony that the soul would find advantage and relief in death (St.
> John of the Cross, 1949, 408).

Soren Kierkegaard

In Soren Kierkegaard Lake also finds one who "needed to go no further than himself to uncover his source material" (Lake, 1964, 595). Indeed, Lake calls him "incomparably the most perceptive diagnostician of
the tortuous paradoxes of the schizoid person" (Lake, 1964, 595) who
"went further into the understanding of the schizoid position than any
man who has ever written about it" (Lake, 1964, 901). Lake understands

Kierkegaard as referring to the schizoid position variously, as "sickness unto death", as his "thorn in the flesh" or his "incurable melancholy", associating "it closely with dread and the abnormal, paradoxical wish to die and be annihilated, in order to escape the mental pain of it" (Lake 1964, 558).

In Kierkegaardian nomenclature, what gives rise to this final paradoxical wish to die? Lake cites Kierkegaard's use of the terms "dread" and "despair" to describe the fetus' or the child's reaction to either abandonment or "the invasion of distressingly bad maternal emotions" (Lake, 1981d, T19). But what is at the root of these is some type of "disrelation" between mother and fetus/infant, the opposite of "interpersonal bondedness". Lake quotes Kierkegaard from *The Sickness Unto Death* at this point, arguing that "ontological anguish, identification with non-being, [and] dread" arise from disrelation:

Despair is the dis-relationship in a relation which relates itself to itself. . . . In the synthesis is . . . the possibility of . . . disrelationship. . . . If he were not a synthesis, he could not despair, neither could he despair if the synthesis were not originally from God's hand in the right relationship.

Whence then comes despair? From the relation wherein the synthesis relates itself to itself, in that God who made man a relationship lets this go, as it were, out of His hand . . . herein, in the fact that the relation is spirit, is the self, consist the responsibility under which all despair lies (Kierkegaard, 1946, 148-149).

This Kierkegaardian passage is hermeneutically profound for Lake. In it he sees Kierkegaard's explanation not only of the genesis of despair, which he envisions as the "outcome of dread" or "identification with non-being", but also its cause, the inability of the fetus/infant "to be identified with the source-person in an indissoluble synthesis" (Lake, 1964, 713). Lake writes that "dread is the state of needing a personal object and being objectless. To put it ontologically, it is non-being" (Lake, 1964, 714). Despair and dread are bound up together here. In another important Kierkegaardian passage for Lake, he cites the resulting dynamics of "disrelation" and "non-being":

Despair is the sickness unto death. It is indeed very far from being true that, literally understood, one dies of this sickness, or that this sickness ends with bodily death. On the contrary, the torment of despair is precisely this, not to be able to die. . . . So to be sick unto death is, not to be able to die-- yet not as though there were hope of life; no, the hopelessness in this case is that even the last hope, death, is not available. When death is the greatest danger, one hopes for life; but when one becomes acquainted with an even more dreadful danger, one hopes for death. So, when the danger is so great that death has become one's hope, despair is the disconsolateness of not being able to die (Kierkegaard, 1946, 150-151).

Thus stated, despair and its concomitants are the "ultimate form[s] of mental pain" (Lake, 1964, 715).

A third passage of Kierkegaard's, this time from the *The Concept of Dread*, is particularly crucial for Lake's appropriation of Kierkegaardian categories to explain the transmarginal and schizoid response. Lake writes that "this language of Kierkegaard's is straining to express the nature of life and its catastrophes in the earliest and most determinative months of existence. This is precisely how schizoid persons . . . tend to relate their complex dilemma" (Lake, 1964, 726):

One may liken dread to dizziness. He whose eye chances to look down into the yawning abyss becomes dizzy . . .

Thus dread is the dizziness of freedom which occurs when the spirit would posit the synthesis, and freedom then gazes down into its own possibility, and grasps at finiteness to hold on to it. In this dizziness freedom succumbs, sinks to the ground. Further than this, psychology cannot and will not go. That very instant everything is changed, and when freedom rises again it sees that it is guilty. Between these two instants lies the leap which no science has explained or can explain. He who becomes guilty in dread becomes as ambiguously guilty as possible (Kierkegaard in Lake, 1964, 725-726).

To Lake, this language, however tortured, clearly expresses the exigencies of a transmarginal break. He summarizes the parallels in the following passage from *Clinical Theology*:

The fall away into detachment from the source-person was not wished for . . . [and] this disastrous denouement was not intended. Therefore, the fall, which occurred in anguish, and as a result of anguish, can only most ambiguously be said to incur guilt. . .

The "freedom" which dread compelled the baby to seize upon, probably at a moment of ultra-maximal mental pain or anguish, was not primarily a choice. It was first a dizziness, a swoon, a fall, a confused catastrophic happening in which the spirit of life by relatedness to a source-person died (Lake, 1964, 726).

Lake continues:

> The detached, spiritless ego does not and cannot go free. It is in a state of "bound freedom" . . . The ego cannot tear itself away from the synthesis, even if it should spend the whole of life trying to stretch or break or cut the "umbilical cord" of the original synthesis. This cannot be done . . . the "qualitative leap" has taken place. The relationship is not as it was before. It is broken. At the same instant, everything is changed, and when freedom arises again is sees that it is guilty. It is in the wrong. It is living a lie . . . [It] feels itself guilty. In part, this is the invariable schizoid feeling of "unconditional badness". The awful question "Why did this happen?" is answered in such a way as to defend the mother's goodness at the cost of one's own. . . . This is not guilt but affliction, but it feels exactly like guilt; not moral guilt so much as ontological guilt. It says, "I ought never to have existed" (Lake, 1964, 726-727).

Real moral culpability, indeed sin, arises when alienation from the actual source of being is retained. Lake writes:

> The continued state of detachment from, and independence of the real source persons (God and the parents become indistinguishable here) which, if the soul maintains it, becomes a state of sin. . . . The direction dread takes, as fear, is no longer dread of the evil of separation (the hysterical position) but dread of the good (the schizoid position) with its dread of the goodness of human bonds (Lake, 1964, 727).

Thus, this person is born and lives his life "painfully aware of the effects of dereliction" but very often unaware of the "actual moments of agonizing mental pain in which the splitting took place" (Lake, 1964, 701). Lake writes that the "victim does not know where this uncanny and unpleasant state of mind comes from" but that "Kierkegaard is explicit about" its origin in the "infantile states of mind and their return to consciousness" (Lake, 1964, 701).

For Lake, Kierkegaard also presents us with a typical example of defense against the despair of the transmarginal break: introversion and intellectualization. Lake explains:

> When the invasion of distressingly bad maternal emotions has entered and overwhelmed the foetal body, the embryo takes refuge in the head. Thought, split off from the rest of the body . . . becomes the sole source of a private joy. Introversion provides the main defense, facilitated by a good intelligence (Lake, 1981d, T19).

Lake then cites a passage from Kierkegaard he sees as descriptive of this process:

> Inwardly torn asunder as I was, without any expectation of leading a happy life, . . . as it naturally springs from and lies in the historical continuity of family life-- **what wonder then that in desperate despair I grasp as naught but the intellectual side in man and clung fast to it** [emphasis Lake's], so that the thought of my own considerable powers of mind was my only consolation, ideas my one joy, and mankind indifferent to me (Kierkegaard, 1938, #244).

Simone Weil

In Simone Weil Lake also finds someone well acquainted with the dynamics of first-trimester transmarginal stress. Referring to Job, Lake writes about Weil that she suffered in this "same way [i.e. "affliction", the schizoid position] and described this condition of spirit minutely" (Lake, 1964, 558).

Lake saw in Weil's three-fold "nail of affliction", including the bodily, mental and social elements, an accurate "alternative nomenclature" very descriptive of transmarginal and schizoid states. He writes:

> We are able to recognize that many elements of these classical descriptions of affliction, such as those of Simone Weil, refer decisively to the first trimester. . . . For instance, Simone Weil's recurrent metaphor of the nail piercing the naval, sees [sic] as being like a moth, pinned alive into an album as a specimen. . . . The nail, or spear or dagger metaphor, as descriptive of the sensation of the foetus as the mother's sharp distress penetrates its vulnerable body, is exceedingly common when the subject is reliving a distress-invaded first trimester (Lake, 1982b, 44).

Another example of correspondence between Weil and Lake and one that he specifically cites is what he perceives to be Weil's description of transmarginal stress:

> Continuously mounting pain produces one kind of struggle against it for a while. Then suddenly, the switches are flung in the opposite direction. Paradoxically it is now death that is longed for, not life. She [Weil] speaks of the co-existence of continuity and separation-- which is represented by the co-existence of hysterical, "come closer", with schizoid, "go away" reactions (Lake, 1981d, T13).

Lake cites a passage from Weil epitomizing this dynamic:

> There is both a continuity and the separation of a definite point of entry, as with the temperature at which water boils, between affliction itself and all the sorrows which, even though they may be very violent, very deep and very lasting, are not afflictions in the strict sense. There is a limit; on the far side of it we have affliction but not on the near side. This limit is not purely objective, all sorts of personal factors have to be taken into account. The same event may plunge one human being into affliction and not another" (Weil in Lake, 1981d, T13).

Weil's essay "The Love of God and Affliction" is particularly salient for Lake. He cites long passages from this essay in several of his works, commenting on Weil's "alternative nomenclature" with a running commentary on how her words apply to transmarginal states.

According to Weil, while affliction includes physical suffering, it is far more than merely physical suffering:

> In the realm of suffering, affliction is something apart, specific and irreducible. It is a quite different thing from simple suffering. It takes possession of the soul and marks it through and through with its own mark, the mark of slavery. . . . Affliction is the uprooting of a life, a more or less attenuated equivalent of death, made irresistibly present in the soul by the attack or immediate apprehension of physical pain. There is not real affliction unless the event that seized and uprooted a life, attacks it, directly or indirectly in all parts, social, psychological and physical (Weil, 1952, 117-118).

The totality of Weil's "nail of affliction" resonated with Lake's understanding of the totality of the schizoid state. "Affliction" Lake wrote, "is like a curse in every cell and tissue, organ and function of the body. The affliction, by our hypothesis, takes place when the organism is just emerging into embryonic and foetal existence. Later on, when born, bits of us can get hurt while most of us escapes. Not so here, every part is attacked" (Lake, 1981d, T12).

Lake paraphrases Weil's description of the three-fold nail of affliction:

1. The social scorn. The nail of affliction. A sense of social degradation with self-scorn, self-hatred. Revulsion is turned inward. A horror of the self as "bad", "black", "inanimate", sub-human. Feels disinherited, no family, no past, no future. A persistent sense of worthlessness. Guilt that I exist. Being at all is bad.

2. The mental pain. A horrible or terrible splitting or tearing apart of the whole self, spirit, soul, mind and body. A cleavage, cracking-up or falling into fragmentation. This can be experienced as madness or loss of wholeness. Disintegration. Detachment of the ego. Feelings of unreality of the self and others.

3. The physical anguish. Agonizing physical distress, bodily wretchedness, muscular tension, pain in abdomen especially at or above the navel, bowels, etc., with nausea, retching, fear of vomiting, diarrhea, palpitation, blurred vision, headache, sweating (Lake, 1981d, C41).

While the physical component of Weil's "affliction" is important, the social and psychological are more so. Commenting on the social dimension, Weil writes that the "social factor is essential. There is not really true affliction where there is not social degradation or the fear of it in some form or another" (Weil, 1951, 119). Lake picks up this theme as referring to the sense of social alienation that the foetus has when s/he is cut off from acknowledgment, approval, and indeed, an ontological sense of being from the defining social relationship, that of the mother. Lake, in commenting upon the social dimension of Weil's nail of affliction writes:

> The sense of social degradation, alienation and rejection is often inseparably hard to get rid of, because the afflicted person has turned in on themselves. In terms of this hypothesis, this individual, as a foetus, sensed their mother's horror or disgust at getting pregnant, which is to say, her hatred of its own being there at all. The foetus was overwhelmed by this maternal revulsion and comes to share it. His own innate sense of being good, and of having been provided with a shopping list, entitling it to come into the maternal womb with an expectation of finding something good enough on the shelves, is totally overturned and destroyed. It begins to be apologetic for having come into the shop at all. The shopkeeper, who might be expected to be behind the counter to welcome the new customer, is not aware that she has any obligation to be there. When the bell rings, telling her that a new customer has indeed stepped into the shop, she appears behind the placental counter only to scream at him, or to beseech him with bitter tears to go away. He may be kept waiting for 20, 24, or 28 weeks, hoping against a rising tide of despair for due recognition, and then be violently extracted, through a door he didn't know existed, left to kick for a few agonizing minutes in panic, until physical death overtakes the many deaths he has already died. He is not buried with liturgical rites or mourned by many. Incineration ends this aborted life.
>
> The afflicted are those who continue to live, who come to term and are born. But the "red-hot iron" continues to sear their souls throughout life, unless some merciful repression for a while obliterates the now self-

destructive impulse, and the death-wish, dominant at depth, is forgotten by living superficially (Lake, 1981d, T12).

That this experience of the most important social relationship is projected onto "god" is only logical. A fetus' primal experience of the "cosmos" as mediated by the mother is determinative for a post-natal conceptualization of the entirety of existence. Lake quotes Weil once again contrasting suffering with affliction:

> The great enigma of human life is not suffering but affliction. It is not surprising that the innocent are killed, tortured, driven from their country, made destitute, or reduced to slavery, imprisoned in camps or cells, since there are criminals to perform such actions. It is not surprising either that disease is the cause of long sufferings, which paralyze life and make it an image of death, since nature is at the mercy of the blind play of mechanical necessities. But it is surprising that God should have given affliction the power to seize the very souls of the innocent and to take possession of them as their sovereign lord. At the very best, he who is branded by affliction will keep only half his soul. . . . Affliction makes God appear to be absent for a time, more absent than a dead man, more absent than light in the utter darkness of a cell. A kind of horror submerges the whole soul (Weil, 1951, 119-121).

Weil goes on to write that there are many who suffer from such affliction all around us. She writes that "we only notice that they have a strange way of behaving and we censure this behavior" (Weil, 1951, 119). Underneath the external surface of "differentness", a "constricted confusion" exists; an internal paradox of the transmarginal break, wherein the desire for "being" is transmuted into a profound desire for "nonbeing". Weil's description of affliction continues:

> Like a half-crushed worm, they [those who suffer from affliction] have no words to express what is happening to them. . . . Affliction is something specific and impossible to describe in any other terms, as sounds are to anyone who is deaf and dumb. . . . Affliction hardens and discourages us because, like a red hot iron, it stamps the soul to its very depths with the scorn, the disgust, and even the self-hatred and sense of guilt and defilement that crime logically should produce. . . . Evil . . . is felt in the heart of the man who is afflicted and innocent (Weil, 1951, 121).

Thus Lake sees Weil's account of affliction as an "authentic account of schizoid affliction" (Lake, 1964, 706).

The Theodicy

Lake's thinking regarding the value of a theological theodicy addressed to psychological suffering did develop and evolve somewhat, but remained surprisingly constant throughout his career. What did change was its application. Early on, Lake spoke of the "innocent suffering" caused by the traumas of early infancy and birth; later on he spoke of the traumas of the primal period, especially the first trimester of intrauterine life.

Early Thought

The component parts of the theological dimension of Lake's M-FDS, especially his theodicy, can be discerned earlier in his writing. As with the other facets of the M-FDS, there seems to be an evolution of sorts regarding his thinking. For instance, as early as 1966, Lake was writing about a paradigm of theodicy regarding the "treatment" of human suffering. In *Clinical Theology*, Lake wrote that the "incalculable riches of Christ" (Lake, 1964, 16), particularly those demonstrated on the cross, are available to all:

> This is what I mean by the need for research into **what** the correlations are between Christ's sufferings and ours, and into **how** these can be effectively communicated to sufferers now. Whether the group members are church-related in the going-to-church-regularly sense, or, because of their affliction are people rejected by and rejecting the existing institution, Christ's sufferings and death are for them. Our research is for them, and so is our pastoral care. . . . For my part, unless we claim, in practice, that Christ's sufferings, death and resurrection are for **all men** we betray both his Lordship and our proper ministry (Lake, 1979a, 2).

Thus Lake contextualizes his work:

> I have always considered that my . . . task was to proclaim the Christ, the Son of God. The focus of the whole proclamation is His Cross, leading as it did to His Resurrection, to His glorified presence "at the right hand of God", and always with us through the Holy Spirit in the common life of His earthly Body. His Cross is my central theme (Lake, 1964, 24).

Lake continues:

It is this event [i.e. the cross], and our proper relation to Christ who undertook it, that is the primary resource for the ultimate transformations of human personality (Lake, 1964, 17-18).

Instructive of Lake's early understanding of theodicy is his citation in the first few pages of *Clinical Theology* of Taylor Caldwell's book *The Man Who Listens*. About it he writes:

> The whole book illustrates the way in which persons in a wide variety of human difficulties, speaking to a man behind a curtain, whom they cannot see, do in fact talk themselves round to the place where they are stating their complaint against the universe. If at that point the curtain opens, they see the Author of the Universe, not as one standing aside in complacency, but as crucified upon the Cross. Their whole attitude to life and to themselves changes profoundly (Lake, 1964, 7).

It is this identification of the suffering God in Christ with those who suffer which "gives Him the right to be called the greatest listener to all suffering. It is this which gives His listening its redemptive quality" (Lake, 1964, 14). Lake continues by writing:

> It is an astonishing fact that the events of the crucifixion of Jesus Christ portray every variety of human suffering and evil, especially those crucial and decisive forms which suffering takes during the first year of life, where mental pain weakens the foundations of character and determines its distortions. Whether we speak about it or not, it is to this centre of the universe, where its Creator identifies Himself with the evils of His creation, that all our dialogue in the end returns (Lake, 1964, 18).

As mentioned above, Lake saw the relationship between the physiological and theological paradigms of the M-FDS as "something shown side by side with something else, inviting comparison of the correspondences" (Lake, 1980b, 3). Specifically, Lake writes about two profound "correspondences" between the experiences of Christ and the experiences of those who pass through the two most basic and common "peri-natal catastrophes." The first is the apparent congruity between the "terrible, asphyxiating crushing affliction during the birth process" and Christ's experience of the "crushing affliction of Gethsemane" (Lake, 1989, 224). The second congruity relates the "separation anxiety which pushes the newborn to the limits of solitary panic-- and beyond, over the edge of the abyss into dereliction and a falling apart of the self in dread and non-being" with Christ's "loss of all friendly faces, the pinioned anguish which cannot in any way find relief from the mounting pain, the sense of social alienation and shame, the 'concatenation of confusion' as to who in this hell he is, the totally condemned, cast out by a righteous God because of the sin with which he is identified, or the perfectly righteous and obedient Son, and finally the rising sense of awful dereliction, which ended with the great cry from the cross, 'My God, my God, why hast Thou forsaken me?" (Lake, 1989, 224).

Lake writes that both the affliction and anxiety of the birth process, as well as the events of early life that bring affliction and anxiety serve to give rise to a deep inner horror of a *deus absconditus*. The child attributes the "badness of an unbearable situation" (Lake, 1989, 225) to himself, since it is both incomprehensible and dangerous to attribute the badness to either "the gods" or his parents. So his mind and heart echo with the reverberation of an "indelible badness in its own very being" (Lake, 1989, 225).

According to Lake, it is exactly to this person in this "constricted confusion" that the paradox of *deus crucifixus* is so profoundly important. It is the "dark continent" of this person that is so ripe for "missionary evangelism". Lake uses the dark continent/missionary metaphor to describe the necessary need to communicate a theodicy to these sufferers. He writes:

> In every human being therefore, a new "dark continent" has opened up, ripe for missionary evangelism. This continent was simply not imagined or known about at the turn of the century. In one sense, Kierkegaard understood it well. Because of his understanding he had already begun to highlight those aspects of theology. But his influence on mainline Anglican and Catholic theology was almost nil until a hundred years after his death. If these "dark continents" are allowed to remain unevangelised, we are warned that from these human jungles, dark forces will emerge, often in "psychic epidemics", to invade and disrupt cultures based on that precarious epiphenomenon, consciousness. (Lake, 1989, 228).

The "gospel" brought to the sufferer is the suffering of Christ on the Cross. For Lake, this is first of all indicative of the fact that "God has not only spoken through His Son; what is perhaps more important, He has listened through his Son" (Lake, 1964, 14). The cross is not only significant for the salvation of sinners, but is also crucial for the reconciliation of sufferers. Indeed, as Lake writes, Christ came to "set the captives free" not only from sin, but from the consequences of "innocent suffering" (Lake, 1964, 14).

Thus, a theology which "merely" proclaims the forgiveness of sin to sinners is inadequate. Lake writes:

> The old paradigm of the work of Christ for men was almost entirely centred on the problem of culpable sin. It had no word to speak clearly to those who, while innocent infants, were victims of parental and social evil. I need to know and do know, that Christ is identified with me, as a highhanded sinner at times, reconciling me in my sinfulness, to God, whose holiness made this provision. The same holiness of the Father set forth his innocent suffering Son, to be identified with the innocent victims of the sins of others. The defenselessness of the "Lamb of God" puts him alongside them (Lake, 1980b, 3).

Lake explains:

> The Cross is my central theme, but the half has not been told if I confine the effects of that redemptive act merely to "the forgiveness of sin", infinitely great as I know that liberating message to be.
> The very powers of evil, standing in the shadows behind "the mystery of iniquity" and "the mystery of suffering", were dethroned by Christ's active, obedient submission to their onslaught. Therefore, he reconciles to God by His Cross not only sinners, but sufferers. Not only the memories of culpable sin which condemn the conscience, but the deeper memories of intolerable affliction which condemn faith as a delusion, these too are confronted by the fact of Christ's Cross. These passive evils, which are not of the soul's own making, are not accessible to a pastoral care which can only talk in terms of the forgiveness of sins (Lake, 1964, 24-25).

Thus Christ's work on the cross is twofold:

> In the presence of sin, high handed and culpable, I need to know that the cross of Christ is the ground on which my justification, God's gift of righteousness, depends. In the presence, however, of unmerited cruelties, catastrophic in their destructive impact on the growing person right at the beginning, which lie like a heavy black cloud across the sky from horizon to horizon from birth to death, for ever afterwards the constant source of intense mental pain, irremediable guilt and inescapable social badness the cross speaks another message, that of a theodicy. This theodicy reinstates the goodness of God, and is in this sense, his justification of himself, when the innocent afflicted, like Job, accuse him of bungling his creation, loading the world with cosmic evil before man arrived on the scene. This theodicy proclaims the Lamb slain from the foundation of the world (Lake, 1989, 229).

Writing in *Clinical Theology* he elaborates:

> Only by making "sin" a synonym for man's state of contradiction and for the fallen human family into which the innocent baby is born, can we speak of "the forgiveness of sin" as the sovereign remedy. What if-- as often happens-- the near-fatal injuries of transit from the womb have produced in the infant an irremediable horror of existence itself, from which all its other interpersonal and ontological evils have stemmed? Can we meet this ultimate anomaly *simplicitor*, with the forgiveness of sins? Whose sins, ask the afflicted from the womb? Ours? How is this our sin? By whom does the offense come? Surely, so far as the child is concerned, the offense is its creator's. Now if (pardon the exegesis) we see that woe does come to that creative Man by whom the offense seems to come, the woe of the Cross itself, as He actively subjects Himself to the dual mysteries of iniquity and suffering, then by His Cross, the offended are made potentially believers. The bondage of the will to trust, the immobility in relation to commitment, the paralysis of faith in face of the awful truth about their origins, all these are resolved by the presence of the crucified Christ with them in their wretchedness (Lake, 1964, 26).

This is where Lake's "therapy of theodicy" is grounded; namely, the communication of God's love and identification through Christ on the Cross to those suffering from pain through no fault of their own. This is "the crux of [all] therapy" because it is not enough "to merely bring the ultimate forms of mental pain to the doors of consciousness, you also must endow the ego with the supernatural fortitude to endure them" (Lake, 1964, 27). This can ultimately be done only because the "Spirit of Christ, in spite of flinching, did bear all the extremities of persecution and affliction" (Lake, 1964, 28) and thus makes available to each sufferer the benefits of his passion, the "incalculable riches of Christ." These benefits are metaphorically expressed by Lake as the "'release of captives', the recovery of sight as insight, the untying of the tongues of those who are struck dumb in the face of shameful parental cruelty, the healing by tears of those who are too terrified to weep at the time when the terror struck" (Lake, 1989, 229).

The "Innocent" Sufferers

As with the Lake's early thought, "the not-as-yet-searched-out riches of Christ in Scripture" and theology are the answer to the need for an "exacting theological paradigm of reconciliation and reparation" in response to "the harshness of the affliction which an innocent foetus has often to endure" (Lake, 1981d, T1). These "basic, original injuries take place during embryonic and foetal life" (Lake, 1981d, T2) and give rise to an early experience of the cosmos which is "so painful as to destroy the innate capacity to trust" (Lake, 1981d, T1). Thus the result is a paradoxical switch from the will to live to a profound desire to die. The fetus, alone within the tomb-like womb is gradually "nudged to the edge of the abyss of non-being . . . and eventually falls over the edge into the nothingness which is the abandonment of hope, love, desire for life, and expectation of access to humanity" (Lake, 1989, 232).

These early primal experiences give rise to the basic definition of "god" and what it is like to live in his world. The resultant cry will echo Job's, "Why was I not taken from the womb to the tomb?" "My experience of your world is such that your only mercy is to take me out of it into oblivion" (Lake, 1989, 233).

This is the situation, according to Lake, to which God must address himself "if God is to make himself understood by the innocent afflicted" (Lake, 1989, 234). There is the need for "God's Proper Man [to] work within constricted confusion," to come "under human conditions hedged about with multiple constrictions" (Lake, 1981d, T1). This is the only way to "speak well of God in the face of all the evil in his creation," that God sends forth "His Son to pioneer a 'ford' through the river of pain." In this way, according to Lake, the Father is "justified."

It is here that Lake finds resonance with the ideas of several thinkers, but particularly so with Jürgen Moltmann and the ideas in his book *Der gekreuzigte Gott*. Lake writes:

> Moltmann clearly interprets the death and resurrection of Christ as both a theodicy and a justification. It is a theodicy because it enables innocent sufferers to experience God's presence with them in their suffering, and by that act to reverse its impact on them, from Job-like accusations against the horrors of God's providence, to Paul-like praise at the divine *paraklesis*. Under a like *thlipsis* or intolerable pressure, the Lamb of God, who is the Lord of Life, suffers alongside his creatures. This makes a joyful bearing possible (*hypomone*), a "sticking it out under" the affliction in the power of the one who is alongside. It is upon Jesus that the greater weight lies. This is the glorious possibility open to the interpretation of the cross as theodicy. As justification it speaks also to culpable sinners of the unmerited mercy of God in imputing righteousness, that is, the gift of rightly-related sonship to them. The innocent afflicted do not feel themselves to be sinners while they are merely automata, dust, weeping stones, worms and the lower forms of life. It

is the theodicy that makes their suffering human and turns them, for the first time, into sinners. Only human beings can be sinners, worms and dust cannot be guilty of sin, and such they feel themselves to be (Lake, 1989, 234-235).

Thus, once the mediatorial work of theodicy has been completed, once the sufferer has sensed the presence alongside of the One who suffered, the One who has penetrated "every tortured cell of the sufferer with the once and for all time agonized cells of his own divine-human body," (Lake, 1989, 238) then the more familiar substitutionary and reconciliatory work of justification can take place.

The "Murder of the Truth"

Before the multi-faceted riches of Christ's work on the cross can be applied, spiritual and emotional poverty must be acknowledged. Standing in the way is the existence of the "vital" or "pervasive" lie; the "murdering of the truth" that took place "in the beginning" which is bolstered and supported by some very influential factors. The biblically-based doctrinal fact of the solidarity of the human race and the individual family in sin "allows for the sins of the father and the mothers [to] descend upon [their] innocent children" (Lake, 1989, 231). This can and does affect them for life. And this results in the fact that "some suffering in later life takes its origin, not in the culpable sin of the sufferer, but from his involvement, while in a state of total dependency, in the sin of others" (Lake, 1989, 231). The afflictions of adult life which "drive people to despair and suicide are faithful reproductions of crises first encountered in the earliest weeks of life" (Lake, 1989, 231).

Whatever the cause of the innocent foetus' or neonate's suffering, whether it is the umbilically-communicated rejection, neglect or hate of intrauterine life, or the possible "brain-destroying, suffocating, twisting, tearing, crushing torture" (Lake, 1989, 232) of birth or the later experience of neglect and abuse, this "truth" must be quickly "murdered." Lake writes that "as soon as the tragedy of human life impinges upon the infant, indeed upon the foetus still within the womb, the truth of what has happened is immediately murdered by repression and turned into a lie which denies that it ever happened" (Lake, 1978c, 118). The truth, however, remains to be uncovered. "Though split off from consciousness, dissociated and repressed, no detail of the incident has been obliterated" (Lake, 1981d, T2).

Hindrances to the "Spirit of Truth"

Once the vital lie is in place, once the "truth has been murdered" and guile is entrenched, several obstacles conspire to prevent the recall of the truth. Lake identified the two main obstacles when he wrote that "religion, in the broadest sense of 'piety' and 'loyalty' to parents . . . obstructs a realistic recall" (Lake, 1981d, T2). The fact that the original experience of the "cosmos" in the person of the mother and subsequently, the father, is generalized onto "god" results in reaction formation on a grand scale. The experience of "god's" "bad universe" as mediated by the foetus' or child's mother is incomprehensible and is therefore repressed and replaced by an idealization of "mother" and "god".

Parents

Regarding parents, Lake writes that they often "have a vested interest in retrospective falsification of incidents they are ashamed of, and 'didn't mean' or 'didn't want' to happen. It is as if obliterating from their record everything that didn't 'go according to plan' and was far from their own 'ideal' of parenting, could obliterate it from the intra-uterine and peri-natal record of their offspring" (Lake, 1981d, T2).

Ironically, Christendom often aids in this falsification because the biblical injunction to honor parents and submit to existing authorities has been recommended for unilateral observance. But this is certainly not the true Christian faith. Christians are to be not only "as harmless as doves," but also "as wise as serpents". "Submission of one's person must never include submission of one's duty to reflect on basic justice, on what is right and wrong whoever does it, on how power is being used, either to enhance humanness or to dehumanize others" (Lake, 1981d, T2). If this duty is relinquished, as it often is, then people are condemned to condemn themselves just because their parents condemned them. These parents, acting in contravention to God's law of love, force the child to repeat and eventually believe the following:

"You are worthless. You are an unfortunate mistake. You are an embarrassment, a source of shame. You were not wanted. It is wrong for you to be her, (at this time, or with the wrong sex, or at all). Honour your mother who transfused you with this terrible truth, long before you took to breathing. Honour your father, whose every glance and rude words impressed this despairing identity upon the tender wax of your infancy and childhood. Honour the authorities who could find no decent room for them to live in, but condemned them and your young spirit to hovel-dwelling. Honour the God who created a world in which such things regularly happen and won't hear criticism of the set up he's responsible for." Say after me; "all is for the best in the best of all possible worlds." This does not honour motherhood, fatherhood, authority or God-head but mocks them (Lake, 1981d, T2-T3).

Lake writes that above all else, this moralism requires a denial of the founder of Christianity, Jesus Christ.

Collusion to this retrospective falsification by the adult sufferer often adds to the "murder of the truth" because it is pleasant to remember our earliest relationships as idyllic. But this cover-up cannot negate the consequences; rather, it generates the very distrust and confusion it was meant to vanquish. Thus, "the mental health of the average man . . . is a life lived over the top of a tissue of closely woven lies, a fabric of falsehood" (Lake, 1978c, 118). And contrary to the conventional wisdom, "the line between the 'normal' person and the 'neurotic' is not that the normal personality can function without intrinsic falsehood whereas the neurotic person cannot" (Lake, 1978c, 118). Rather, it is the "neurotic" person who is discovering the cover-up of the "strenuous denial"; the repression of which has become "normal" for the rest of us. Lake explains:

We call a person "normal" if the self-deception that he uses to repress, deny, displace, and rationalize those basic wounds that are ubiquitous in human beings from babyhood works quite well. He is "normal" in so far as his defenses against too much painful reality are as successful as (all unbeknown to the person himself) they are meant to be (Lake, 1978c, 118).

True health in the human spirit often appears unhealthy and neurotic because it is dealing with the "murder of truth" and is in the process of restoring "truth in the inmost parts." Lake describes this using the metaphor of the physical body:

The first response of the tissues to a deep shrapnel wound is to wall it off *in situ*, so that it cannot spread infection and death to the whole body. But then, as years pass, and health is restored to a high pitch, the tissues will work this foreign body to the surface, until it presents under the skin, and asks, as it were, for removal. Similarly, in abundant health, the attics and basements of the human spirit are being emptied of old junk. This is a phenomenon both of nature and of grace. It is certainly the Holy Spirit's work (Lake, 1967, 19).

The "Helping Professions"

Ironically, the "Holy Spirit's work" is "hindered" by those in the so-called helping professions who are "normal"; by those whose function it is to promote spiritual and emotional health. Their reaction to their own "primal wounds" is repression and therefore, their reactions to other's "primal wounds" is similar:

> Too many ministers, hearing a hint from this or that parishioner of strange, disturbing feelings and fantasies that are tumbling out into the front hall of his mind, can only interpret such "dreadful" dark or dirty contents as evidence of backsliding under the old terminology or a nervous breakdown under the new. Treating his parishioners as he treats himself, the minister insists that Christians don't have such thoughts. They must be returned to the attics and basements from which they emerged. That it is the very nature of sanctification, as a process of eradication of evil of every kind, first to insist that it be looked at steadily, accepted as one's own, and then dealt with under the cross, of this the minister seems to have no knowledge.
>
> If his anxious exhortation fails to effect the cure of re-repression, he hands the patient over to his general practitioner. This good doctor, pressed for time, and maybe also uninstructed in the differential diagnosis between breakdown and breakthrough, will attempt to seal up the attics and basements of the mind with pharmacological glue. Minister and doctor are here acting in collusion with Western man's fear of the unknown dark continent within him, where death of the self in dread sits like a bird of prey, blindfolded, for the time being, by the owner, but biding its time, waiting its chance to attack again (Lake, 1967, 20-21).

Religion

Religion, in the broad sense of the term as inculcating duty, piety, and loyalty to parents, also serves as an obstruction to realistic recall of the primal truth. Christianity, when identified with the "ruling or privileged class" instead of the New Testament identification with the oppressed and under-privileged, also colludes with the repression of the truth. This interpretation of Christianity contains within it the assumption that the prevailing order is a good one. Those who don't feel "good", who, indeed, feel "bad", by their very existence implicitly question the "goodness" of the prevailing scheme of things, and as such, constitute an offense. Lake writes:

The Christian faith, denying its Founder and origins, has culturally assimilated its teaching and assumptions to this folk religion. Insofar as it has done this, a betrayal of the poor and the weak, the sick and the imprisoned, has invalidated Christ's attitude of identification with the socially broken and disowned, joining his critics and murderers (Lake, 1981d, T2).

At this point Lake reiterates the content of Mary's Magnificat. Lake paraphrases the content of Mary's words, who, pregnant with Jesus, declares to her cousin Elizabeth, pregnant with the future John the Baptist:

The necessity, if justice is to be established in the earth, that a certain leveling process must take place. . . . It is for those "of low degree," hardly mentionable among the many classified orders of a "High Grid" society, for whom this crazy God is revealed as "the Suffering Servant", as the "Lamb slain from the foundation of the world" (Lake, 1981d, T2).

This "crazy God" then, stands as a contradiction to and critic of the existing oppressive power structures, be they parents, authorities, religious hierarchies, or "god". The Creator God, far from flinching from responsibility for the "cosmos", sends "the suffering servant" to "condemn their condemnation." Lake, writes that raising the issue of pain and injustice, "far from being disloyal to the Creator, is the only way of being faithful to the truth, to that justice which his image as our creator has impressed upon us indelibly" (Lake, 1981d, T2).

Self-accusation

The paradox of transmarginal state, wherein the desire for life and being is transformed into a desire for death and non-being, makes the recall of the primal truth that much more difficult. Self-accusation and self-hate are the responses of the schizoid state; not other-accusation and other-hate. Lake writes that the effect of victimization of the transmarginal variety does not make them "seek victims for their retributive rage" but rather they "seek ways of prolonging the big person's aggression" against themselves. "They seem to be vindicating the original parental victimizer, continuing to honor the primal hostile verdict by energetically pursuing the same policy now in self-destructiveness" (Lake, 1981d, T2).

God, though, identifies with this self-accusation, with this self-hate, with this self-wrath. Isaiah 63 prophesies that the "object of the crushing affliction and the direction of the wrath seem, at times to be interchangeable with the subject" (Lake, 1981d, T3). God pours out his wrath upon God. God forsakes God. God has "judged" God. Judgment, as Lake notes, has begun with the very household of God. Lake writes:

> God sent forth his Son, as the Lamb slain before the foundation of the world, in order that the final authority should be seen to be sensitive to the criticism that it is a victimizing world into which historical man and his offspring are introduced at conception. It is God himself who, in sending forth His Son to be the world's Redeemer, Restorer, Reconciler and Justifier, justifies . . . the cry of pain torn from the heart of the afflicted. God himself restates the justice of the anguished complaint of the Psalmist, "My God, why have you forsaken me; Why are you so far from helping me?" in that that very complaint becomes Christ's own, within the household of God (Lake, 1981d, T3).

The Way Back

It is this distinctly Christological resource which provides hope for any sufferer of pre-natal and primal affliction. While this "resource" may not be always be so explicitly stated, it is the only "answer", even if implicitly:

> The focal point of all the questions of theodicy: "How could a good God let such evil as this happen in a world in which he takes responsibility?" These probing questions are answered by the presence of Christ alongside in equivalent catastrophic pain. . . . He takes the whole constricted confusion on himself and uses it. He uses pain of all intensities as a prime medium in which he himself grew and enables us to grow (Lake, 1981d, T3).

Because Christ has put the basic fault of the "cosmos" right by the active "bearing of pain . . . and death", this theodicy, this justification of God in the light of suffering becomes a vital bridge between the innocent suffering of the fetus which provoked the primal breach to the use of this suffering as a means for growth. The paradoxical conversion from life to death provoked by transmarginal stress in now righted by a paradoxical conversion from death back to life by means of suffering. Lake states that "this is the royal road to the discovery of the depths of self, of others, and of God. It is as joyful in its conclusion as it is in its passage" (Lake, 1981d, T4).

This occurs because the cross of Christ constitutes the "essential bridge-head . . . between the nightmare of intra-uterine and peri-natal pain, endured in offended innocence, and the resolution of the long-fixated affliction in a day-spring of uninhibited praise of a Creator who, because of his strange work in Christ, is now vindicated, acquitted, exonerated and . . . justified" (Lake, 1981d, T4). Thus, theodicy is defined as follows:

> The facts about God that turn the offense of innocent sufferers into growth, the Cross showing that their cry is heard, as the crucified Son of God utters it, in identification with all victims like him (Lake, 1981d, T4).

Once stated, Lake sets out to cull the Christian theological corpus for any "alternative theological nomenclature" that would lend its weight to his definition of an "exacting theological paradigm of reconciliation and reparation" (Lake, 1981d, T1). He surveys "the whole pharmacopoeia" (Lake, 1989, 227) of Christian theological reflection and applies what appears to correlate to the various components of the M-FDS.

Aurelius Augustine

Lake begins with Augustine, particularly with his *Confessions*, which, he observes, serve to prompt his readers to honesty by "telling of his own abysses" (Lake, 1981d, T15). Augustine writes:

> When they read or hear these confessions of my past sins, which You have forgiven and over which You have drawn a veil . . . then their hearts will be aroused. They will no longer lie in the slumber of despair, saying, "I cannot", but will awake in the love of Your mercy, tasting the sweetness of Your grace (Augustine, 1963, X:3).

It is in his *Discourses on the Psalms*, however, that Lakes sees Augustine displaying a profound understanding of human suffering as tragic, senseless and irremedial and "linked with the significance of the suffering and death of Christ" (Williams, 1979, 78). This suffering is permitted by God primarily to draw persons closer to him. Here, Christ's suffering serves as an exemplar:

> We find our own weakness in pain and dereliction, but are saved from despair by the knowledge of Christ's weakness. Christ suffers real mental anguish, sorrow and fear. . . . The dereliction of Christ on the cross, where,

"God cries out to God for mercy", is repeatedly taken as the moment in which Christ shows himself paradigmatically human and gives voice to all human suffering, but especially to the sufferings of his Church, the body of those whose lives are lived under the sign of the strange *Deus crucifixus* (Lake, 1981d, T15).

Commenting on Psalm 141:7, in *Discourses on the Psalms,* Augustine makes the statement that the two Biblical texts which provide the key for the understanding of the entirety of Scripture are Acts 9:4 ("Saul, Saul, why do you persecute me?") and Matthew 25:40 ("What-ever you did for one of the least of these brothers of mine, you did for me"). Lake cites Rowan William's comment on Augustine's observation:

> In these sayings is affirmed the absolute unity of Christ with his suffering people; and this principle of God's identification with humanity is the clue to the whole of revelation. What is said of God in Christ can be applied to God. Christ suffers in our sufferings, and we in his-- "we too were there." The pattern of Christ's cross is the meeting place of God and humanity. To become Godlike is to accept crucifixion by the destructiveness of the world (Williams in Lake, T15).

Martin Luther

Lake sees Luther's *theologia crucis* as based solidly upon verses 18-30 of chapter one of Paul's first letter to the Corinthians where Paul's summary of the power and wisdom of God is "Christ crucified." The *theologia gloria* that Luther saw as the opposite of the *theologia crucis* was attacked by Luther in Thesis #21 of "The Heidelberg Disputation" (Luther, 1962, 290-292) in 1518. Luther writes that "the theologian of glory says bad is good and good is bad. The theologian of the cross calls them by their proper name" (Luther, 1962, 291). Again Lake cites William's summary when he writes:

> The *theologia gloria* looks on outward forms only, and so fails to perceive the strange and contradictory reality of God's working. The *theologia crucis* is accurate vision, which is prepared to confront without flinching the terror of God's judgment, to look at the "evil" of doubt, dereliction and fear and call it good. Without the theology of the cross man misuses the best in the worst manner (Williams in Lake, 1981d, T16).

Rather, the true "theologian" must recognize, as Luther clearly states in Thesis #20, that "the visible and manifest things of God [are] seen through suffering and the cross" (Luther in Lake, 1981d, T16). Thus Christ has revealed himself paradoxically, by hiding himself beneath suffering and the cross. Strength is manifested in weakness. This paradox is also true of the human condition. Lake writes:

> Our problems in living derive from the fact that our "strength and prosperity" are usually expressive of the "strength and prosperity" of our repressive defenses. . . . We give the impression of being most positive when we are the most able to negate the fact that we are negating primal negations, avoiding the fact that we are avoiding the void (Lake, 1981d, T16).

Thus the cross become the place where God is truly made known; where God abandons God to reach down to the abandoned. In seeking for indications of what is authentically God, including His "life, activity and presence, we shall find them only in their contradictories, in our death and hell, as in Christ's" (Lake, 1981d, T17). This basic paradox can be seen in Luther's often misunderstood statement *simul justus et peccator*. Williams writes:

> Faith begins in the experience of *accusatio sui*, alienation from the self, guilt, the sense of condemnation: an experience which becomes *metanoia* when it is seen as a taking of the cross, standing where Christ once stood, under Law, under wrath. . . . The duality of Christian experience --wrath and grace found together in the cross-- persists throughout life, and there is no grace without the prior stripping away of illusory self-complacency. Every moment of grace and forgiveness rests upon the experience of *accusatio sui*; before you can be reconciled, you must see your alienation. . . . To know forgiveness in the midst of hell because of the cross of Christ is the criterion of true Christian faith.   . . . Quite pragmatically, the believer is upheld and supported by the knowledge that Christ himself passed through this hell and thereby consecrated it to God (Williams, 1979, 148-149).

Luther describes this clearly:

> Having entered into darkness and blackness I see nothing; I live by faith, hope, and love alone and I am weak, that is, I suffer, for when I am weak, then I am strong (Luther, 1892, 176:16).

Lake quotes Luther writing in summary describing the theologian of the cross:

He does not . . . flee sufferings. . . . To all that is humble and lowly he turns in love; that is the "love of the cross, born of the cross, which turns in the direction where it does not find good which it may enjoy, but where it may confer good upon the bad and needy person." For as one "reduced to nothing through the cross and suffering," he knows that "sinners are attractive because they are loved; they are not loved because they are attractive" (Luther in Lake, 1981d, T17).

St. John of the Cross

That Lake viewed Juan de la Cruz as both an example and an insightful detailer of the dynamics of the schizoid state has already been affirmed previously. Lake further writes that "where St. John of the Cross is so poignantly observant is in his description of the troublesome disturbances which, in some Christian people, accompany those particular stages, of maturation or of growth in obedience to the Holy Spirit's prompting, involve a letting go" (Lake, 1981d, T8).

Lake utilizes three elements of St. John's diptych, the first being the short poem "The Dark Night":

1. One dark night,/Fired with love's urgent longings/--Ah, the sheer grace!--/I went out unseen,/My house being now all stilled; 2. In darkness and secure,/By the secret ladder, disguised,/--Ah, the sheer grace!--/In darkness and concealment,/My house being now all stilled;/3. On that glad night,/In secret, for no one saw me,/Nor did I look at anything,/With no other light or guide/Than the one that burned in my heart;/4. This guided me/More surely than the light of noon/To where he waited for me/--him I knew so well--/In a place where no one appeared./5. O guiding night!/O night more lovely than the dawn!/O night that has united/The lover with his beloved,/Transforming the beloved in her lover./6. Upon my flowering breast/Which I kept for him alone,/There he lay sleeping./As I caressing him/There in a breeze from the fanning cedars./7. When the breeze blew from the turret/Parting his hair,/He wounded my neck/With his gentle hand/Suspending all my senses./8. I abandoned and forgot myself/Laying my face on my beloved;/All things ceased; I went out from myself,/Leaving my cares/Forgotten among the lilies. (John of the Cross, 1987, 55-57).

Lake also utilizes two of John's commentaries, including *The Dark Night*, which examines the first four stanzas of the poem in detail and the poem in general, and *The Ascent of Mount Carmel*, which makes allusions to the final four stanzas of "The Dark Night" but is not, strictly speaking, a commentary on the poem (Kavanaugh, 1987, 43-54; 157-

161). The two commentaries complement each other, with *Ascent of Mount Carmel* focusing more on human initiative, or the "active night", while *The Dark Night* deals with divine initiative, or the "passive night" (Kavanaugh, 1987, 46).

For Lake, the active phase of the dark night of the senses corresponds to the period when the sufferer "keeps down inner badness" (Lake, 1981d, T8). Indeed, "negative dynamic drives compel us to deny the effects of 'memories' of a 'bad' 'God'" (Lake, 1981d, T11). The "fact" that "god" allowed deprivation, desertion, hunger, pain, cold, humiliation, and hell must be denied.

The beginning of the healing process, according to Lake, only comes when we realize that we must "let go of our sensory satisfactions, including comfortable [and not so comfortable] emotions [which] . . . have become part of our habitual defense against fears" (Lake, 1981d, T8). The "active night of the senses" begins when we act on our realizations; we are in charge; but all we can really deal with is conscious material. Lake writes that "our major problems are rooted in the unconscious, in primal grief, rebellion, despair and dread. These cannot be shifted by will-power" (Lake, 1981d, T8). Thus, eventually, "the over-active, restless, never-ending struggle [to] actively purge 'badness' out of the character, is seen to be what it is, and given up" (Lake, 1981d, T11).

Thus, the switch from the active to the passive night of the senses begins (Lake, 1964, 842-851). This passivity is not to be "quietist", but an "active attentiveness to what emerges when we let the latent self emerge from the cellar" (Lake, 1981d, T8). "We offer to God our rage against 'god'. We open our lusts to Him. We come to rest in Christ's work" (Lake, 1981d, T11).

All this is simply a necessary preliminary to the bodily, mental, and emotional distresses which accompany the "dark nights of the spirit." The passage from the "senses" to the "spirit" marks the passage from the "Illuminative Way" to the final goal, the "Unitive." Drawing on John's descriptions, Lake describes this transition:

> As the senses are purged of their attachments to persons and things that intrinsically lack permanence, while the Spirit is leading us into detachment, we may fall into fearful darkness, or lonely emptiness. In letting go what we have clung to, these false fears are tested, and found to be liars. Instead, we move into what proves to be an illuminated place, indeed a kind of "dazzling darkness" so much is there to be learned in it (Lake, 1981d, T8).

Once we have passively learned what this dazzling darkness shows us about ourselves, the "Unitive" way ferrets out the deepest anxieties the individual has incurred in his whole life. These experiences have made any commitment to closeness a hazardous endeavor. Indeed, for Lake, the severity of the dark night, the "degree of psychosomatic distress", is in direct relation to the actual primal distress suffered by the individual (Lake, 1981d, T8). Lake continues by writing:

> If, in the womb or later, dependency on others has proved too risky, especially in situations so intimate that it is not possible to get away from them, the recoil into non-attachment resists any call back into closeness and dependency. This applies to God as much as anyone. This call to trust, in depth, the steadfast love and reliable supplies that are "supposed" to come from God, is felt to be particularly menacing if the primal experience was of a bad maternal input which had an overwhelmingly evil power of invasion (Lake, 1981d, T8).

But finally, "in loving attention and active abandonment to God in Christ, we endure the pain" and finally reach down and re-own the roots of primal pain. Kavanaugh describes the result:

> The point of arrival to which the night leads is "the new man," divinized in being and operation, living a life of faith, hope, and love, now fortified and without taint (Kavanaugh, 1987, 160).

John Bunyan

Lake also sees John Bunyan's allegory of *The Pilgrim's Progress*, especially the segment pertaining to the Valley of the Shadow of Death, as paradigmatic of "the journey of growth in faith seriously." Regarding this journey, Lake writes that Bunyan "has this whole situation summed up accurately" (Lake, 1964, 883). Like the dark night, this valley is as "dark as pitch":

> We also saw there the Hobgoblins, Satyrs, and Dragons of the Pit; we heard also in that Valley a continual howling and yelling, as of a People under unutterable misery, who there sat bound in affliction and Irons: and over that Valley hangs the discouraging Clouds of confusion: in a word it is every whit dreadful, being utterly without Order. . . . About the midst of this valley, I perceived the mouth of Hell to be (Bunyan, 1856, 94).

After various attacks, some effective and others warded off by various weapons and prayer, Christian is disconsolate until he finally hears a voice stating Psalm 23's "though I walk through the valley of the shadow of death, I will fear no evil, for thou are with me." This brings him immediate comfort for several reasons:

> First, because he gathered from thence, that some who feared God were in this Valley as well as himself. Secondly, for that he perceived God was with them, though in that dark and dismal state; and why not, thought he, with me? Though by reason of the impediment that attends this place, I cannot perceive it (Bunyan, 1856, 98).

Finally, day broke and Christian reminds himself of two passages of Scripture; "He hath turned the shadow of death into the morning" (Amos 5:8) and "He discovereth deep things out of the darkness, and bringeth out to light the shadow of death" (Job 12:22).

Jean-Pierre de Caussade

In his book *Self-Abandonment to Divine Providence*, Jean-Pierre de Caussade echoes St. John of Cross when he commends a "passive fidelity" in the face of "dark solitude". Lake sees here a correlation with the vicissitudes of the M-FDS and it's therapeutic "cure". Regarding de Caussade, Like writes that "after St. John of the Cross, [he is] the clearest writer in this same tradition" (Lake, 1981d, T18).

The book's first section, titled "The Virtue of Self-Abandonment" includes discussions on the limited effect, apart from God's direct channeling action, of "spiritual reading, . . . exercises of piety" (de Caussade, 1971, 38-41) and "the mind and other human means" (de Caussade, 1971, 41-43). But God does directly bring to sanctification "repugnant" souls, hence the second and larger part of the book, "The State of Self-Abandonment." This begins with a long chapter describing the end result; souls totally abandoned to God. De Caussaude writes that "this state presents nothing but sweetness when attained, but many agonies have to be passed through on the road" (de Caussade, 1971, 100). Lake relates these quoting de Caussade:

> The life of Faith is nothing else than a continual pursuit of God through everything that disguises, misrepresents, and so to speak, destroys and annihilates Him. . . . in the same way souls of Faith pass through and beyond a continual succession of veils, shadows, appearances, and as it were, deaths,

all of which circumstances do their best to make the Will of God un-recognizable, but they pursue and love the Divine Will unto the death of the Cross. . . . Darkness become light and bitterness sweetness.

When the event of the present moment terrifies, starves, strips and attacks all the senses, it is just at that moment that it nourishes, enriches, and vitalizes Faith. God leaves her [the soul] without any other support than Him alone. Her dwelling place is in darkness, forgotten and abandoned by creatures, in death and nothingness . . . the darker it grows, the more numerous the abysses, the snares, the fears, the persecutions, the famines, the troubles, the despairs, the purgatories and hells that line our path, the greater shall our faith and confidence be.

In the midst of her affliction at the [seeming] loss of her Beloved, something tells her that she is in possession of him.

God keeps a soul alive in the state of self-abandonment by methods seemingly more adapted to bring her to death. . . . We must allow ourselves to be plunged into it (de Caussade in Lake, 1981d, T18).

Soren Kierkegaard

Kierkegaard, according to Lake, "explored with unprecedented subjective accuracy of observation" the dynamics not only of the state of transmarginal stress, but also, "believing passionately in Christ, he descended into the saving dialogue between Christ crucified and the afflicted individual" (Lake, 1981d, T19). This "saving dialogue" begins with the recognition, that humanly speaking, no possibility of escape from an oppressive intolerable self-hood exists. Indeed, a "man is brought to the utmost extremity."

It here that Kierkegaard, in the climax of *The Concept of Dread*, begins to explicate dread as a saving means of faith. Quoting Kierkegaard, Lake writes:

By the aid of faith dread is absolutely educative, for it lays bare all finite aims and discovers their deceptions. In this sense "the greater the dread, the greater the man". Christ was in dread even unto death. When a man learns that he can demand of life absolutely nothing, and that "terror, perdition, annihilation, dwell next door to every man, and has learned the profitable lesson that every dread which alarms him may the next instance become a fact" he may learn by faith in God to accept the situation of being squeezed out of every secure foothold or handhold in the finite world. He learns from the loss of all things to trust absolutely in the infinite, in God Himself. . . . The man who has passed through the curriculum of misfortune and lost everything receives everything back again. But he does not receive it in a finite sense but in an infinite. "He sank absolutely, but then in turn he floated up from the depth of the abyss, lighter now than all that is oppressive and dreadful in life" (Kierkegaard in Lake, 1964, 735).

This "test" is a severe one and is illustrated by the patriarch Abraham in *Fear and Trembling*. It requires a "double movement", the first being an "infinite resignation of all hope of natural fulfillment of natural wishes in the finite order of things" (Kierkegaard in Lake, 1964, 757). Paradoxically, because with God all things are possible, the second movement is "infinite faith", which "by virtue of the absurd", solely through the means of faith "claims back again everything in the temporal order that God chooses to give" (Kierkegaard in Lake, 1964, 758). God takes the things "which are not" and fills their admitted emptiness with his Fullness.

Regarding Kierkegaard, Lake wrote that he claimed a "close affinity between 'the Sickness unto Death' or 'Affliction', and the Christian Faith with the Cross of Christ at its centre. Christ's presence with us, crucified in a like distress, is hint enough, or ought to be, to make us sharply observant of it. The Christ whose Passion alerts us to its likelihood, is the way to its healing" (Lake, 1981d, T19). Thus, "the possibility of this sickness (of despair) is man's advantage over the beast; to be sharply observant of this sickness constitutes the Christian's advantage over the natural man; to be healed of this sickness is the Christian's bliss" (Kierkegaard, 1946, 148).

P.T. Forsyth

Regarding P.T. Forsyth's essay "The Taste of Death and the Life of Grace" Lake writes that "his metaphors for the misery he detects in man, which Christ savingly shared, are those which emerge when the afflictions of the foetus in the womb are being re-lived and reconciled" (Lake, 1981d, T20).

Forsyth's essay, which is a commentary on Hebrews 2:9 ("that he by the grace of God should taste death for every man"), begins with this statement which Lake quotes:

> Jesus Christ not only died, but he tasted death as incredible bitterness and penury of soul. I would dwell on the psychology even more than on the theology of it (Forsyth in Lake, 1981d, T20).

Forsyth follows this by noting that the "taste of death today" is not so much death but pain, which is an intrusion into the "ideal order of things." Modern man has internalized pain so that we "have fewer wounds but more weariness. We are better cared for but we have more cares. There is less agony, perhaps, but perhaps also more misery" (Forsyth, 1957, 48). Forsyth illustrates his point:

> It is the moral horror of death that comes home to us today. It is not the writhing agony . . . but the mute, lonely, soulless misery of a faithless, hopeless, loveless, round of drudgery, failure, and lacerated life. . . . It is not the horror of a bleeding frame, of a crucifixion, but the horror of a gray, void, lampless, deep, unpeopled world. The color of death is not red, but gray . . . it is the horror . . . whose chief trouble is not pain but the fear of it, not acute agony but dull and stony woe, not furious despair, but incurable melancholy (Forsyth, 1957, 60-61).

So more than ever, it is "only faith in God that can master it in its ultimate form, its most desolate, squalid, benumbing and panic form, death in amoral waste, in spiritual solitude, impotence and failure, death with just enough feeling left to feel itself dead" (Forsyth, 1957, 51).

This is where Christ's pain and death are so salient: "he experienced the worst of it, touched the bottom of it, the godforsakeness of it, the earthiness, the deadness of it. . . . It was a dreary hell, a dismal swamp, an icy grave. . . . Christ sounded and tasted death to the uttermost" (Forsyth, 1957, 51-52). He also knew the worst kind of despair; becoming "sin" for us, tasting death as "it can only be tasted by . . . the High and Holy One, who feels Himself in the atmosphere of base, revolting sin, of moral atheism, ashiness, mustiness, torpor, dust. . . . His was the death of death . . . because he tasted the death in death, and visited the caverns of horror that underlie the soul, and are seldom entered even by the dying man . . . [and finally,] he bruised the serpent-- a thing of slime" (Forsyth in Lake, 1981d, T20).

To Lake, this serpent is the "slimy, loathsome Satan," a poisoner of wells who envelopes and invades, who is hideous, monstrous, mean, and filthy. "It is just these unnerving wretched insinuations of constricting and invasive evil that Christ in his Passion and Cross most rigorously reaches down into the terrors of the first trimester in the womb" (Lake, 1981d, T21):

> All sin runs out at last to mean sin. And it is the mean sinners that are hardest to save, the last tax on a Redeemer, perhaps hopeless, intractable, in the end,

even to his death. Their element is death at its deadliest. They haunt a miry suburb in the soul's black country, of mean houses, half built and then deserted, "bog, clay and rubble, sand and stark black death." To encounter them, to enter such benumbing, belittling, inert, penurious air is to taste the death in death (Forsyth, 1957, 55).

Thus Christ literally experienced "death for a million"; this is not just "a parable of moral sympathy," or the "beholding of death as being in every man," but rather "He tasted death for every man" (Forsyth, 1957, 56). Thus, it was "death made cheap, death for a million" (Forsyth, 1957, 55).

This death becomes the gift and grace of God, not only to us through Christ, but also to Christ himself. God the Father withdrew His face from His Son, but never His grace. It could not be any other way. If God's grace failed Christ, how could it save us? Forsyth concludes that "this bitter, dismal taste of death . . . was God's grace to Christ. When He tasted death He tasted how gracious the Lord was" (Forsyth, 1957, 64). This is important to note because Christ's experience of death and grace is paradigmatic for all who follow. Lake summarizes Forsyth's point:

God the Father gave his son an immense gift of grace, in inviting him to represent him in person, to all who would become his sons and daughters, by the obedient humiliation that carried the cross to his death in shame. This grace, of dying while representing, in person, the truth of the cost of bridging broken relationships, was given to Christ. This same grace is transmitted through him, into all those who, in the afflictions they suffer while so small as to be weak, vulnerable and innocent of any ill-will, endure to the death of the spirit while striving to maintain love, under impossible conditions (Lake, 1981d, T24).

Simone Weil

In her book *Gravity and Grace*, Weil wrote that "the extreme greatness of Christianity lies in the fact that it does not seek a supernatural remedy for suffering but a supernatural use for it" (Weil, 1952, 73). In an essay from the book titled "The Love of God and Affliction", she continues:

Affliction is a marvel of divine technique. It is a simple and ingenious device which introduces into the soul of a finite creature the immensity of force, blind, brutal and cold. The infinite distance which separates God from the creature is entirely concentrated into one point to pierce the soul in its very centre.

The man to whom such a thing happens has no part in the operation. He struggles like a butterfly which is pinned alive into an album. . . . He whose soul remains ever turned in the direction of God while the nail pierces it, finds himself nailed on to the very centre of the universe. It is the true centre, it is not in the middle, it is beyond space and time, it is God. . . . This nail has pierced cleanly through all creation, through the thickness of the screen which separates the soul from God. . . . It is at the intersection of creation and its Creator. This point of intersection is the point of intersection of the branches of the Cross (Weil, 1952, 135-136).

Indeed, it was here that Christ was made a curse for us. It was not only Christ's body that was accursed, but his soul as well. Weil writes that "in the same way, every innocent being in his affliction feels himself accursed" (Weil, 1952, 122. Thus, Christ is able "to be alongside the innocent afflicted, the victims of constricted confusion, to help them bear the injustice of this, because he has himself been its victim" (Lake, 1981d, T12).

Karol Wojtyla

Frank Lake's last book, published in 1982, was titled *With Respect* and carried the intriguing subtitle of "A Doctor's Response to a Healing Pope." In his preface to the book, Lake related that the discoveries that lead to the formulation of the M-FDS had put him out on a professional and theoretical "limb" of sorts and "any measure of support from medicine or theology becomes particularly reassuring" (Lake, 1982c, xvi). It is in the verbal and written work of Pope John Paul II that Lake finds theological reassurance for several dimensions of the M-FDS.

The first is the general affirmation of Pope John Paul II, perceptible in many of his speeches and sermons, of the profound importance he attaches to the maternal-fetal relationship. In an address on "Mother-hood", John Paul affirms that Mary's "spiritual motherhood" is con-comitant with her "physical motherhood" to the fetal Christ. He stated that "this motherhood filled the nine months of waiting for the moment of the birth" (Wojtyla, 1979a, 9). The Pope also spoke of Christ remembering his mother as "the one to whom he owed, together with life, everything that constitutes the beginning and structure of the history of his spirit" (Wojtyla, 1979a, 10). In another speech, this time to medical personnel, the Pope predictably condemns all abortion. Lake, however, was gripped by the underlying awareness he discerns in these words related to the need for positive acceptance of pregnancy:

The medical service needed "adequate operational structure, which will encourage the joyful acceptance of life about to be born." He [John Paul] showed himself to be aware of the importance of the mother's joyful and tranquil acceptance of the embryonic and foetal person growing within her. There could be, said the Pope, a "therapeutic ministry of doctors affirming and defending human life in all those particular contingencies in which life itself can be compromised through the positive and wicked intention of human will" (John Paul II in Lake, 1982c, xvii).

Lake continues:

I was unaware of any other theologian anywhere saying clearly what I now know to be a fact with devastating implications, namely that every "human being, from the moment of his conception under his mother's heart, bears within him this divine stamp, which makes him a subject capable of opening up responsibly to God and others" (Wojtyla, 1980a, 16). That the fetus "opens up responsibly" to the mixed good and bad input from the pregnant women in whom he or she is fortunate or fated to be developing . . . is an empirical fact based on evidence we cannot nullify. To have a theologian, and a Pope at that, affirming the same reality from another angle, could not fail to engage my grateful attention (Lake, 1982c, xvii-xviii).

A second area of "reassurance" that Lake senses from the Pope relates to John Paul's poetry. As a young Polish priest, Karol Wojtyla would often submit poetry for journal publication under a pseudonym. Lake recounts that he was astonished to find one poem, "one of the most perceptive of them", entitled "Schizoid". Lake writes that while several unusual theologians, including Kierkegaard and Weil, have attempted to grapple with this paradoxical and life-negating condition, "nowhere else had I discovered a theologian willing to employ the psychiatric diagnostic term and go on to show how accurately he comprehended its dynamics and how skilled he was at counselling the sufferer" (Lake, 1982c, xvii-xviii). Wojtyla's (1979) poem follows:

There are moments, hollow without hope;/will I ever light up a thought,/ ever strike warm sparks from my heart?/Don't push me aside, don't recoil from my anger./This isn't anger - no, no -it's only an empty shore.

The slightest weight is too much for me,/I walk on and feel I'm not moving at all./You never stand still, remember, your strength/recharges in silence; it will find its way./Your strength will explode.

And then without violence, not instantly wholly yourself,/you must give heart-space to your moments, space to the pressure of will./There is growth in hollow stagnation;/your fever-shot eyes must not/burn it to ashes.

Lake writes that he was not surprised, "having proof of Karol Wojtyla's poetic empathy into the schizoid affliction, to discover his meditations on the meaning of the Cross and Passion of Christ are rich in this rare and matching insight" (Lake, 1982c, xxi). Primarily the cross is where God declares his solidarity with all sufferers:

Jesus Christ went forward towards death in full awareness of his messianic destiny. He knew that the destiny of all humanity and the whole world lay with him and his cross. Scourged, mocked with a crown of thorns, he carried to Mount Calvary together with the weight of his cross the truth of human suffering, humiliation, scorn, torture, agony, death. . . . On the day of his death Jesus entered into the fullest and deepest communion and solidarity with the entire human family, and especially with all those who throughout history have been the victims of injustice, cruelty and scornful abuse. And in shouldering all this in his true human nature, he, the sign of contradiction, was above all the Lamb of God who takes away the sin of the world (Wojtyla, 1979, 86).

The cross, although designed as an instrument of torture and disgrace, becomes "the point in history when all men are so to speak conceived afresh and follow a new course within God's plan . . . no longer dependent on human conditioning" (Wojtyla, 1979, 87). For Lake, this becomes a metaphorical contrast to being "born again", which is not enough; rather "Christ has to be conceived afresh [in each person], so that the blight of human conditioning can be reversed" (Lake, 1982c, 36).

This represents the only hope of true change, and indeed, because of this "the suffering of Christ speaks in a special way to man and not only to the believer. The non-believer also will be able to discover in him the eloquence of solidarity with the human lot" (Wojtyla, 1980b, 39). That this should be so is not surprising because the cross is where "God comes alongside those who, in innocence and total vulnerability, have been victims of violence [or] sufferers on account of others' sins" (Lake, 1982c, 40). The Pope continues:

He won us back for God by shedding his blood. . . . Why the blood of Jesus? Why the cross? . . . The mystery of the cross cannot be assessed by studying it from one angle alone. The mystery implicit in the cross is far beyond man's intellectual grasp, far beyond human understanding. Yet it constantly recurs whenever man reflects on the world, on God, on himself, on good and evil, on eternity. And always we find fresh aspects of this ineffable mystery to contemplate . . .

In the cross there lies, concealed, power to redeem the world and justify men before God; but in the cross another power too lies concealed, and therefore another meaning. How often man turns to God to confront him with demands! God is expected to relive sufferings, to correct injustices, even to put an end to all the world's evil. But when a man turns his eyes to the cross, his thoughts make an abrupt about-turn. It's very strange; it's as if the one hanging from the cross, Jesus, has justified everything; it's as if at that moment . . . he had justified God to himself before man (Wojtyla, 1979b, 89).

In an encyclical titled *Dives in Misericordia*, the Pope relates some similar thoughts:

In this way the Cross of Christ, on which the Son, consubstantial with the Father, renders full justice to God, is also a radical revelation of mercy. . . . The cross is the most profound condescension of God to man and to what man-- especially in difficult and painful moments-- looks on as his unhappy destiny. The Cross is like a touch of eternal love upon the most painful wounds of man's earthly existence (Wojtyla, 1980b, 42-43).

"The Healing of Memories"

In his book *Tight Corners in Pastoral Counselling*, Lake, commenting upon the various psychological systems that existed, wrote that he had "no loyalty to any one of these methods. . . . Eclecticism is the correct theological stance" (Lake, 1981g, 13). Several years before he wrote these words, Lake's theological eclecticism was beginning to embrace certain components of what he called the Charismatic Renewal Movement. In a letter dated from 1973, Lake wrote that while he was "personally at the edge of the charismatic movement" (Lake, 1973, 5), nonetheless, "his nose" combined with a great deal of evidence, was telling him that something very important was occurring. In the same letter he wrote:

In 1966 I had to write "What the LSD-assisted abreaction makes possible, the Holy Spirit, communicating Christ's indwelling personal courage, makes bearable to the central self in Christ." I would now say, without any fear of contradiction, that the Holy Spirit, in the charismatic prayer group, is making the first part available as well as the second (Lake, 1973, 6).

What convinced Lake of the importance of the charismatic prayer group as it related to his own understanding of counseling was a combination of his own observation, and in particular, an international charismatic conference that was held in Nottingham in the summer of 1973, to which he was invited as one of the speakers. At this conference he was exposed to the thought of several prominent Charismatic thinkers, specifically Graham Pulkingham and Arnold Bittlinger (Lake, 1973, 7).

Particularly important for the evolution of Lake's ideas regarding the M-FDS was the charismatic "inner healing" movement that collectively is identified by Agnes Sanford's term "The Healing of Memories" (Sanford, 1966, 105). Sanford's methodology when counseling someone with "deeply embedded psychological hurts" focused upon first listening prayerfully and intently to the rehearsal of the harmful memories from childhood. She writes that as the counselee was speaking, she was "praying that the Spirit of Christ will bring up from his memories whatever needs to be brought up, will guide him to say the key words and will help me to recognize the key when I hear it" (Sanford, 1966, 105). The process of sharing the memory, of sharing the hurt, allows for the "sharing of the life of Christ with them" (Sanford, 1966, 106). The "healing" of these memories would take place through prayer. Sanford wrote:

> I simply pray, usually with the laying on of hands, for the love of Christ to come into this one and forgive the sins and heal the sorrows of the past as well as the present-- the little child who used to be, as well as the grown person who is now. I begin at the present and go back through the memories, mentioning every sin and every grievous incident that has been told me. Indeed, I go further back than this, and pray for the healing of those impressions of fear and anger that came upon the infant far beyond the reach of memory. I carry this back to the time of birth and even before birth and pray for the restoration of the soul, for healing of the soul-- the psyche-- of the real, original person (Sanford, 1966, 107).

Given Sanford's willingness to affirm the potential detrimental effects of pre-birth events, it is understandable why Lake identified with her ideas. But perhaps more important than Sanford in Lake's theology and methodology of the "healing of memories", was Francis MacNutt's book *Healing*. MacNutt, a Catholic priest in pastoral ministry, heard Sanford's phrase "healing of memories" and it immediately had an effect on his thinking:

It was as if a whole wall of an unfinished building suddenly went into place. It made sense not only because Christ came to free us from the evil that burdens us, but also because it was in accord with what psychologists have discovered about the nature of man: that we are deeply affected not only by what we do, but by what happens to us through the sins of others and the evil in the world (original sin) (MacNutt, 1974, 181).

MacNutt divided "healing" into four basic categories: repentance for personal sin, inner healing for the full range of emotional and psychological problems, physical healing, and deliverance from demonic oppression. Like Lake, he envisioned the first "healing" of repentance as insufficient for those suffering from emotional problems "innocently". Very often these subconscious, deeply-rooted and imbedded problems result as a consequence of events that occurred pre-verbally and because of someone else's "sin". Advising repentance to those who are innocent provides no "healing". Thus, MacNutt saw the crucial need for an inner healing, whereby painful memories from the past are brought to light and then committed to healing prayer. He continues:

Some of these hurts go way back into the past; others are quite recent. Our experience coincides with the findings of psychologists: that many of the deepest hurts go way back to the times when we were most vulnerable and least able to defend ourselves. There is a good deal of evidence that some hurts go back even before birth while the child was still being carried in the mother's womb. Just as John the Baptist leapt in Elizabeth's womb when she heard Mary's greeting, so every child seems sensitive to it's mother's moods. If the mother does not really want the child or is suffering from anxiety or fear, the infant seems somehow to pick up the feelings of the mother and to respond to them. . . . These earliest memories up to the time we are two or three years old seem to be the most important in setting the patterns of our future behavior (MacNutt, 1974, 183-184).

What allows inner healing to take place, according to MacNutt, is the fact that "Jesus, who is the same yesterday, today and forever, can take the memories of our past" and in the place of wounds from the past fill them with his transforming love.

Thus Sanford, and MacNutt in particular, were influential on Lake's thinking with regard to the place of prayer and "inner healing" in a counseling ministry to those suffering from primal trauma. But Lake also went beyond and differed significantly from both. For Sanford and MacNutt, prenatal memories are one possible source among many of pain and hurt; for Lake they are central and catastrophic.

Relative to Sanford and MacNutt, Lake relates his methodology:

> Our own practice is to begin, as always with prayer for the Holy Spirit's guidance, and then to facilitate the person in **making their own search** [emphasis Lake's] into the prime occasions on which the feelings they are complaining of were felt with total intensity. Consistent deep breathing (so symbolic of the Spirit's fullness) enables the "adult" to go down into these experiences which were overwhelming to the foetus or the baby with being overwhelmed or scared by them now (Lake, 1978a, 2).

Lake was also critical of several of the characteristics that he observed among Charismatic prayer groups. The first was their tendency to ignore and deny the more "negative" emotional states and over-emphasize the more "positive". For instance, in his critique of a textbook on how to run a seminar in the Holy Spirit, Lake relates that "it says that the group leader must be cheerful and smile pleasantly. That's rubbish. The only thing you want are leaders who are real" (Lake, 1991a, 23). Elsewhere Lake wrote:

> It is regrettable that the Renewal movement has become associated in people's minds with an unbalanced emphasis on the joy and praise which well up from within. The same dynamic inflow of the Holy Spirit's power, applying the work of Christ throughout human personality, reaches as much into the depths as it does into the heights, as much into the despairing heart as into the dancing one (Lake, 1978c, 47).

Along with this overemphasis on the positive, Lake also recognized among some in the Renewal movement mistaken notions about healing, both in terms of who and how the process of healing would take place. Lake related these criticisms in a seminar:

> Sometimes I get very troubled when some of my friends who are in the healing movement are presented with somebody who is suffering from cancer, or somebody who has some long-standing character disorder, and they say, "All things are possible with God. Only believe and it will happen." Now this is true, but it worries me when I hear them saying it, because often they have no idea of the suffering and the waiting that is often necessary. . . . What we are saying is that yes, all things are possible for God, but the sovereignty of God determines in any given case whether it is good for this person or that to receive this or that kind of healing . . .
>
> Healing is what the whole of counselling is really about, isn't it? Sometimes, in charismatic circles, they want to do the healing in isolation

from all the other things. Their idea of healing is of something coming across that will send away, dismiss, and obliterate the whole of the pain in [an instant]. But that kind of thing is unworthy of the [Holy Spirit] (Lake, 1991a, 134-135).

As has already been noted, central to Lake's endeavor is the communication of Christ's identifying work on the Cross to the sufferer, particularly the primal sufferer. The connection between this dimension and "inner healing" is the Holy Spirit, which, in the context of trust, brings to mind the trauma of the past and then applies the work of Christ to these wounds. Lake explains:

Christian pastoral care can now, potentially, do more than merely trim the more rampant offshoots of twisted behavior. The root of the briar is laid bare. Our concept of the Holy Spirit's inreach, in applying the reconciling work of Christ, as our fellow-sufferer and Saviour, to the early sources of trouble in man, cannot stand still. . . . The Holy Spirit, bringing to bear the work of Christ, has now given to his Church the means to relieving the severest and the most permanently damaging bonds of all, those tribulations which are imprinted so deeply on the minds, bodies and spirits of his little ones as to destroy their joy (Lake, 1978a, 3).

Lake relates the "healing" ministry and the ministry of the "cross" as complementary. Christ's work on the cross is preceded by the years of his Galilean ministry of healing; but in a very real sense they are inseparable from each other and it is only in considering them together that a full understanding of Christ's ministry can be achieved. Similarly, Lake ties the ministry of the communication of theodicy with the ministry of the healing prayer group. He concludes his essay "The Work of Christ in the Healing of Primal Pain" by writing that "the ministry entrusted to us glorifies Christ in making available to the sufferer the power of the Holy Spirit who sustains Christ in the crushing terrors of Gethsemane and the agonizing loneliness of Golgotha, enabling him to become reconciled to what had hitherto been totally unbearable. Christ is glorified in either way, in joy . . . or in joyful suffering" (Lake, 1989, 241).

Chapter Four

Analysis and Critique

Having presented in detail Lake's formulation of the M-FDS along with evidence regarding its psychological and theological applicability, to what extent can his model be maintained as paradigmatic in the manner previously discussed? Lake's designation of the M-FDS as a "new paradigm" (Moss, 1986, 52) in two somewhat overlapping senses corresponds with the two main lines of inquiry addressed by this work, those of chapter two and chapter four. As a scientific paradigm connoting "a generally accepted system of ideas which defines the legitimate problems and methods of a research field" (Moss, 1986, 53) does Lake's M-FDS pass muster? Based on the existing data, do Lake's formulations allow for the M-FDS to be "generally accepted as a system of ideas?" In response to these queries and based upon the evidence previously presented, five major questions seem to emerge. The first addresses the issue as to why the ideas contained in Lake's M-FDS have not in the recent past and present been "generally accepted as a system of ideas". Secondly, how is the "evidence" that Lake based his theory upon to be evaluated? Specifically, given the problems regarding the fallibility of human memory and the potential suggestibility of clients, how can the data regarding prenatal and primal integration be evaluated with regard to its veracity?

Thirdly, does the existing evidence reasonably allow for the affirmation of the M-FDS as a paradigm in terms of the fetal period generally, particularly the second and third trimesters. The fourth question relates to Lake's stress upon the paramount importance of the first trimester, or embryonic period, in particular. Lastly, much of Lake's "evidence" is based upon the assumption that the "memories" recalled by his subjects by means of deep-breathing or LSD abreaction are substantially accurate and represent real biographical events that actually transpired. This assumption is examined in light of the current evidence.

The second manner in which Lake affirmed the M-FDS to be paradigmatic was in a comparative sense in which the scientific paradigm was paralleled to certain theological considerations. In this sense, "paradigm" was utilized more broadly as "a pattern, something shown side by side with something else, inviting comparison of the correspondences" (Lake, 1980b, 2). Based upon the evidence presented in chapter three regarding Lake's utilization of the M-FDS as a paradigm of comparison with the theological realm, the major question that arises touches on the M-FDS as a theodicy and the relationship between this theodicy and the "other" great work of the cross, atonement.

Thirdly, Lake's whole project was devoted to an integration of the biblical and theological on the one hand with the psychiatric and psychological on the other. To what extent does he achieve this with the M-FDS, and achieve it legitimately? What are the implications of the convergence of these two lines of inquiry?

Lastly, to what extent does Lake's thinking and the research evidence that presently exists allow, however tentatively, for the discussion of a "prenatal psychology"?

Critique of the M-FDS as a Scientific Paradigm

The "Old" View

At its very simplest, the M-FDS can be viewed as a simple extension of commonly held and accepted developmental psychological principles into the realm of the prenatal period. In a similar manner, it can be affirmed that this process of "extension" has occurred over the last several centuries into first the period of early childhood, then infancy, then the neonatal, and subsequently the perinatal periods. Each "extension" was initially resisted and only gradually accepted as the research evidence accumulated supporting the affirmations of the significance of each period for later psychological functioning.

A clear example of this can be seen regarding the changes in the perception of neonatal capabilities. Prior to the 1960's, the neonate was regarded as a purely physiological being (Rau, 1982, 131). The introduction of Brazelton's "Neonatal Behavioral Assessment Scale" in 1970 for the purpose of "better understanding the child's 'interactive behavior'" (Schindler, 1988, 24) had a profound effect of changing attitudes towards the newborn. By 1973, William Jame's description of the neonatal world as "blooming, buzzing confusion" was being replaced by the concept of the "competent newborn" (Stone, Smith & Murphy, 1973). This notion is now fairly widely accepted. Rau, writing in 1983, described the change:

> And so arose the picture of a baby that incorporates the essential and psychologically important characteristics-- even if they are still only rudimentary-- which also form the older child and adult, respectively. It is the picture of an active organism, one which contributes to its own development in interaction with the world around it. As a result, it can now even be described in terms of subject, not only in objective terms which are already well-known (Rau, 1983, 83).

It can be noted that the acceptance of the criticality of each developmental period is greatest for the later stages, with acceptance gradually lessening for each subsequent earlier period. Thus, hardly any resistance presently exists regarding the crucial impact of early childhood on later functioning; but resistance increases respectively for the affirmation of the impact of the infant period, the neonatal interval, the perinatal experience, and finally, intrauterine life on subsequent psychological functioning. Because of the difficulty in accumulating "evidence" for the earlier as opposed to the latter stages, more "evidence" exists regarding the critical importance of the later periods and thus, a greater acceptance of the "evidence".

Because of this, the dominant prevailing view of prenatal life continues to be one of viewing the fetus as relatively passive and inert physiologically and devoid of meaning psychologically and psychodynamically. Thus, for instance, "psychoanalysis does not really ask, 'When did it begin?' Instead, it asks a rather different question, 'When after birth did it begin?'" (Peterfreund, 1971, 74). Freud envisioned intrauterine life as similar to sleep, a condition of "absence of stimulation and avoidance of objects" (Ridgeway, 1987, 17). With this underlying attitude widely accepted, the physiological and psychological capabilities of the fetus have been unknown, minimized or disregarded. A similar disregard and gross underestimation for the capabilities of newborns and infants has also existed, although, as mentioned above, research has gradually illustrated the amazing capabilities of infants and neonates. Even despite the evidence, many still regard infancy as somewhat devoid of psychological significance. For instance, Stone, Smith and Murphy (1973) list a series of statements from published books regarding infant capabilities. All have since been shown to be in error. A partial list follows:

> "Visual pursuit is absent for the first two weeks of life." (1930); "Until [cortical] development occurs [at almost a year] the motor behavior of the infant resembles that of the precordate animal." (1942); "It is even incorrect to say that the child sees, hears, feels unspecifically at birth. . . . The greatest part of everything which is going on does not reach the delicate system of the newborn. Only a few and very strong stimuli reach the infant's psyche at birth." (1948); "Behavior observable during the first two weeks of life [consists wholly of] different types of reflexes." (1952); "Newborn infants do not show sensory discrimination in any modality." (1961); "Consciousness, as we think of it, probably does not exist in the newborn. . . . The newborn child in unable to fix his eyes on objects." (1964); "The newborn has been considered largely a reflex organism, primarily controlled by his internal environment and organic processes, but responsive to a number of external impacts" (1966) (Stone, Smith & Murphy, 1973, 3-4).

This faulty understanding of fetal life continues to exist, and has existed, for a variety of reasons, including the fact that interest in embryology extending as far back as the Middle Ages and before, has been primarily oriented towards anatomy and the "mechanics" of pregnancy and birth and not towards a fetal perspective. Thus, the legacy of this outlook has been to view the fetus, "apart from some aimless kicking which began in the fifth month . . . [as] placid, fragile vegetable who developed quietly in preparation for a life which started at birth" (Liley, 1991, 192). Although interest in the intrauterine life has greatly expanded, there is still the tendency to begin with adult functioning and work backwards, eventually arriving at the prenatal period. Intentional or not, this "comparative" mentality has contributed toward the regard of the preborn and neonates as inadequately functioning adults rather than well functioning fetuses and babies.

Another reason why a false understanding of fetal life continues is suggested by deMause who has pointed out that many of those who subscribe to the "older view" of fetal life very often cite one study by Langeworthy in 1933 as evidence (Langeworthy, 1933). This study made the assertion that "incomplete myelinization of sensory tracts" resulted in the inability of the fetus to receive neural messages from its specialized sense receptors. However, research subsequent to Langeworthy's study has clearly shown that full myelinization, which occurs only after birth, is not essential for sensory functioning. While full myelinization does increase the rapidity of conduction, well-organized neural activity and sense receptivity is possible long before the nerve fibers are completely myelinated (Bekoff & Fox, 1972, 323-341). DeMause writes that Langeworthy's "incomplete myelinization" misstatement "continues to be used to deny the ability of the fetus and the newborn to feel pain in many areas of medicine, from the use of aborted fetuses as subjects in painful medical experiments to the denial of anesthesia during circumcision and surgery of the newborn" (DeMause, 1987, 253).

Further, the modern discussion of the notion of "consciousness" as it relates to adults, and the difficulty in defining the term adequately, has lead to the view that the term itself is taboo. As Chamberlain points out:

> It is unfortunate that for all concerned that these specialties [obstetrics and pediatrics] came to prominence in during as era of psychology when the subject of consciousness was taboo and neonates were considered essentially decorticate. Therefore, virtually all the routines of modern obstetrics and pediatrics presuppose an infant who is without personal thought, feeling, or memory-- a position which, I think, can no longer be reconciled with the facts (Chamberlain, 1983, 3).

Further, various ethical issues related to human embryological and fetal research have been raised which prevented certain types of investigations and thus certain data was simply unavailable. This lead to a reliance on comparative animal studies, which, although somewhat applicable, proved ultimately to be wanting due to the great variation between human and animal, and even human and mammalian, reproductive physiology, psychology and embryology. While still important, especially as it relates to research on various teratogens, animal studies obviously prove less than satisfactory when seeking data on specifically and uniquely human characteristics.

The lack of technology which would have allowed better observation and monitoring of the fetus "in utero" has also contributed toward a faulty understanding of fetal functioning. As technology, including intrauterine sonography, photography, sound spectrography, electroencephalography, x-ray and other forms of fetal monitoring, have become more and more sophisticated, they have opened up a window on the embryological and fetal life of human beings heretofore unavailable. In addition, various forms of medical technology has pushed the threshold of "viability" earlier and earlier, in a sense allowing external observation of the entire "third trimester."

Commenting on the confluence of these variables, Davies has written that perhaps study of fetal life has been lacking due to the fact that the fetus itself was so "inconveniently tucked away in a most inaccessible situation. This area of medicine offered little opportunity for discovery, and did not attract much talent. Why study a creature so passive, so dull, so small, and technically so difficult" (Davies, 1973, 965)?

Further, very often those who have made claims regarding the importance of the prenatal period have been on the fringes of "scientific credibility". Many of the important early modern thinkers' reliance on what many have considered suspect procedures and methodology have been generalized to their results. For instance, Francis Mott's heavy reliance on the analysis of dreams and Stanislav Grof's utilization of LSD both introduce a certain amount of doubt into the credibility of their claims regarding intra-uterine life. Furthermore, the association of descriptions of the prenatal period and affirmations of its cruciality with extensive use of hypnosis, age-regression, birth-reenactment, and primal techniques also constitutes a perceived credibility gap, however fair or unfair.

Lake himself, while aware of the problems of perception, was not immune to such speculations. In a paper written near the end of his life, he relates that initially he did not expect any memories of the first trimester stage to extend any earlier than the blastocystic phase, around 4 to 10 days after implantation. And yet, to his astonishment, when, in the process of primal integration, people were given the opportunity to "become an ovum" or "become a sperm" many did express a strong identification with a memory of this time.

In light of these findings, Lake wrote:

> I am painfully aware this openness to change, in the wake of the evidence derived from the same sort of 'therapeutic regression' as enabled us to discover the Maternal-Foetal Distress Syndrome in the first place, comes to look more like a *reductio ad absurdum* (Lake, 1977a, 4).

Lake continues and states that to ask people to accept first the reality and importance of pre-natal events, then first trimester events is hard enough for some to countenance. He proceeds:

> But to push the matter earlier is to risk being laughed out of court. The temptation to suppress the indications of 'transmissions' from pre-zygote states can also be picked up, so as to limit the required paradigm change to embryonic and foetal life, and hope to have that accepted as a first stage, has not gone beyond the temptation. Having determined to proceed in the wake of the evidence, one might as well be hung for a sheep as a lamb (Lake, 1977a, 4-5).

Given all of the above, it is not surprising that some of the claims made by Lake with regard to his M-FDS were greeted and continue to be greeted, with incredulity and skepticism. This was and continues to be the case even among some of the members of the Clinical Theology Association which Lake himself founded in 1966 and directed up to his death in 1983. Many have made criticisms as to the reliability of the "data" which Lake used to formulate the M-FDS.

Methodology

Part of the problem with the "data" that Lake's sets forth as foundational for the entire M-FDS is that it is riddled with difficulty as to how it was obtained and how it should be interpreted. While Lake wants his theories to be accepted as "scientific" and towards that end uses the "terminology of science-- evidence, hypothesis, syndrome" (Campbell, 1982, 25), he seems to gloss over the necessary distinction that the M-FDS, at its very root, is incapable of being tested experimentally in the sense of being able to relate cause and effect. The M-FDS is a theory which Lake has formulated which attempts to make sense of the data (MacInnes, 1977, 12) collected through the residential primal workshops.

However, Lake addresses the issue of replicability in "Mutual Caring":

> The immediate "scientific" question is, "Is it replicable elsewhere?" The answer is, "Yes, so long as you don't try to cut any corners. It would be fatal to replication to omit, for instance, the deep togetherness that happens in the group, as a result of the two days of leisured introductions, in which each person has had opportunity to speak of the life-problem that brought them here, with total freedom to be emotionally honest, and then to recollect and

speak of the bodily sensation patterns and specific feelings which take hold of them when the ancient affliction strikes.

To say to a group of scientific workers, totally unused to having that quality of intimacy and *mutual* openness with the subjects of their highly "controlled" experiments, "you cannot cut this corner or you are failing to replicate the ground rules of the workshop", is to state firmly a limitation they probably would find difficult to overcome.

If there are serious investigators, honestly concerned to know whether these things are as we have reported, I would advise against trying to replicate this in a "scientific establishment." It simply would not be a replication of the experiment, but something totally lacking in too many respects. But there is nothing to prevent their joining, as an unpretentious member of a workshop, open to the same constraints on loose criticism, and fully ready to share themselves and grow through the basis of this, coming to a scientifically reliable validation or refutation. To be scientific in these fields requires a stringency which the "scientific method", as practiced in laboratories, has always strenuously evaded. I would guess that "unconscious" roots to do with foetal experiences that have made "knowing-by-emotional commitment" too painful and hazardous, and "knowing-at-an-emotionally-neutralized-distance" the only tolerable stance, have a decisive part in determining that deliberate subjective impoverishment that calls itself "scientific", but is not (Lake, 1982b, 73-75).

When Lake writes that the hypothesis of the M-FDS "continues to resist attempts to nullify it" (Lake, 1981g, 38) the question inevitably arises: "How could one nullify it?" The M-FDS is a theory partially made up of impossible-to-substantiate or refute tenets. For example, Lake infers a perceptual capability to the first trimester fetus that is sophisticated enough to be able to distinguish his mother's recognition or lack of it, regard or disregard, notice or lack of it (Lake, 1981d, C41). Lake writes elsewhere that "before she knows that she is pregnant, the foetus *knows* what sort of person this is" (Lake, 1981g, 15).

That this may or may not be true is not the point, rather the simple fact of the matter is that this cannot be "proved" or "disproved". The fact that some persons "relive" these subtle perceptions as adults in a simulated primal experience of sorts is not "proof". Too many other variables potentially intervene, including fantasy, imagination, projection, and suggestion.

Thus, Lake states as "scientific fact" what cannot be verified as such. He writes, regarding the M-FDS, "These are not theories, they are facts" (Lake, 1989, 232). Lake seems to shade the difference between an observable verifiable "fact" which can be corroborated by others with an assumption based upon such a "fact". As Hutchinson points out, this is the difference between a statement such as "the fetus responds with increased movement to music" and the statement "the fetus attributes a badness of the unbearable situation to some inexplicable but indelible badness in his own very being" (Hutchinson, 1977, 18). Many of Lake's "scientific facts" are in fact unsubstantiable assertions such as these.

Thus, Lake's M-FDS ends up being somewhat of a self-authenticating system (Hutchinson, 1977, 17) not unlike Freud's, whereby the theories set forth to explain behavior are buttressed with "evidence" of whatever sort available. Those who question or refuse to accept the "evidence" are categorized as deluded. Lake writes that many, "particularly among the members of the helping professions, do experience deep, emotionally charged resistances even to considering this as a possibility, for themselves or others" (Lake, 1989, 253). One critic of Lake makes the point that the problem with such untestable "grand theories" is that "they can easily become a kind of religion or metaphysic which positively inhibits the practitioners openness to re-examine them" (MacInnes, 1977, 12). Certainly this could be said of Lake.

Birth and Pre-natal Memories

Birth and the Fetal Period

Given the concerns regarding Lake's "evidence", the question of the veracity of the "evidence" which first gave rise to the M-FDS in Lake's mind remains. As was previously noted, the originating phenomena which subsequently resulted in the M-FDS as a theoretical paradigm consisted of birth and pre-birth "memories" in many of Lake's patients as a consequence of the abreactive use of LSD. Lake writes that starting in 1954 he was given " full time for two years, no other jobs [but] to pick out patients, [give them LSD,] and sit with them for four hours, six hours, as long as was necessary" (Lake, 1976a, 2-3). He seemed to discover that when used in the presence of a trustworthy therapist, LSD-25 seemed to serve effectively to de-repress the "forgotten" memories of the patient which he later noted, quite frequently included memories of birth traumas of various types (Lake, 1964; 1978). Following a switch in abreactive technique from LSD to Reichian deep-breathing in 1969, he continued to find similar results, particularly in the context of the small group residential seminars that the CTA was running. During the period between 1979 and 1982, over 500 persons attended these seminars at

Lingdale, some lasting as long as 7 days (Moss, 1990, 3:1). Another 700 persons went through the workshops at other locations, including Brazil, Australia, India and Finland (Lake, 1981c). The recorded audiotapes and written transcripts of these sessions provided much of the hard "evidence" for Lake's formulations of the M-FDS. In addition, Roger Moss, a co-researcher of Lake's during this period, completed a follow-up survey of those who had attended the residential workshops at Lingdale between October 1979 and April 1982 (Moss, 1984). The survey, consisting of 52 main sections covering 11 sides of paper, was sent out to 500 of the total of 516 (Moss, 1984, 8). A return rate of 56.2% (N=281) was achieved and these were analyzed in light of the data and evidence already at hand, which included abundant anecdotal evidence consistent with Lake's previous work indicating a strong connection between the primal experience and the actual facts of the pregnancy. Moss (1990) notes these consistencies under several broad headings, including "conception", "threatened abortion", "deaths", "good feelings", "mother's depression", "traumatic birth", "incubators", and "removal from mother after birth".

As far as "primal experiences" go, almost three-fourths (71.2%; N= 200) were judged to have had a valid primal experience of some sort. Further, 12.8% recounted being in touch with some deep feelings which they couldn't clearly identify as definitively "primal" in nature (Moss, 1984). Of the 200 who did report a "primal" experience of some sort, almost half (47%; N=94) stated that in subsequent sessions of primal work they uncovered further information regarding their early life. Some 89 (31.6%) participants discovered confirmation of components of their primal experience when checking with their parents or relatives regarding the facts of their prenatal and antenatal life (Moss, 1984).

How is this "evidence" to be understood, particularly in light of the very real problems related to the fallibility of human memory (Hilgard, 1980; Loftus & Loftus, 1980) and the suggestibility (MacInnes, 1977) of subjects both in terms of the recall of "eyewitness" memories (Brewer & Treyens, 1981; List, 1986; Loftus, 1979a; 1980) and in hypnosis (Barber, 1962; Evans & Kihlstrom, 1975; Orne, 1962; 1979; Putnam, 1979; Sarbin, 1950)? Research has shown, for instance, that the "memories" of adults for events which transpired only short periods of time previously can be altered by time, new information (Loftus, Miller & Burns, 1978), and leading questions (Loftus, 1975; Loftus & Palmer, 1974), so long as the "memory" remains plausible (Loftus, 1979b; Loftus & Greene, 1980). While there is not universal agreement with the specifics of these research results (McClosky & Zaragoza, 1985), there is general agreement that "memory" is subject to error. Given the difficulties that exist with adult memories of events in adulthood, any conclusions regarding the M-FDS which are based on the veracity of fetal memories recalled in adulthood must be made very tentatively.

However, it is interesting to note that Lake is far from unique in the recounting and reporting of such "memories". Indeed, many therapists report that birth and pre-birth "memories" are quite pervasive, even if they themselves have grave doubts about their veracity and reliability. For instance, Freud encountered them but interpreted them in the same light as many early memories; namely, as fantasies (Freud, 1933).

Numerous others have taken the reports of such memories, whether obtained as simple recollections of memory, or through the mechanisms of hypnosis, "conscious imaging" (Neighbour, 1981), gestalt methodology, dream recollection, deep-breathing regression or LSD, more at face-value. Beginning with Rank's *The Trauma of Birth*, many have reported extensively on birth and pre-birth memories, including Nandor Fodor (1949), D.W. Winnicott (1957; 1958; 1972), Francis Mott (1964), Stanislav Grof (1975; 1977), Phyllis Greenacre (1945), Melanie Klein (1975), M.L. Peerbolte (1951; 1954), Arthur Janov (1970; 1971; 1972; 1983), Gustav Graber (1924), R.D. Laing (1978; 1982), and others (Chamberlain, 1981; Ducasse, 1961; De Rocha, 1911; Feher, 1980; Kelsey, 1953; Orr & Ray, 1977; Ploye, 1973; 1976). While the sheer quantity of reported birth and pre-birth material is not evidence of its credibility or reliability, it certainly raises questions as to why its report seems to be so ubiquitous.

Like Lake, many of the above mentioned researchers have stumbled upon these reports quite reluctantly and only came to accept their basic reliability after correlating many of the reports with hospital records and reports from parents and other observers. For instance, Cheek, in a study using hypnosis with 10 subjects, reported that all were able to demonstrate the exact sequential movements of their heads and shoulders during birth. Cheek reported that none of the individuals involved had any conscious knowledge of the mechanisms and combinations of movement during birth usually known only to those with specialized obstetrical training (Cheek, 1974, 261-266).

Lake himself reports in several places that he only reluctantly came to the conclusions he did (Lake, 1977a, 6-7). He wrote that the M-FDS has "so far resisted our attempts to nullify it" (Lake, 1981g, x) and that after an initial biased incredulity was overcome, he was determined simply to listen to the evidence. He made several corrections as the evidence revealed that certain assumptions were flawed. He writes that his willingness to countenance changes in the theory shows that "it has been built up in a way that continually invites self-correction, because it is at every point inductive, based on actual findings, not deductions, [not] based on prior intuition, rule, authority or dogmatic assertion. Once the possibility was broached and the technique developed the evidence rolled in and the theory inevitably formed itself" (Lake, 1977a, 5).

In a series of studies designed to differentiate true "memory" from suggestion, Raikov (1980) examined the ability of adults under hypnosis to exhibit genuine neonatal reflexes. The results proved interesting: 100% of the subjects showed the typical uncoordinated eye movements and sucking reflexes typical of neonates, 60% demonstrated the foot-bending reflex, 50% displayed the Babinski reflex and tearless crying, and 40% manifested the grasping reflex and spontaneous movements of the arms and legs. In a follow-up study (Raikov, 1982), using suggestion alone without hypnosis on highly hypnotizable subjects, only a small number of "neonatal" behaviors could be observed. The same was true when professional actors attempted to duplicate neonatal behaviors, being correct only 15% of the time. Raikov concluded that "neither acting, suggestion nor imagination could account for all the phenomena observed" (Raikov, 1982, 116), and that the information acted out in the original subjects was being recalled from memory.

In a similar study designed to "shed light on the reliability of birth memory retrieved in hypnosis" (Chamberlain, 1988, 61), David Chamberlain (1986) studied 10 mother-child dyads. The children, who ranged in age from 9 to 23, all stated that they had no conscious memories of their births, while the mothers all claimed that they had never shared details of their children's births with them. Chamberlain reported that the "mother and child reports were remarkably detailed and reflected individual interests, experiences, and perceptions. Their two stories interlocked and formed a coherent whole rather than veering off in different directions. Stories matched or dovetailed at as many as 24 different points while direct contradictions of fact in the separate narratives where quite rare. Children correctly reported many details such as "time of day, locale, persons present, instruments used, position of delivery, behavior of nurses and doctors, first feedings of water or formula, room layouts and details of discharge and home-coming. Sequences were usually accurate: moving in and out of cars, rooms, on and off of certain beds or equipment, nursing from the bottle and/or breast in correct order, and the appearance and disappearance of doctors and fathers" (Chamberlain, 1986, 34). Although Chamberlain did find one case of "a limited pattern of fantasy" he re-ports that "judging strictly from my sample of ten pairs, it appears that birth memories are quite likely to be real not fantasy, true not false and within reasonable limits, a reliable guide to what actually happened (Chamberlain, 1983, 62).

However, the fact remains that clear and certain falsehoods regarding early memories do often emerge under hypnosis, thus casting at least a hint of suspicion regarding the truth of such "data". One possible explanation for this was stumbled upon by Hilgard. He found evidence that in some cases, the "facts" about what happened can be known by one segment of "consciousness" but unknown by another, resulting in what Hilgard called "divided consciousness" (Hilgard, 1977). Thus, lack of memory about a certain event may indicate that the segment of consciousness under hypnotic consideration may be unaware of the memory, while another segment may have total recall.

Buttressing this contention was the discovery by Cheek (1959) and others (Bennett et al, 1979) that many patients under general anesthesia, who were supposedly unconscious, were indeed perceiving and reacting to comments made by medical staff. Indeed, researchers discovered that patients under general anesthesia were not only sensitive to the words spoken, but also to various nuances, inflections and tones in the voices.

The connection between early birth and pre-birth traumas and adult manifestations of neuroses is one of the main assertions of Lake's M-FDS. Lake is, of course, not alone in the affirmation of this connection. Many of the above cited researchers would concur. Specifically, Leslie Lecron (1954; 1963) and David Cheek (1975), using an "ideomotor" technique in hypnosis, have connected early birth trauma with peptic ulcers, oesophageal spasms, spastic colon, asthma, emphysema, hyper-ventilation syndrome, sterility, dysmenorrhoea, failed analgesia in labor, premature labor, toxemia, frigidity and habitual abortion. Barnett (1979), using the ideomotor technique asked a series of questions of 876 different hypnotized patients and found that 28% reported negative birth experiences. He, like Lake, Cheek, and Lecron, found strong connections between these experiences and the presenting problems. Cheek, in his re-search has gone one step further. Like Lake, he has also discovered that clients under hypnosis report many prenatal "memories" (Cheek, 1986).

Other "evidence" for the credibility of birth and pre-natal memories can be found in the spontaneous memories of children when asked about the circumstances surrounding their birth and pre-birth experiences (Chamberlain, 1988; Rhodes, 1991). Given the limited vocabulary of younger children, many are able to point to parts of the body, act out, and give accurate motions and sounds of early experiences (Laibow, 1986).

First Trimester

Perhaps the most criticized component of the M-FDS is Lake's contention that memories from the first trimester, indeed from the blastocystic phase and even earlier, exist at all. While Lake initially believed that the blastocystic phase was almost always experienced and remembered as positive (Lake, 1977a, 3), he later came to see this stage, like the ones that followed, as potentially disastrous psychologically. Representative of Lake's descriptions of "blastocystic bliss" (Lake, 1981d, C41) include such characterizations as " a good experience of non-attachment, even of unitive and quite 'transcendent bliss'" (Lake, 1981g, 15), a "monistic sense of 'union with the Absolute'" (Lake, 1981d, C41), a "delightful dialogue of being and awareness with joy" (Lake, 1976c, 1).

But near then end of his life, Lake modified this initial understanding to include negative memories of the blastocystic period:

> We now have a significant number of cases in which the moment of conception itself has been registered with horror and recoil, as a total disaster - the beginning and origin of a negative evaluation of the life process and self-identity that has persisted through the blastocystic stage and through it to implantation and beyond (Lake, 1977a, 2).

Lake's assertion that memories from as early as four days after conception even exist and that they are accessible to the adult provokes credulity. The process of neurulation, where the neural plate begins to develop from the ectodermal cells thereby providing the primitive nerve cells for the brain and spinal cord is not complete until the 18th day. The continued development of the neurons, particularly the process of myelinization, and the synaptic junctions between neurons was thought to be necessary for any type of "memory" to remain.

Lake was quite aware of the neurology of memory. In order to address this seeming paradox, of memories seeming to exist before the morphological structures necessary for the formation and retention of those memories, Lake turned to the work of Karl Pribram. In several works (Miller et al, 1960; Pribram, 1969; Pribram & Broadbent, 1970), but particularly in *Languages of the Brain* (1971), Pribram has argued that long-term memory exists due to a two-process mechanism. The first is the neuron itself, while the second is the neural junction. The activity of the neural junction is part of an overall organization which is not specifically dependent upon any given single neuron. Pribram called this the "slow potential microstructure" (Pribram, 1971, 25). This microstructure is composed of the "aggregate of slow potentials present over an extended location at any moment" (Pribram, 1971, 19). Thus, the neural junctions are more than just merely transmitters of neural impulses, they can also serve as functional retainers of memory traces. Pribram writes:

> It is in the junctional mechanism that the long lasting modifications of brain tissue must take place. . . . Long-term memory therefore becomes more a function of junctional structure than of strictly neural (nerve impulse generating) processes (Pribram, 1971, 47).

The reason this is true is that the neurons themselves do not replicate, rather it is the neural junctions or synapses which "not only multiply but are also replete with active chemical processes, any or many of which are candidates for the evanescent, temporary, and long term modification upon which memory must be based" (Lake, 1981g, xv).

What is significant to Lake is that the neural junctions or synapses can store hologram-like patterns which could provide the basis of a distributed memory system independent of particular neurons (Pribram, 1971, 143). It is said to be holographic due to the way optical holograms produced by laser light work. When a camera records a visual picture of an object, each point on the film records information which arrived from the corresponding point in the visual field and thus produces an image that "looks like" the object. But when properly exposed by a coherent light source, a holographic record results when an image is taken and information from each point of the visual field is stored throughout a filter. The information stored on this filter does not resemble the visual image at all since the information does not correspond directly to the various points in the image. Rather, "the optical filter is a record of the wave patterns emitted or reflected from an object". Thus, the filter serves to "freeze" the wave pattern, and it re-mains so "frozen" until the process is reactivated, and the waves are "read out of the recording medium" (Pribram, 1971, 145-146).

The properties of holograms make them "potentially important in understanding brain function". Pribram cites Leith and Upatnicks (1965) when he writes:

> First . . . the information about a point in the original image is distributed throughout the hologram, making the record resistant to damage. Each small part of the hologram contains information from the entire image and therefore can reproduce it (Pribram, 1971, 150).

The same would be true for a neural holographic process. Perceptions and memories can be stored as "spatial interactions among phase relationships of neighboring junctional patterns" (Pribram, 1971, 166), thus allowing for the possibility of memory traces as early as synaptic junctions exist. Thus, there could be chemical storage of memory traces within the spatial junctions.

That this hypothesis may be true, according to Lake, might account for "memories" in the first trimester. These memories, stored holographically, are said by Lake to become "unfrozen" by the process of primal integration, or earlier in his research, by LSD. But this still does not account for memories of the zygotic and blastocystic phases because synaptic junctions do not exist.

Lake here takes Pribram's principles and extends them earlier in what he calls the "holographic principle". While he realizes that the synaptic junction is required for holographic memory, he states that perhaps "similar but simpler recording is feasible on the basis of properties resident in the protein molecule" (Lake, 1981g, xv). Regarding this, he writes:

> The hologram principle means that the whole is somehow present in every part, that is to say, in the single cell. We are familiar enough with this in so far as the nucleus which contains the genetic recipe for each individual is repeated identically in every cell. The same seems to be true in the case of certain protein molecules in the cell, which are now regarded as the probable basis for long-term memory (Lake, 1983, 2).

The principle that Lake is referring to is "multilevel redundancy", wherein the reduplication of the genetic and chromosomal information contained in the original germ-cell or zygote occurs in every single one of its descendants. Regarding this possibility, Lake writes that "even if, by mitotic division, that one cell has now increased numerically to the 10(62) cells of the adult human body, each of these cells carries a nucleus identical with that of the first cell' (Lake, 1976c, 2). Lake then asks the question, "Could there be reduplication and transfer of memory in the cytoplasm?" In answer to his question he quotes Richard Dryden's *Before Birth* (1978):

It is possible that the zygote contains information in addition to that stored in the nucleus. There is indeed evidence that the cytoplasm of the fertilized egg contains information that is essential to at least the early stages of development. . . . There are several sites where cytoplasmic information may be stored. The abundant free ribosomes may carry developmental information. . . . The mechanism of protein synthesis lends it self to analysis by information theory, with . . . the ribosomes helping to convert the coded message into a protein molecule (Lake, 1981g, xvi).

Lake would see here the possibility of micro-storage of early memories. Elsewhere he describes how this memory would originate and then how its residue might remain:

> If, at any stage, a restricted group of cells is delightfully excited or terribly traumatized, it is the descendants of that groups of cells which will, according to the holographic principle, continue to store and resonate to similar experiences. . . . The psychological and physiological basis of long-term memory is in the hologram which exist, at infinitesimally small potentials, in the protein molecular substance of every cell that is a descendent of the ones that were excited or distressed in the first place (Lake, 1976c, 2).

There is, then, according to Lake, a compulsion of sorts, to repeat the experience in adulthood "so as to be able to feel it again, enjoy it again, or ward it off again more successfully, or suffer it again in order to replenish the rationale for bitterness" (Lake, 1976c, 2). This is especially true if the experience was a positive one. The compulsion to regress back to an ideal state in light of the present pain is strong. Thus to recover this sense of participating again in a state of unitive bliss can be a resource in therapy, because it promotes an original sense of oneness which the person can strive for. Lake writes that "as a find on an archeological dig it is a great treasure" (Lake, 1983, 2).

Thus, while there seems to be a limited amount of evidence for at least the possibility of birth and pre-birth "memories" of some sort, the questions of their veracity and indeed, their access years later is problematic. Lake is not ignorant of the problems inherent in the report of these "memories" and he attempts to control for such variables as "suggestablity" and a selective culling out of supportive evidence while ignoring opposing evidence. For instance, on the topic of holographic memory storage Lake is somewhat tentative:

My interest in the biological existence of pre-verbal memories is not to demonstrate the legitimate existence of our findings but to indicate their biological feasibility, and to guard against dismissive criticism based on an antiquated neurology when they are reviewed (Lake, 1981g, xvi).

The M-FDS as a Paradigm

The Fetal Period

The huge wealth of research regarding the importance of prenatal life on subsequent functioning has accumulated mostly in the past 20-30 years. Based upon the evidence presented in earlier, it seems quite clear that the previously accepted conventional understanding of fetal life as inert, hypoxic, and pain-insensitive is incorrect. Far from this view, fetal life is intensely active and reactive; far from being an inert dependent passenger in pregnancy, the fetus is, to a great degree, actually in control. As Liley has clearly stated:

> It is the foetus who guarantees the endocrine success of pregnancy and in-duces all manner of changes in maternal physiology to make her a suitable host. It is the foetus who, singlehandedly, solves the homograft problem-- no mean feat when we reflect that, biologically, it is quite possible for a woman to bear more than her own body weight of babies, all immunological foreigners, during her reproductive career. It is the foetus who determines the duration of the pregnancy. It is the foetus who decides which way he will lie in pregnancy and which way he will present for labour. Even in labour the foetus is not entirely passive (Liley, 1991, 192-193).

Indeed, one researcher in the area has stated that "present available data would suggest that the mature human being in utero is neither in a stupor nor in an hypoxic coma and that it will respond to various extra-uterine stimuli and to maternal emotions" (Goodlin, 1979, 1).

The pivotal assertion of Lake's M-FDS was that "powerfully im-pressive experiences from the mother and her inner and outer world . . . reach the foetus, defining its relation to the intra-uterine reality in ways that persist into adult life" (Lake, 1981c, 5). Confining for the moment our discussion to the second and third trimesters, roughly corresponding to the fetal period, does the evidence allow for an affirmation of this assertion? Based upon the evidence presented previously, the answer is a qualified yes.

The qualifications necessary for answering in the affirmative result from several important points. The first is the gradual morphological and psychological development that results over the span of the fetal period. The increasing sophistication and complexity of the central nervous system in conjunction with the specialized sense receptors is concomitant with an ever-increasing complexity in fetal behavior (Richmond & Herzog, 1979, 15). Thus, morphologically and psychologically speaking, what might be manifestly obvious and observable at 32 weeks after gestation is less obvious and observable early on. Thus, our conclusions regarding the viability of Lake's M-FDS as a paradigm must be more tentative for earlier dates and can be less tentative for later ones.

Nevertheless, speaking generally regarding the fetal period, one can affirm that the requisite structures and capabilities are present which allow for a profound influence upon the developing fetus by the immediate environment of the womb. That this environment, to a great degree, is dependent upon the mother and her immediate environment is the essence of what Lake was saying.

What are these requisite structures that allow for influence of this sort? Regarding the fetal period, they are the similar to the structures and capabilities necessary for environmental effects that are post-natally influential. Of primary importance are the various morphological components of the nervous system: the cerebral cortex, the spinal cord, the tactile, visual, auditory, gustatory, vestibular, and gustatory sense receptors and their corresponding areas of the brain. The capabilities stemming from these structures and often promoting their further development are also present: movement, tactile sensitivity, REM sleep, crying, vision, hearing, tasting and hearing. Further, the intermodal fluency between senses and the "higher-level" processes of learning, habituation, conditioning, imitation, memory, cognition, however rudimentary, are all indications of the ability of the fetus to apprehend "powerfully impressive experiences from the mother and her inner and outer world" (Lake, 1981c, 5).

The second qualification necessary within the general framework of affirmation of the M-FDS for the fetal period relates to affect. Whether fetal or even neonatal emotion exists in the same or similar manner of infants or adults is impossible to determine due the inherent subjectivity of experienced affect. Research with both preborn and newborns, however, has shown clear evidence for at least the external behavior normally associated with internal emotion. For instance, crying and smiling, of both the intra-uterine and extra-uterine varieties, have been connected to the internal states of pain and satiation respectively. Research with prematurely born and neonates seems to find that certain facial expressions are indicative of affect states such as sadness, fear, disgust, happiness, surprise, anger, interest, distress, and shame. Using videotape of neonates in the first week of life, Eisenberg and Marmarou (1981) revealed of full range of clear-cut expressions of emotion. Thus, the research again seems to indicate that if "powerfully impressive experiences from the mother and her inner and outer world" do "reach the foetus" (Lake, 1981c, 5), that the fetus can, at least in a rudimentary manner, respond emotionally to these experiences.

Absolutely key to the affirmation of Lake's M-FDS is the concept of "umbilical affect". Lake's understanding is essentially that of Mott's, who conceptualized a bi-directional flow of blood from mother to fetus as mediated by the placenta through the umbilical cord, which gives rise to various physical "feelings" such as aggression, submission, emptiness, fullness, giving and taking that are the basis for subsequent psychological "feelings". Lake picked up on Mott's term "umbilical affect" to designate this exchange, defining it as the "feeling state of the fetus as brought about by blood reaching him through the umbilical vein." (Moss, 1987, 203). As both Lake and Mott define this exchange, the umbilical vein not only conveys nutritive resources and as such could be experienced as a "life-giving flow, bringing . . . renewal and restoration" but could also "be the bearer of an aggressive thrust of bad feelings into the foetus if the mother herself was distressed and 'feeling bad.'" If the mother felt emotionally unsupported , then "this feeling of deficiency, lack of recognition and the failure of looked-for support, would be just as specifically felt by the fetus. It became distressed by the failure of its immediate environment to provide the expected acceptance and sustenance, not so much at the level of metabolic input . . . but to nourish the earliest beginnings of the person in relationship" (Lake, 1976b, S1).

Certainly the biological morphology for this exchange is present at the very beginning of the fetal period. The morphological structures which allow for "natural" exchanges to occur also allow for the passage through the placental barrier of various teratogens, including drugs, viruses, and significantly neurohormones.

As previously noted, a large body of research evidence exists which has clearly shown the impact, both positive and negative, of a mother's environment on her fetus. Numerous studies have correlated various maternal affect states such as anxiety during the fetal period with newborns who suffer from higher heart rates, lower birth weight, irritability, poor sleep patterns, gastrointestinal difficulties, hyperactivity, excessive crying, and who are perceived by their parents as having a difficult temperament, score lower on mental and motor skills tests, and have a much higher incidence of birth complications of all types. Various studies have also connected higher rates of spontaneous abortion, birth complications and preterm delivery with fear, anxiety, guilt, negative attitudes toward the pregnancy, emotional immaturity, difficulty in accepting the pregnancy, and husbands who offered little or no support.

Neuroendocrinological studies done over the last decade are illustrating more and more why and how the above results occur, namely, the physiological mechanisms which allow "umbilical affect" to occur. The neuroendocrinological interactions of the mother's endocrine and nervous systems in response to the environment profoundly affect the fetus within her.

But what of Lake's contention that the "umbilical affect" flow sets up reaction patterns that persist into adulthood? For instance, persons who early on reacted "hysterically" tended to react hysterically as adults and persons who adopted the typical "depressive" defense patterns early on, tended to utilize them as adults. Is there evidence that the reaction to early emotional stress tended to set up a pattern of similar reacting that is life-long?

As previously cited, numerous correlational studies have found a strong connection between fetal "stresses" and later dysfunctional behavior. Research studies have associated maternal anxiety during pregnancy with offspring who have much higher rates of childhood autism, psychosis, schizophrenia, emotional and behavioral disorders, and psychiatric disorders in general.

What appears to be causing these long-term dysfunctions is nothing other than "umbilical affect". While the effect of the various neuro-hormones released by the endocrine system seem to be reversible in infants and adults, they seem to be less reversible in the fetal period; indeed, they appear to be more-or-less irreversible at certain critical periods in development during the embryonic and fetal stages. What seems to be produced is a psychophysiological predisposition to respond that some researchers have traced into adulthood. While there is not yet a precise understanding as to how the psychological and physiological dimensions interact to cause long-term psycho-physiological behavior changes, it is clear that something is going on. Recent evidence seems to indicate that the hypothalamus, as the "emotional regulator" of the body is key in this transaction.

Lake described the fetus' response to these experiences as follows: "the tendency is to feel identified with all of these invading maternal emotions in turn and to react to each" (Lake, 1981g, 21). It is this response, according to Lake, that is so determinative for subsequent functioning, especially when the fetus is responding to an emotive flow of severe distress. The result, depending upon the specific intrapsychic dynamics, is an emotional "colouring of a person's life" (Lake, 1978a, 3); the appearance of a particular group of symptoms and signs that characterize a particular psychopathology. Thus, "this intra-uterine interaction is the source of images, perceptions, meanings, values and personality defenses to cope with them" (Lake, 1981f, 65).

In addition to Lake and other early researchers such as Mott and Lietaert Peerbolte (1951), others have more recently also broached the notion of predispositions to respond stemming from the fetal period, terming them engrammes (Ployé, 1976, 667), imprints (Lake, 1981g, 16), or patterns (Turner, 1988, 309). Ployé suggests that three categories of engrammes or imprints exist: imprints of early threats to the pregnancy such as attempted abortion, etc.; imprints related to toxemia or poisoning, and imprints related to later threats to the pregnancy. Ployé gives an example of how these "biological imprints", some from the first trimester, often manifest themselves later on as dreams:

> Comme type d'engramme possible, on pourrait cite l'exemple hypothétique suivant: Un enfant rêve qu'il escalade la berge abrupte d'une rivière et a très peur dans le rêve quand il se sent en danger de lâcher prise et de tomber à l'eau. Les rêves de chute, surtout quand la présence d'eau aggrave le danger, sont souvent interprétés comme étant des rêves de naissance. Si cependant la mère de notre enfant hypothétique présentait nettement une histoire de menace de fausse-couche pendent les deus premiers mois, et si par ailleurs la naissance elle-même s'était pratiquement passée sans incident, ne pourrait-on pas considérer ce genre de rêve comme l'engramme possible de l'anxiété biologique éprouvée par l'embryon en face de cette menace à son existence?
>
> Je suggèrerais qu'il pourait y avoir grand intérêt à suivre ces rêves d'enfants quand ils présentent le thème de quelqu'un qui se cramponne des pieds et des mains à une paroi verticale sans attachement à aucune corde, ou qui se fait déloger de quelque niche ou cravasse où il avait pris refuge. On pourrait alors s'enquérir, par exemple, au sujet d'une menace possible de fausse-couche ou d'une tentative d'avortement pendent les premières semaines, période où l'embryon est implanté dans la muqueuse utérine et s'accroche ensuite à la paroi utérine, sans l'intermédiaire d'un cordon ombilical non encore développé (Ployé, 1976, 668).

Interestingly, Lake's formulations and language would correspond quite exactly to Ployé's suggestions. For instance, the idea of the imprinting effect of an experience akin to being poisoned can be readily found in Lake's writing. In *Tight Corners in Pastoral Counselling* he describes a negative experience of umbilical affect flow as an "invasion of the fetus in the form of a bitter, black flood . . . of incompatible . . . and alien emotions" (Lake, 1981g, x) or as the "foetus being 'marinated' in his mother's miseries" (Lake, 1981g, 141).

An intriguing suggestion to explain imprints or predispositions has been proposed by Hepper as similar to "learned helplessness." According to Hepper:

> The foetus has little control over the stimulation it receives and it is unable to escape from it. A number of stimuli may be aversive, for example, loud noises, nicotine, or perhaps most interesting, stress. The foetus responds to maternal emotions, including stress, reactions which may be mediated by substances (e.g. hormones, catecholomines) crossing the placenta, by increased maternal arterial pressure, or by increased maternal muscle tone reducing the available space for movement in the womb. . . . It may be that the foetus in highly stressed mothers experience a situation very similar to that of animals in learned helplessness experiments. Such experiences may contribute specifically to the onset of particular disorders, for example depression, or, perhaps most likely, will predispose the individual to respond in certain ways that increase the likelihood of suffering from psychiatric disorders in later life (Hepper, 1989, 292).

Based upon the broad evidence presented regarding the physiological and psychological capabilities of the second and third trimester fetus, Lake's M-FDS could be commended as a paradigm, a "generally accepted system of ideas which defines the legitimate problems and methods of a research field." The one important qualification would relate to memory. If "umbilical affect" causes some type of "proto-memory" or physiological alteration in the nervous system, which sets up later predispositions to respond to stress, then the M-FDS can be legitimately utilized as a conceptual scheme, "a set of concepts (abstracted by generalization from particular clinical experiences) which is interrelated by hypothetical and theoretical propositions" (Lake, 1977a, 1). Thus stated, the M-FDS does not depend upon the veracity or even the accessibility of early fetal "memories", but rather on the negative effects of maternal stress on the fetus within her and the correlation of that experience with later psychopathology.

Perhaps the single most controversial aspect of Lake's M-FDS is his strong emphasis upon the first trimester of intrauterine life. He affirmed that the developmental process, not only in the physiological dimension, but also psychological, emotional, cognitive, and spiritual dimensions, begins not in early infancy or at birth or even in the second or third trimesters of fetal life. Rather, Lake asserted that "we must begin at conception, through the blastocystic stage, to implantation and the events of the first trimester. It is here, in the first three months or so in the womb, that we have encountered the origins of the main personality disorders and the psychosomatic stress conditions" (Lake, 1981g, ix). In the introduction of *Tight Corners in Pastoral Counselling*, Lake wrote the following:

> We have always known, whether taught by St. Augustine, Soren Kierke-
> gaard or Sigmund Freud, that infants suffered abysmally, and that human
> beings crawling out of their abysses into life have damaged perceptions,
> distorted goals and a lifetime bondage of primal fears. What we had not
> known, and even now are somewhat terrified to know as clearly and
> rigorously as we in fact do, is the contribution to this soul-destroying pain
> and heart-breaking suffering that comes from the distress in the womb when
> the mother herself is distressed. **The focus for psychopathology is now, for
> us, the first trimester of intra-uterine life** [emphasis Lake's]. These first
> three months after conception hold more ups and downs, more ecstasies and
> devastations than we had ever imagined (Lake, 1981g, vii-viii).

Lake was certainly aware of the various problems associated with this claim. In a paper addressed to medical colleagues and researchers titled "The Internal Consistency of the Theory of a Maternal-Foetal Distress Syndrome" he sought to address some of the issues inevitably raised by his propositions. The first issue, and the one for which the paper was named, was to address testability of the central hypothesis of the M-FDS, which he defined as "the de-repression of aspects of fixated foetal experience, i.e. to foetal distress of various kinds, incurred as a result of the passage to the foetus of maternal distress-- of the same kinds. The placental-foetal or umbilical circulation is involved in this, though *telepathic* communication between mother and foetus is not ruled out" (Lake, 1977a, 1). Perhaps an illustration of what Lake was describing can be found in Lester Sontag's early study titled "War and the Maternal-Fetal Relationship" (1944). He observed that the babies of women whose husbands were serving in the armed services and thus daily threatened with death tended to be crankier and have an array of physical problems.

He theorized that the intra-uterine environment of constantly worrying mothers would have a deleterious effect on a whole generation of infants. Sontag coined the term "somatopsychics" (inferring the mirror process of "psychosomatics", which refers to the way in which psychological processes effect physiological ones) to describe the way "basic physiological processes affect the personality structure, perception, and performance of an individual." Thus, the developing fetal morphological apparatus is influenced by the intra-uterine environment in such a way as to predispose certain psychological processes following birth.

Lake saw the M-FDS as empirically testable by defining two independent variables and one dependent variable. The first independent variable is the "actual nature of content of the mother's distress" (Lake, 1977a, 1), namely, what is transfused into the fetus, and the second is the "nature and content of the foetal response to the distress, as it is being relived in deliberate 'therapeutic regression'." The dependent variable is the "actual symptomolgy which the subject is 'complaining of', or 'reporting' together with those 'signs which can be elicited on questioning'" (Lake, 1977a, 1).

Lake was confident that the data for the two independent variables could be gathered relatively objectively. The data for the first could be gathered by a combination of precise history taking, along with reliable inferential data regarding the mother's personality and stress reactions at the time of the first trimester. The data for the second, Lake believed, was accessible through "pre-natal or primal integration work" of the sort described earlier. These two variables are not independent of each other, since the second, to a great degree, is based on the first.

Lake's prediction that the dependent variable of present functioning is highly correlated with the independent variable of maternal stress is due to his conceptualization of "patterning" (Lake, 1981e, 4) or "imprints". This notion is central to the M-FDS as a predictive tool relating to etiology and as a beginning for the therapeutic process. Lake writes:

> We have consciously and systematically pursued the relations between isomorphic (similar-patterned or same-shaped) elements (1) in the present history of signs and symptoms, (2) the mother's environmental pressures and *her* reactions, signs and symptoms, during the first trimester when she was carrying this individual, and the signs and symptoms manifested by the subject during the re-experiencing of the events of the first three months in the womb (Lake, 1977a, 2).

One example of "patterning" that Lake clearly delineated as originating in the first trimester of intra-uterine life was homosexuality. In *Tight Corners in Pastoral Counselling*, Lake related his views on the psychogenesis of homosexuality:

> Insofar as we are now looking confidently at the first trimester for the origins of schizoid affliction, it is the same first trimester that we will look to discover the origins of homosexuality in men and possibly also in women . . .
>
> The question arises, why, in association with feelings of intense distress and revulsion at being invaded and surrounded by so much female misery, there should also be this heartache for the intimate love of a man. The answer, given at this moment of the reliving of experience early in the womb, by a sufficient number of homosexual men . . . is that this yearning is a result of the transfusion of exactly that state of mind and emotional longing in the mother, from her to the foetus, through the feto-placental circulation. . . . It is this combination of the mother's emotional distress at their life situation plus her yearning for the intimate love of her man that are transferred into and impressed upon the foetus, early in intra-uterine life (Lake, 1981g, 149-150).

Lake continues his discussion by relating his theories regarding the etiologic dynamics of lesbianism and then follows with an affirmation, that although he views the origins of homosexuality to be in the first trimester, later environmental determinants also play a part:

> I conclude that though the psychogenic roots of homosexuality in men and women in the first trimester can now be taken as a workable hypothesis, rooted in and related to the maternal-foetal distress syndrome, the dynamics of each person are quite individual and specific. They will certainly have gathered later determinants in subsequent trimesters, in difficult births and in all the successive stages of psycho-sexual development (Lake, 1981g, 152).

Lake was certainly willing to subject this conceptual scheme to investigation. He wrote regarding the two independent variable cited above:

> The hypothesis is nullified if there should be, over a series of well-investigated cases with reasonably informative parents, no significant correlation between the feelings and background emotional colouring and the sex drive of the subject with that of his mother, overt or suppressed, in the early months of pregnancy.
>
> It would also be nullified if pre-natal integration work did not lead to a reliving of the complained-of symptoms . . . when focusing on the first

trimester. So far, the hypothesis has not been nullified on either count (Lake, 1981g, 152).

Some recent research finding have lent support to some of Lake's hypotheses regarding the psychogenesis of homosexuality. Several retrospective studies (Dorner et al, 1975; 1980) have found correlations be-tween stressful maternal life events which occurred during pregnancy and the incidence of adult male homosexuality. Dorner and his colleagues found that out of 800 homosexual males, "highly significantly more homosexuals were born during the stressful war (World War II) and early post-war period than in the years before or after this stressful period. This finding suggested that stressful maternal life events, if occurring during pregnancy may represent in fact, an etiogenetic risk factor for the development of sexual variations in the male offspring" (Dorner, 1988, 426).

Another study (Dorner et al, 1983) compared the answers of 100 heterosexual men with 100 bi- and homosexual men of the same age to questions relating to maternal stress during their prenatal life. The highest significant correlation was found in homosexual men (followed by bi-sexual men) and maternal stress. One-third of the homosexual men reported severe maternal distress while they were in utero (i.e. death of someone close, rape, severe anxiety, abandonment by partner), and one-third reported moderate maternal stress. Compared with this data, none of the heterosexual men reported severe stress and only 10% reported moderate stress.

What might explain such results is the effect of neurohormones re-leased under the aegis of the hypothalamus on the developing fetus during the first trimester in response to the environmental stresses that the mother experiences. Lake seemed to anticipate that corroboration of his theory of "umbilical affect" and "patterning" might best be done through animal studies. Regarding homosexuality he wrote:

> I am not well informed as to research in animals. It would be surprising if no studies had been done on the effect of stress applied to pregnant mammals on the behavior and psychological reactions of their offspring. I am open to in-formation on this point (Lake, 1981g, 153).

Indeed, the emerging field of psychoneuroendocrinology has cor-roborated some of Lake's ideas regarding the etiology of homosexual behavior. In a series of studies by Dorner (1967; 1968; 1969; 1970) and his colleagues (Dorner et al, 1968; 1969; 1979; Dorner, Docke & Mustafa, 1968a; 1968b; Dorner & Fatschel, 1970; Dorner & Hinz, 1968; 1971; 1978; Dorner & Staudt, 1968; 1969) on various animals, permanent alterations in adult sexual behavior were produced by neuroendocrine changes during critical brain organization stages during the embryonic period. Since the same basic neuroendocrinological systems are functional in human beings as in the experimental animals, Dorner made the following hypothesis:

> Primary hypo-, bi- or homosexuality produced by androgen deficiency in males and androgen excess in females during sex-specific brain differentiation might correspond etiologically to primary hypo-, bi- or homosexuality in human beings (Dorner, 1988, 423).

Thus, a neuropsychoendocrinological process occurs, whereby certain psychosocial influences in the mother's environment cause an intrauterine environment that in turn causes hypothalamic predispositions in the fetal morphology to respond psychologically in particular ways. As this relates to sexuality, Dorner writes that "prenatal psycho-social influences, which are able to affect the levels of systemic hormones and/or neurotransmitters, should . . . be regarded as possible etiologic factors in the development of sexual deviations" (Dorner, 1988, 425). Several studies (i.e. Stahl et al, 1978) have clearly demonstrated this in rats, finding that prenatal stress tended to demasculinize males rats in terms of testosterone levels and observed behavior. Dorner cites another study that distinguishes the prenatal stress as crucial:

> We have observed bi- or even homosexual behavior in prenatally stressed male rats after castration plus estrogen treatment in adulthood, whereas prenatally non-stressed but later equally treated males displayed heterosexual behavior (Gotz & Dorner, 1980). Hence, prenatal stress can predispose to the development of bi- or even homosexual behavior in males (Dorner, 1988, 425).

Research into other environmentally caused hormonal fluctuations in the prenatal period have also shown the deleterious effect of the postnatal predisposition. For instance, research on overnutrition (Franková, 1970; Dorner et al, 1976; 1977) and undernutrition (Ravelli, 1976) resulting in changes in the insulin and/or glucose levels during critical periods of fetal brain development have been found to alter irreversibly "the function and tolerance ranges of hypothalamic control centers for glucose metabolism" (Dorner, 1988, 426). This has been cited as a predisposing risk factor in obesity (Dorner, 1973; 1978), diabetes mellitus (Dorner & Mohnike, 1973; 1976; 1977; Dorner et al, 1973; 1975; 1984), and atherosclerosis (Dorner, Haller & Leonhardt, 1973).

Interestingly, the predisposing effects of neurohormones and other endocrinal effects does not end at birth. Rather, the source of the hormones changes from mother to child himself, but the effect can be just as profound. For instance, the postnatal psychosocial effects of extended handling, electric shocks (Denenberg, 1964), maternal deprivation (Dorner et al, 1982), overnutrition (Dorner & Grychtolik, 1978), and malnutrition (Hinz et al, 1976; Rodgers, 1978; Ryan, 1977), and the administration of various neurodrugs (Dorner, 1976; Dorner et al, 1976; Hecht et al, 1978; Hinz et al, 1978) all resulted in permanent neuro-chemical changes in the brain and/or permanent alterations of emo-tionality, exploratory behavior, learning capability and memory capacity. This certainly would correspond to Lake's statements regarding the ongoing pre-natal and post-natal determinants to various behavior states.

Dorner has proposed (Dorner, 1973) two ontogenetic organization rules for the neuroendocrine system, the second of which clearly has application to Lake's notions of "patterning":

> During the pre- and/or early post-natal life, systemic hormones and neuro-transmitters are capable of acting as organizers of the brain, which is the controller of the neuro-endocrine-immune system. Thus, the quantity of the systemic hormones and neurotransmitters co-determines during a critical period of brain development, the quality, i.e. the responsiveness, of their own central nervous system controllers and hence the functional and tolerance ranges of their own feedback systems throughout life. . . . Abnormal levels of systemic hormones and neurotransmitters, which can be induced by abnormal conditions in the psychosocial and/or natural environment, can act as teratogens and lead to permanent physiological and/or psychological dysfunctions in later life. Thus many malfunctions of reproduction, metabolism, information processing, and immunity called up to now idiopathic, essential, cryptogenic, primary or genuine can be explained by pre- and/or early postnatal psycho- and/or physiological processes. Therefore, "structural teratology" (teratomorphology) . . . [must be] supplemented by [a] "functional teratology" (teratopsychophysiology) (Dorner, 1988, 429).

That Lake affirmed this "functional teratology" is obvious. The source of the "abnormal conditions in the psychosocial environment" were, for

Lake, variable. He writes that the "influx of maternal distress" (Lake, 1981d, C41), which Dorner refers to as "abnormal levels of systemic hormones and neurotransmitters", may result from her "distress in relation to the world. It may be due to her marriage, to her husband's withdrawal rather than more intimate supporting when he is asked urgently for more than his personality can easily give. It may be due to the family's economic or social distress in a distressed neighborhood. . . . If she is grieving the loss of, or nursing a still dying parent, the sorrow overwhelms her and overwhelms her fetus" (Lake, 1981f, 66). Whatever the cause, "the pain of the world, picked up by the family, is funneled by the mother into the fetus" (Lake, 1981f, 66). Included in this dynamic then, is "both the registering of the intrusion of the mother's condition, of yearning, anxiety, fear, anger, disgust, bitterness, jealousy, etc. into the fetus, and its own emotional response to this distressed and distressing invasion" (Lake, 1981d, C41). This is exactly what a teratopsycho-physiology describes.

The Problem of Memory

The fifth and final question regarding the M-FDS as a scientific paradigm relates to the question of memory. While this issue has already been touched upon briefly, it is important to note that Lake's assumption of the authenticity and verity of fetal memories as they present themselves in recall of whatever type is certainly open to question.

The term "childhood amnesia" was coined by Freud (1951) to account for the paucity of conscious memories of early childhood. Indeed, several researchers have found that the mean age of their earliest memory is between 39 (Cohen, 1989) and 42 months (Dudycha & Dudycha, 1941). This would not present a problem for Lake, due to his belief that most of the "memories" of the fetal period, and indeed, birth, are unconscious, and thus need to be elicited by means of hypnosis, LSD, or deep-breathing.

Since much of the "evidence" that Lake uses to buttress the M-FDS consists of reported "memories", the question of the content of these memories remains. Unfortunately, Lake makes no distinctions between the various dimensions of memory, thus confusing the issue. Researchers have suggested that "memory" is divided up into multiple systems, each operating according to separate principles. One early distinction between two types of memory was made by Tulving (1972), who distinguished episodic memory of an experiential nature from semantic memory involving language and information. Memory of a semantic type is dependent upon language and is described by Tulving as follows:

> It is a mental thesaurus, organized knowledge a person possesses about words and other verbal symbols, their meaning and referents, about relations among them and about rules, formulas, and algorithms for the manipulation of these symbols, concepts and relations (Tulving, 1972, 380).

Episodic memory, according to Tulving, is autobiographical and involves the particular combinations of sensations, feelings, thoughts and behavior unique to the individual. Included in this memory sub-system would be the further sub-systems of memory related to sensation, perception and affect. Episodic memory thus contains representations of an individual's experiences "according to their temporal and contextual relations to those of other events" (Gregg, 1986, 24).

Tulving later added a third memory system, called procedural memory (Tulving, 1983), which consists of connections between stimuli and responses. Also included are various motor memory skills such as turning over, sitting up, and operating equipment.

When we examine the "memories" that Lake reports as evidence, they mostly consist of the episodic type, although procedural memory is also present. For instance, Lake reports that many persons "reliving" their prenatal and perinatal experiences, make various motor movements quite representative of those developmental periods. Very few memories of the semantic type are reported, this being consistent with the fact that the language skills necessary for encoding such memories are not yet present.

The evidence regarding the reliability and verity of autobiographical and episodic memories is mixed. In one study, Field (1981) analyzed interviews of individuals carried out on people at age 30, and again at age 47, and lastly, at age 70. Regarding questions about education, family, occupation and relationships, the average correlation for factual questions over the 40-year span was .88, while questions regarding attitudes and emotions were less, .43.

Other studies have shown that episodic memories tend to be grouped together according to similarities, often forming a composite memory (Linton, 1982; Means et al, 1988) and that chronological information is thus often lacking (Wagenaar, 1986). Both recency (Rubin et al, 1986) and primacy effects (Holding et al, 1986) have been observed with episodic memories, and research shows that they tend to get less accurate over time (Cohen & Faulkner, 1986; 1988a; 1988b). The major determinants of memorability seem to be the presence of a significant temporal event (Brown et al, 1986; Loftus & Marburger, 1983), the relative emotionality and perceived importance of the event, and rehearsal (Rubin & Kozin, 1984).

Lake's report of "memories" of fetal and embryonic life are essentially episodic. While it is conceivable that such memories do indeed exist, they must be interpreted in light of the difficulties described above. Certainly the retention of such "memories" is consistent with the finding that high emotionality and importance tends to be correlated with retained memories. Perhaps those who do not have such memories did not experience these events as emotionally charged. Thus, Lake's finding that extremely negative fetal experiences seem to be best and most vividly remembered correlates with the evidence.

Critique of the M-FDS as a Theological Paradigm

In Frank Lake's issue-long article "The Theology of Pastoral Counseling" published in *Contact* in 1980, he cites three general theological goals: the thorough theological grounding for everything he does, the communication of a cross-based theodicy, and finally, the development of a theodicy which can even incorporate fetal suffering. As was noted above, a full analysis of Lake's theological method is beyond the scope of the present work, but a critique of Lake's exegetical and hermeneutical methodology relating to the M-FDS is needed. Secondly, central toward an understanding of the M-FDS as a theological paradigm is Lake's theodicy. Simply put, "*what* are the correlations between Christ's sufferings and ours, and *how* can these be effectively communicated to sufferers" (Lake, 1979a, 2)?

As has previously been cited, Lake's use of the term "paradigm" relating to the theological dimension of the M-FDS was defined as "a pattern, something shown side by side with something else, inviting comparison of the correspondences" (Lake, 1980b, 3). What he sought to imply by this was the close parallel between "the agony of the human spirit as it endures ultimate injuries and the agonies of Christ in his crucifixion" (Lake, 1964, xvii). But underlying this paradigmatic relationship were Lake's assumptions regarding the integration of the psychological and theological realms. That a theological understanding of Christ's sufferings could be not only correlated, but also integrated with the psychological trauma of a first trimester fetus is assumed by Lake.

Lake's Methodology

Theological and Biblical Method

In an article titled "The Work of Christ in the Healing of Primal Pain" Lake described his theological method:

> My task is to approach the "work of Christ" from the limited aspect of an inductive, strictly 'clinical' theology. I am not, as I understand my task, required to give a full and rounded account of the whole body of soteriological doctrine as such. I am not here a teacher of theology, responsible to stress this or that aspect in direct proportion to the stress it receives in the Scriptures, and argue deductively that what must follow is such and such.
>
> Approaching the theological task inductively my concern must be . . . to take up "an issue in the present situation". . . and then analyze it in depth, to see what is at stake in it and how Christian truth may be related to it (Lake, 1989, 226).

He continues by affirming that he does not see it as his task to "declare the whole counsel of God" on every occasion. Rather, he says, "the whole pharmacopoeia of the gospel medicine is open to us to use. . . . What we do stands or falls by its faithfulness to the juncture between the particular human need and a particular God-given resource at whatever level" (Lake, 1989, 227).

The attempted integration of "God-given resources" and the "pharmacopoeia of the gospel" with the various facets of "human need" is both the strength and weakness of Lake's entire project. The division of the human person into physiological, psychological and spiritual dimensions while often practical, arbitrarily and superficially violates the essential unity of what it means to be a human being. Lake's stated attempt to integrate the various bodies of specialized data into a unity, grounded in a Christian theology informed by the Bible, is certainly commendable. But he succeeds only in a superficial manner and often at the expense of seeming to violate the original meaning of various passages.

Also estimable is the distinctly Christian therapy that this attempted integration gave rise to. "Clinical Theology" was defined by Lake as "the theology of pastoral care of a person in trouble, sorrow, weakness, confusion, affliction, anxiety, depression and the like" or "the theology that informs a 'clinical meeting' where actual cases and concrete problems are being presented, analyzed and discussed with a view to 'treat-ment' or the 'conduct of the case'" (Lake, 1989, 226-227). Certainly these overlap and from the standpoint of the seeming inadequacies and weaknesses of both traditional Christian pastoral care and traditional psychotherapeutic models, both were and continue to be needed.

Further, Moss makes the point that Lake's therapeutic system has the advantage of making clearly apparent, up front, its religious undertones. These undertones were, for Lake, not simply implicit in a minor way, but rather foundational. Lake's intention was that psychology and therapy are always to be judged by and answer to a Biblically-informed Christianity.

But the weaknesses of Lake's attempted integration of "God-given resources" and the "pharmacopoeia of the gospel" with the various facets of "human need" are also readily apparent. His so-called inductive theology (Campbell, 1982; van de Kastelle, 1984) manifests itself practically as a hermeneutic theory in which both the biblical and theological resources are used in the service of certain psychological observations (Atkinson, 1982; MacInnes, 1977). Lake's stated theo-logical task of "taking up an issue in the present situation" and then going to the "pharmacopoeia of the gospel" to see what applies to "particular human need" is the essence of how he utilizes both the Bible and various theologians.

While Lake would certainly disagree with this criticism, the very manner in which he uses the Bible, which is quite often, illustrates his sometimes flawed exegesis. For instance, Lake very often ignores basic grammatico-historical exegetical principles in *Clinical Theology* when he uses biblical personages to illustrates various clinical psychiatric descriptions, categories and treatments. For instance, Lake would see Ahitophel, Ahab and Elijah (Lake, 1964, 102-103) as exhibiting the classic behavioral signs of depression. Simon the Pharisee, Peter, and Paul all exhibit dissociative behavior (Lake, 1964, 461-470). According to Lake, Jeremiah evidences paranoid symptomology (Lake, 1964, 1107) and Abraham, Jacob, and Job all evidence schizoid characteristics (Lake, 1964, 752-763; 866-869; 581-588).

Perhaps typical of Lake's problematic exegetical method regarding the use of Biblical figures is his understanding of Mary Magdalene as the prototypical hysteric and Jesus as the prototypical counselor of an hysteric (Lake, 1964, 446-458). According to Lake, while Jesus affirms Mary, he affirms her not just as a person, but as a person of worth. Because of Mary's "hysterical" dependence upon Christ, his death is an "appalling cataclysm", because while the disciples may have lost their leader and Peter may have lost his self-respect, Mary had lost her personality. She goes to the tomb and refuses to leave. Christ appears to her and Mary unwittingly thinks she is speaking with the gardener. According to Lake, the two questions that Jesus asks Mary ("Why weepest thou?" and "Whom seeketh thou?") are the two questions fundamental to every hysteric. The hysteric is seeking someone who will give them a reason to stop crying. According to Lake, Jesus then begins to teach Mary that her dependence upon him must change; not the fact of it or even the incarnational element to it, but rather the limitedly human element of it. She must give up clinging to the humanity of Jesus (i.e. she tries to cling to his feet) because she now becomes a member of the new humanity, in which the Holy Spirit dwells within.

It could be argued that Lake's exegesis here and in numerous other places is really an eisegesis. While this is certainly not always true regarding his handling of the biblical sources, he does frequently read into the text rather than derive meaning from the text. Mary's relationship with Jesus apparently began when he cast seven demons from her (Luke 8:2). That it was a close relationship is seen in the fact that Mary, along with several other women, traveled with Jesus' entourage and supported his ministry financially. She is next mentioned at the foot of the cross with Jesus' mother Mary (Mark 15:40; John 19:25). Finally, she is mentioned in all four gospels as one of the women who first discovers the absence of Jesus' body at the tomb (Matthew 28:1-7; Mark 16:1-8; Luke 24:1-10; John 20:1-2).

Based perhaps on Mary's "clinging" behavior following Jesus appearance to her, Lake reads into her actions and Jesus' response a totally foreign therapist/hysteric relationship. No biblical evidence exists to claim Mary as manifesting an hysterical dependence upon Christ. Indeed, Luke reports that both women "clasped his feet." Mary's presence at the garden tomb is not necessarily indicative of her loss of "personality", but is normal mourning behavior for one who has lost a close friend. Others were also in the garden, including Joanna (Luke 24:10), Salome and Mary, the mother of James (Mark 16:1). Jesus two questions to Mary are not assessment questions, but rather straightforward queries relative to his death and resurrection. While Lake's point that Jesus was telling Mary that their relationship would be changing is legitimate, the reason has to do not with psychodynamic notions of transference and dependence but with Christ's anticipated ascension and the giving of the Holy Spirit. While described behavior may certainly indicate certain parallels between biblical figures and certain personality types, Lake very often ignores the historical, cultural, social context of the various biblical passages he cites.

Perhaps typical of his recurrent faulty exegesis regarding his use of Biblical passages as they related to therapeutic processes was his suggestion that being "born-again" could be understood as relating to re-living one's birth through primal integration. Tom Small writes:

> I can remember when, together with a number of other leaders in the Anglican renewal movement, I met Frank in London to convey to him our concern . . . and to beg him to not to go on suggesting that the text "You must be born again" in John 3 could be validly exegeted as meaning, "You must relive your birth experience." We cannot have convinced him because he went on doing it (Small in Peters, 1989, 84).

Lake's repeated eisegesis is even more apparent regarding some of the theological sources, particularly as it relates to the M-FDS. Lake justified the application of theological sources to psychological categories by stating that "alternative nomenclatures" have been used historically to refer to the same human experiences. Thus, Lake can state definitively that St. John of the Cross' "Dark Night of the Soul", Martin Luther's *theologia crucis*, Simone Weil's "Nail of Affliction" and Soren Kierkegaard's "Sickness Unto Death" all apply, more-or-less to various psychic disturbances, but are particularly applicable to the schizoid experience of dread, non-being, degradation and despair resulting from transmarginal stress at the pre- or perinatal stage. The "alternative nomenclature" scheme, in which Lake connected and paralleled certain similar ideas, language and themes, results in a surface "integration" at the cost of the integrity of the theological sources.

For instance, Lake's appropriation of St. John of the Cross, Soren Kierkegaard and Simone Weil as not only a describers of fetal distress, but also as sufferers is an affirmation fraught with difficulty. What Lake does is to connect in a facile manner the language of theological reflection and description with the language of psychodynamic, psychological and primal descriptions. Since these languages, in his view, are merely "alternative nomenclatures" for the same experiences, he moves back and forth between them with apparent ease, sometimes with total disregard for the historical, social, religious, and political context in which St. John, Kierkegaard and Weil lived and wrote. Several specific examples follow.

As noted previously, Lake describes St. John of the Cross as a severely stressed and, indeed, schizoid personality (Lake, 1964, 593; 842), whose poem "I die because I do not die" is said to illustrate this. The translation that Lake uses of St. John's poem seems, on the surface, to express the paradoxical embrace of death and recoil from life that is so characteristic of the transmarginal states. Yet several other translations (Barnstone, 1968; Nims, 1979) render the language of the poem as less expressive of hate of life and more expressive of longing for God. Indeed, the title of John's poem in one translation is rendered a description, "Coplas about the soul which suffers with impatience to see God" (Campbell, 1951). One example of the varying translations illustrates the point. The translation Lake uses for the first stanza follows:

> This life I live in such a way/Is nothing but life's deprivation,/One prolonged annihilation/Till at last I live with Thee./Hear, my God hear what I say,/I do not want this life of mine;/I die because I do not die.

M.C. D'Arcy's translation (1951) of the same stanza is quite differently evocative:

> This life I live in vital strength/Is loss of life unless I win You:/And thus to die I shall continue/Until I live in You at length./Listen (my God!) my life is in You./This life I do not want, for I/Am dying that I do not die.

Lake's use of this poem as an expression of the despair of the schizoid position is quite different than its seeming expression of longing for God. Indeed, the schizoid position shuns all contact, especially with the mother and then with God as a projection of the dynamics of the mother/child dyad. Thus, Lake's meaning is the diametric opposite; instead of a longing for God which makes this life pale by comparison, it becomes for Lake a rejection of life, including the primary maternal and theistic relationships of life.

In Kierkegaard Lake also finds a schizoid personality, one who was "afflicted with . . . dread and incurable melancholy" (Lake, 1964, 586), and one who also recorded an "alternative nomenclature" for the exigencies of fetal distress and its result, the schizoid position. It is true that many Kierkegaardian scholars would acknowledge that Kierkegaard suffered from some form of dysfunction, if not psychopathology. And one can certainly and plainly see within the Kierkegaardian corpus an insightful and incisive comprehension of the human spirit and its struggles, including the psychological struggles.

Lake is thus right to see Kierkegaard as a theologian who was a psychologist as well, with self-analysis as his main subject of inquiry. While Kierkegaard wrote of his "incurable melancholy" and at times acted in a peculiar manner, Lake's appropriation of Kierkegaard's terminology as expressive of specific characteristics of the M-FDS proceeds too far and reads too much into what Kierkegaard meant.

For instance, in Lake's hermeneutical hands, Kierkegaard's terms "dread", "despair" and "dis-relation" relate specifically to the fetus' or child's reaction to either abandonment or "the invasion of distressingly bad maternal emotions" (Lake, 1981d, T19) resulting is "dis-relation" between mother and fetus/infant. "Sickness unto death" is closely related with the "abnormal, paradoxical wish to die and be annihilated" (Lake, 1964. 558). Lake wrote that Kierkegaard's language in the *Concept of Dread* "is straining to express the nature of life and its catastrophes in the earliest and most determinative months of existence" (Lake, 1964, 726).

Perhaps Lake anticipated the problems of applying Kierkegaard's terminology to the specific components of the M-FDS. Thus, he writes:

> The fact that the terminology is difficult and the expression sometimes tortuous is not entirely the fault of Kierkegaard's too complex intelligence. This is in the nature of the material under consideration, which is essentially pre-verbal, or non-verbal, and paradoxical. He had to invent a language and define his own concepts. Whatever one tries to express in this field of schizoid studies, continued reading of Kierkegaard will show that either in the works he published, or in the posthumous *Journals*, he had said it all 120 years ago, and said it better" (Lake, 1964, 595).

Thus stated, Lake feels free to appropriate Kierkegaard's descriptions of "pre-verbal, non-verbal, and paradoxical" experiences to the M-FDS. Lake writes that "Kierkegaard is explicit about" the origin of the "catastrophes" of the M-FDS in the "infantile states of mind" (Lake, 1964, 701). Further, "Kierkegaard's image of a poisoned environment spreading its poison into him until his own life and whole existence is poisoned, occurs commonly in first trimester transcripts" (Lake, 1982b, 44). Lake then cites an extract from Kierkegaard's *Journals*:

> The whole of existence frightens me, from the smallest fly to the mystery of the Incarnation; everything is unintelligible to me, most of all myself; the whole of existence is poisoned in my sight, particularly myself. Great is my

sorrow and beyond bounds; no man knows, only God in heaven, and He will not console me (Kierkegaard, 1938, #275).

Thus Lake sees in Kierkegaard's description a reiteration of primal distress, a recitation of the "facts" of transmarginal distress. But what Lake ignores is the rest of the journal entry which he quotes from. In it Kierkegaard is clearly referring back to 1836, to a period three years earlier when he had engaged in a period of moral rebellion and sin. Kierkegaard's journal entry, made in the very midst of his peculiar relationship with Regina Olsen, continues:

No man can console me, only God in heaven and he will not have mercy upon me --Young man, you who still stand at the beginning of the way, if you have gone astray, O be converted, turn to God and taught by him your youth will be strengthened to the work of manhood; you will never experience what he must suffer who after having wasted the strength and courage of his youth in rebellion against Him, must now, exhausted and powerless, begin a retreat through the desolate and devastated provinces surrounded on all sides by the abomination of desolation, by burnt towns and the delusive expectations of smoking sites, by trampled down prosperity and broken strength, a retreat as slow as a bad year, as long as eternity monotonously broken by the sound of the complaint: these days please me not (Kierkegaard, 1938, #275).

For Lake, a third and very important originator of an "alternative nomenclature" for the M-FDS is Simone Weil, whom, he believes is also someone well acquainted with the dynamics of first-trimester transmarginal distress. Lake writes:

Simone Weil's account of the three-fold affliction corresponds exactly with the three-fold aspects of severe and undisplaced negative umbilical or intra-uterine affect. Persons re-living a very bad time in their first trimester, speak of themselves, in later life, exactly in these ways. Constricted confusion has been of schizoid intensity, following transmarginal stress (Lake, 1981d, T13).

Perhaps it can be affirmed that Lake's utilization of a very narrow segment of Weil's thought is less problematic than his use of St. John of the Cross or Kierkegaard. Weil's own struggle with dysfunction and pathology (Murray, 1981) resulted in her premature death by anorexia nervosa (McLellan, 1989). Her descriptions of *malheur* were, to an extent, self-descriptions. However, the problem of what Weil meant by her descriptions and how Lake's utilizes them to express the dynamics of the M-FDS still remains. Weil's essay, "The Love of God and Affliction" (Weil, 1951, 117-136) is the major source for Lake's use of Weil. This essay was written in response to an experience in 1938 during Holy Week, where she had gone to all of the Catholic liturgical services. Anderson writes that "in spite of splitting headaches, she had responded deeply to the beauty of the chanting and the words. 'The Passion of Christ' she said, 'entered into my being once and for all'" (Anderson, 1976, 58).

Thus, "The Love of God and Affliction" was a Good Friday meditation which focused on theodicy and the Cross. While Lake certainly saw correspondences between Weil's descriptions of affliction and his own understanding of prenatal distress, there is nothing in this essay which might indicate that Weil intended anything as specific as Lake envisions her to mean. Thus, Lake's use of Weil as a resource for a general theodicy is certainly legitimate. But seeing Weil as describing specifically the M-FDS is not.

Integration of Psychology and Theology

Lake's flawed exegesis of the Biblical and theological resources in the service of certain psychological observations regarding the M-FDS gives rise to the weakness of his attempt to integrate psychology and theology. Perhaps the fact that Lake was never professionally trained as a theologian partially explains his eisegesis; but certainly any attempt to integrate two overlapping, yet disparate fields, brings with it certain problems.

For instance, both theology and psychology have distinct "languages" and "categories" which, in the parameters and context of each well-defined field of study, are intelligible and useful. But when the "languages" and "categories" of one field are used interchangeably with those of another, meaning is often lost or transmuted in the transition (Gravelle, 1990). F.J. Roberts (1972), in a discussion about Clinical Theology, makes the further point that even within the various fields that Lake sought to integrate there are a whole variety of sub-fields with distinct vocabulary and category structures which complicate the task of integration even further. For instance, the challenge of integration that Lake attempts with the M-FDS embraces not only the theological dimension, but also the physiological, psychoneuroendocrinological, and psychological/psychiatric. Melinsky, addressing this difficulty, writes of Lake's attempted integration:

> For theological guidance, Dr. Lake looks principally to Job, St. John's Gospel, St. Paul's Epistle to the Romans, Kierkegaard, Simone Weil and Martin Buber. His psychological mentors are Freud and the neo-Freudians, Klein, Fairbairn, Sullivan and Guntrip. Since there are great divergences amongst theologians and psychiatrists in their own fields, it is hardly to be expected that any one mortal could lead these two contentious disciplines to a happy marriage (Melinsky, 1970, 119).

Thus, Lake's attempt to integrate psychology and theology results in a superficial amalgam of psychologically-interpreted theology and theologically-interpreted psychology. There is a concomitant loss of rigor in both sets of categories, but especially in the theological. Melinsky comments:

> There are flashes of insight sparked off by the high tension between the fields of theology and psychiatry. But there are also links made between the two disciplines which are too simple (Melinsky, 1970, 127).

Lake saw no barrier to using the different categories as if they corresponded in a one-to-one fashion. This often resulted because he was open to new ideas and if they struck his fancy, he sought to "integrate" them immediately into his theoretical constructions. Michael Jacobs, who edited *Tight Corners in Pastoral Counselling*, states that Lake's "failing was the wish to integrate everything he read as soon as he could, without really digesting it, or looking for alternative explanations." Indeed, Jacobs stated that Clinical Theology started to "go wrong" with the "rapid undigested introduction of the newer therapeutic ideas" (Peters, 1989, 86).

Others have criticized Lake similarly (Peters, 1989, 90; 163). The integration of new "ideas" often took place on the basis of a "seeming" similarity between Lake's evolving thinking regarding the M-FDS and the new "idea". Especially toward the end of his life, Lake seemed to be grasping for anything that might buttress his theories of pre-natal distress. Perhaps at the root of this rapid superficial integration was, as one of Lake's colleagues put it, his seeming "inability to reflect critically upon one's own basis of thought" (Peters, 1989, 81). This inability led, in turn, to an inability to countenance criticisms of the M-FDS. In a final riposte to Alastair Campbell's critical review of *Tight Corners in Pastoral Counselling*, Lake wrote:

> Enough. Enough to make my point that the reviewing is tendentious. It is looking to criticize, manufactures some most unjustly on the way, and ends where you would expect. To throw in our direction that most pejorative of smear terms, "Fundamentalist", is in the poorest of taste and quite indefensible. Alastair remains, entrenched where he began, unable to make the effort to understand my world and therefore unjust to it. Of what group are those the predominant characteristics (Lake, 1982, 29)?

Lastly, Lake's attitude toward those who disagreed with his assumptions regarding theology and psychology was often one of condescension. Roberts wrote that very often "the confusion created by the . . . mixing of categories is interpreted by some as an indication of their failure to acquire the secret" (Roberts, 1972, 24). This embrace of the unbeliever's "gnostic ignorance" is evidenced by Lake's introduction to "Mutual Caring":

> I doubt its power to convince where the opposition is itself partly un-conscious and partly deeply invested in current theory and long-established practice, based on Freudian, Kleinian or neo-Freudian "object-relations" theory, all true at their own levels, but whose assumptive fields cannot conceive of foetal experience and learning (Lake, 1982b, Intro:6).

Lake's Theodicy

Perhaps the true confluence of Lake's attempted integration of the physiological and psychological with the theological can best be seen in his theodicy. His absolute belief in the reality of "harsh" fetal affliction in both the physical and psychological dimensions required an "exacting theological paradigm of reconciliation and reparation" and "a corresponding deepening of theodicy to cover it" (Lake, 1981d, T1). This "requirement", according to Lake, is necessitated by the "innocence" of the fetus which is called to endure horrendous suffering although not culpable in any way whatsoever.

Lake's theodicy is within the overall line (Hick, 1966; 1981) of historical and theological formulations such as Augustine (1857), Luther (1962), P.T. Forsyth (1957), Kosuke Koyama (1974; 1977), Kazoh Kitamori (1958), Jurgen Moltmann (1972), and Alvin Plantinga (1974). While differences and distinctions can certainly be found among these theological thinkers, the general strain of thought relates any "justification" of God for the pain and evil of creation directly to the cross. It is the cross and the concomitant "pain of God" which answers and "resolves our human pain" (Kitamori, 1958, 20).

The uniqueness of Lake's paradigm of theodicy is its application to the exigencies of pre-natal suffering, and as such, represents an extension of theological reflection into an arena of human existence previously ignored. But what of the dimension of the M-FDS which seeks to address fetal suffering theologically?

It is important to note that underlying Lake's theodicy is the affirmation of God's attribute as Creator and thus, ultimate responsibility for His creation. Lake writes:

Nothing . . . of the horrors of the foetal-placental cosmos will have come as a surprise to God. Not did he wait till we found out about it before he did something to remedy it, indeed all that needed to be done. He accepted responsibility for setting up this sort of human creation, with all its possibilities of foetal contentment, satisfaction and joy, . . . and the possibility of the total absence of . . . care, plunging the foetus into . . . hell (Lake, 1982b, 79).

Redemption is not a divine reaction or response to an unplanned deterioration of creation, to the "possibility of fetal hell", rather it precedes creation, and is part of the plan. We need not shrink back from attributing responsibility to God, because God has taken responsibility and "answered" the question before it is even asked:

What indications do we have of any sensitive planning on God's part as Creator? What evidence is there that he had already taken steps to be able to meet those unfortunate victims, whom his Creation would sadistically crush, and not be totally ashamed of himself? Because we must admit he did let it go on, with its inevitable monstrous entail of heart-broken distress to the tiniest of his human creatures, embryos and foetuses, before they are twelve weeks on from their conception. The answer centres in that mysterious yet utterly firm assertion, that God's Son, the sharer of his eternal being and his agent in creation, is also the Lamb of God, slain before the foundation of the world. Redemption is therefore the prior and larger reality, containing creation (Lake, 1982b, 79).

But this "answer" remains unknown to those who suffer the "catastrophic trespass" (Lake, 1981f, 67) of profound primal pain. They must deny the truth, "murder the truth" and repress the reality of what has really occurred. And yet, the consequences of this "primal catastrophe" remain:

> A state of infinite, unending, distress exists and is maintained in the primal consciousness of all those who are victims of the Maternal-Foetal Distress Syndrome. They can be no means account for it or understand its origins. Yet it is present in them as the first and total experience of their cosmos, keep up in every moment of each day, month, year, for a life-time (Lake, 1982b, 80).

This "infinite, unending distress" manifests itself in self-blame, self-accusation, and self-hate. Mother cannot be blamed; God cannot be blamed, therefore, the "badness" must be attributed to an inherent worthlessness within (Lake, 1982b, 80). Lake writes:

> The failure of any human being to answer the urgent appeal for a presence gives rise to a deep inner horror of a *deus absconditus*, a "god" who is dead, perhaps killed. The reproach re-echoes in the mind and still reverberates as a pervasive heart break. A basic question of theodicy is avoided only by the infant's attributing badness of the unbearable situation to some inexplicable but indelible badness in its own very being. This is the usual outcome. It is unthinkable that "the gods" are bad. Far better take the blame and leave their righteousness intact (Lake, 1989, 224-225).

The concomitant sense of despair because this "badness" is perceived to be indelible provokes an unending, yet somehow deserved, rejection by "the world", including people and God:

> This victim of the invasion of the adult world's evil, has been indelibly taught, by it's prenatal distress to distrust the world. It perpetuates that perception of the world and projects consistently the same expectation of painful meaning. It concludes, at the end of the first lesson, that as the world was hostile it its life and well-being at the beginning, so it is now, and ever shall be, world without end (Lake, 1981f, 67).

It is to this very sufferer that God through Christ "answers" by his suffering and death on the cross. And it is here where Lake's emphasis of the "innocent sufferer" is so accentuated. Lake writes that for the fetus who "suffers under the weight of the mother's affliction, in the world where she is dependent on the father's care, but where the sins of the fathers descend upon the children, generation feeding affliction into the next below it, until it is funneled into the foetus in a catastrophic trespass"

(Lake, 1981f, 67), to speak of fetal culpability is absurd. In response to this "torture of the innocents" (Lake, 1981f, 67), Lake states provocatively "We don't need redemption by Jesus Christ, [because] there's no sin problem here" (Lake, 1976a, 26). Elsewhere he writes:

> The old paradigm of the work of Christ for men was almost entirely centred on the problem of culpable sin. It had no word to speak clearly to those, who, while innocent victims, were the victims of parental and social evil (Lake, 1980b, 3).

What Lake is addressing is what he sees as the historical over-emphasis upon the work of Christ on the Cross related to the problem of culpable sin to the detriment of the "other" great work of Christ on the Cross; his identification with sufferers. It is the proclamation of this neglected work of identification and "justification" which, according to Lake, must precede the proclamation of the atoning work for the "innocent sufferers" of the M-FDS:

> Before we come to the proclamation of the identification with Christ with culpable sinners, to bring them to forgiveness and a new right relatedness to God as his children, we must, for all the afflicted, speak first of Christ's identification with the innocent who are submerged in this affliction through no fault of their own (Lake, 1980b, 3).

Lake's emphasis upon this "innocent suffering" comes perilously close to denying the doctrine of original sin as interpreted in the Pauline (Romans 5:12-18), Augustinian, Reformation (Calvin, 1960, xv:8) and Reformed tradition (Berkhof, 1939). In his emphasis upon the innocence of the fetus in relation to fetal suffering, Lake at times implies a complete lack of sin, including original sin. This is most clearly illustrated in "Mutual Caring." In a section titled "What would be the consequences of Jesus' 'Freedom from Sin'?" Lake cites Sebastian Moore's *The Fire and the Rose are One* finds three such consequences. The first follows:

> This freedom is present at the deepest level, where a person confronts ultimate mystery. There would be a total, unimpeded intimacy with God. There would be no guilt in the relationship, no holding back and rendering the other fearsome and threatening. The self would flourish in its ultimate companionship with the infinite in a **total, grateful and joyful acceptance of one's being from the mystery** [emphasis Lake's], on which in consequence one casts no "shadow". There is a **consciousness of oneself as**

beloved of the mystery and of the mystery as unshadowed love and beauty [emphasis Lake's]. The sense of "I am not alone" would be overpowering. There would be an almost inconceivable flourishing of the human person (Moore in Lake, 1982b, 14-15).

Lake comments upon this consequence of being "sin-free", presumably also original sin-free, in the following manner:

Foetal life at twelve weeks is only minimally aware of persons beyond the mother, . . . But all that Moore sets out in his first section [quoted above] I have heard many times, when the maternal-foetal tenderness flow has been moving exceedingly well (Lake, 1982b, 15).

If by this Lake is implying that the blastocystic phase or any other phase of fetal life is one of "consciousness of oneself as beloved of the mystery" because of its sin-free quality, then he has denied the traditional doctrine of original sin. Lake does use language similar to that above over and over again to refer to the blastocystic stage (i.e. Lake, 1982c, 85), which, he says, is often experienced as "a unitive and quite transcendent bliss" (Lake, 1981g, 15) or "a glorious ground for mystical experience of unattached 'being, awareness and joy'" (Lake, 1977a, 3).

However, elsewhere Lake seems to affirm, at least tentatively, that the "innocence" of the fetal sufferer is not absolute, but relative. He states that the earlier one goes back for the "sources of trouble", the more "the responsibility for introducing evil must fall, not on the very young themselves, but on the older, adult members of the species" (Lake, 1989, 228). He continues:

Responsibility and culpability, to which the gospel as at present preached addresses itself, so that the conviction of sin may take hold, are minimal in these relatively innocent, because helpless, sufferers (Lake, 1989, 228-229).

Lake seems to infer that "the biblical doctrine of the solidarity of the race and the family" is understood as the effects and consequences of the sin of the previous generations which are experienced by the fetal sufferer. In the same article cited above, Lake writes:

The sins of the fathers and the mothers do descend upon innocent children. This can affect them for life. . . . All this is to say that some suffering in later life takes its origin, not in the culpable sin of the sufferer, but from his involvement, while in a state of total dependency, in the sin of others (Lake, 1989, 231).

Because Lake nowhere explicitly denies the doctrine of original sin, it is difficult to determine that he indubitably does. Certainly he comes close. Numerous times in his writings he speaks of "innocent" suffering, and speaks of it in relation to and as an analogy with the "innocent" suffering of Christ on the Cross. Quoting Simone Weil and then commenting, Lake writes:

> "If the tree of life, and not simply the divine seed, is already formed in a man's soul at the time when extreme affliction strikes him, then he is nailed to the same cross as Christ."
> I would take the "divine seed" to be the experience of blastocystic bliss and the "tree of life" to be the establishment of the umbilical circulation. It is certainly true that affliction experienced at this stage, in total innocence, partakes of the suffering of the Lamb of God (Weil in Lake, 1981g, 29-30).

What Lake is referring to is his "theology of correlation" by which the experience of the "innocent" prenatally afflicted is juxtaposed with the innocent suffering of Christ on the Cross. Lake sees a symmetry and congruity that is "marvelous":

> The more we put the metaphors of salvation and the images of the crucifixion of Jesus Christ under the microscope . . ., requiring that it should speak with manifest relevance, gripping applicability and transforming power, at this hitherto unimagined depth of pre-verbal, pre-propositional panic, the more we discover the Father's marvelous provision and the perfect correlation of the Son's costly and total obedience (Lake, 1981f, 67).

It is not only the "innocence" that corresponds, but the very experiences of the afflicted fetus and the afflicted Savior are also similar. There is the rejection of the Parent, the aloneness of the suffering, "the sweat of blood at Gethsemane . . ., the spitting and the flogging, the crown of thorns that disfigures his face with caked blood, the cross-beam that crushed his shoulders till he fell under the weight, in the nails that were hammered through the palms of his hands and the soles of his feet, and the spear that pierced his side. All these have profound and vivid relevance to those who are reliving foetal distress at the mother's distress" (Lake, 1981f, 67).

But more than the surface similarities, what is so profound about the cross for Lake is not only the fact the sinners are saved, but that sufferers are identified with in the total and absolute sense. Lake cites Isaiah 63, where the "object of the crushing affliction and the direction of the wrath seem, at times to be interchangeable with the subject." God pours out his wrath upon God. God forsakes God. God has "judged" God (Lake, 1981d, T3).

This "theology of correlation", as one critic has stated, while "very poetic", never really goes beyond analogy (Isbister, 1977). Certainly there is much in the suffering of Christ, both in his life and death, to commend itself analogically to human suffering (i.e. Hebrews 2:14-18). But to build into the very definition of theodicy a necessary identification of God with specifically fetal sufferers is to limit theodicy. Lake's tunnel-vision regarding first trimester fetal suffering and his consequent emphasis upon fetal affliction, has the result of ignoring or dismissing the pain and suffering of the remainder of life as secondary and almost incidental.

According to Lake, the innocent suffering of the fetus seems to create a need for God to justify himself. Lake affirms in "Mutual Caring" that while "God is not directly the victimizer" for human suffering, particularly the innocent affliction of the first-trimester fetus, he is, nevertheless responsible. Referring to this distinction, Lake writes:

> In one sense we can take God "off the hook". But in another sense, . . . he, not sins of the fathers for generations impinging on a pregnant mother, would be held to blame. . . . The Cross is God's acceptance of the whole attribution of blame for the searing effects of maternal distress on foetal persons which leads to all the life-long manifestations of the afflicted person (Lake, 1982b, 83-84).

Although Lake makes this distinction between God as victimizer and God as responsible, it is for all practical purposes meaningless in the context of some of Lake's statements. Lake seems to obligate God to send Christ to the Cross if He is not to be utterly ashamed of himself. He cites Christ's question on the road to Emmaus: "O fools and slow of heart, **ought** [Lake's emphasis] not Christ to have suffered these things, and entered into his glory?" Lake answers: "Yes; he ought" (Lake, 1989, 236). This, to Lake, speaks of the "oughtness", indeed, the requirement of God to justify Himself for His creation and to His creation.

Lake uses some very strong language to convey this justification of God. Two examples follow:

> Christ's passion and death is God the Father's **apology** [emphasis mine] to them for the appalling evils they have suffered. God was and is in Christ, reconciling them, by his loving presence alongside them in equivalent innocence and marvelously appropriate suffering, matching the evil world in which their innocence was set (Lake, 1981f, 67).

> If the Cross of Christ says anything to the afflicted, who suffered first, and fatally for their trust, in the first trimester of life in the womb, about the forgiveness of their sins it is that **he is God, begging their forgiveness** [emphasis Lake's] for the hurts caused by the sins of the fathers, funneled into them by the distress of the mothers (Lake, 1981g, 175).

This type of imagery transforms the Cross from an event illustrative of God's love, grace and mercy into an event where God becomes "tolerable" (Lake, 1989, 235). The Cross becomes primarily a justification of God and only secondarily a justification of humankind.

Thus, Lake over-emphasizes what he sees as the neglected work of the Cross to the detriment of what he sees as the previously over-emphasized work of the cross. While he never denies the salvific, atoning, justifying work of Christ on the Cross, the primary emphasis for him is the work of identification in which God is "now vindicated, acquitted, exonerated and . . . justified" (Lake, 1981d, T4):

> This theme, of Christ as the innocent, just man, as the Lamb taken from the flock to have the sins of others laid on his head, sharing the lot of all the innocent, this is the deepest and earliest level of meaning in the suffering of the Son of God (Lake, 1981g, 175).

It is, for Lake, the "deepest and earliest" work of the Cross because, for the afflicted, it precedes the "other work" of the Cross:

> Where this aspect of Christ's mediatorial work is allowed to take place, in establishing justice of a new and costly kind by his presence alongside the sufferer, indeed penetrating every tortured cell of the sufferer with the once and for all time agonized cells of his own divine-human body, the **work of theodicy is over. Then the more familiar work of justifying grace takes over. . . . All along he has also been a sinner** [emphasis Lake's]. He is now free to turn and acknowledge this sinfulness, indeed he is liberated in order to turn from confrontation of the other to self-confrontation (Lake, 1989, 238).

Lake summarizes his theodicy:

> God sent forth his Son, as the Lamb slain before the foundation of the world, in order that the final authority should be seen to be sensitive to the criticism that it is a victimizing world into which historical man and his offspring are introduced at conception. It is God himself who, in setting forth His Son to be the world's Redeemer, Restorer, Reconciler and Justifier, justifies . . . the cry of pain torn from the heart of the afflicted. God himself restates the justice of the anguished complaint of the Psalmist, "My God, why have you forsaken me; Why are you so far from helping me?" That very complaint becomes Christ's own, within the household of God (Lake, 1981d, T3).

Conclusion

Frank Lake can be critiqued for some of his excesses and failings and these have been presented. But Lake also can be commended for a significant contribution to pastoral counseling and pastoral theology. His impact upon these fields in the United Kingdom was extensive, not only through the C.T.A., but also through his books, articles, sermons, and lectures. While this work has not concerned itself with the primal therapy that Lake proscribes as the "cure" for the M-FDS, it is certainly a significant component of his overall project.

Alastair Campbell, in a somewhat critical review published in 1982, described Lake as "one of the most important figures in the contemporary pastoral care scene" (Campbell, 1982, 26). He continues:

> It is obvious that Dr. Lake's ability to synthesize apparently disparate bodies of knowledge makes his work essential reading for anyone interested in pastoral theology (Campbell, 1982, 26).

This is indeed one component of Lake's genius. While at times he tended to synthesize in a simplistic and superficial manner, he nevertheless attempted and at times succeeded in drawing analogies and correlations which were valid and quite helpful for pastoral care. One significant example would be his "Dynamic Cycle", described at length in *Clinical*

Theology and elsewhere. Lake's use of the Gospel of John to construct an anthropology based upon the only "normal" specimen of humanity that has ever existed is simple and yet profound. His exegesis is not strained and the model is truly an integration of the psychological and theological realms. One writer evaluated Lake's work on the "Dynamic Cycle" as an "unusually deep interpretation of a Christocentric model for the understanding of human dynamics in health and in emotional sickness. It seems to integrate a number of valid concepts from secular psychology so thoroughly, they have few contradictions with his theological affirmations" (Eliason in Peters, 1989, 165).

The "input" phases of "acceptance" and "sustenance" coupled with the "output" phases of "status" and "achievement" together give a well-rounded paradigm of explanation of physiological, psychological and theological development. Indeed, the analogy of the "womb" with the "womb of the spirit" is an apt one.

In some ways, this book has critiqued Lake for failing at an impossible task. It is unreasonable to expect anyone to conceptualize an all-embracing theory which somehow accounts for every facet of human experience, and which somehow correlates these with each other. While Lake did not attempt to theorize a conceptual scheme which explained everything, he did latch on to the M-FDS as a theory which could explain quite a lot. His overemphasis upon the prenatal was perhaps a result of what he perceived as an almost total neglect of this phase. In this he is certainly correct.

How is the M-FDS to be evaluated? Certainly it cannot be summarily dismissed. The evidence presented in this work certainly allows for a M-FDS to exist, with some qualifications. That embryological and fetal life may not be "just like" Lake described them does not change the emerging research evidence descriptive of a prenatal organism that is quite sophisticated.

Apart from some of the more extreme affirmations that Lake makes regarding the perceptual and memory capabilities of fetuses and embryos, and even sperm and ova, the M-FDS does have significant evidence to warrant its acceptance as a paradigm in the sense of "a generally accepted system of ideas which defines the legitimate problems and methods of a research field." The parameters of the "research field" that Lake is defining are those of the beginning and end of intra-uterine life. The problems, restrictions and methods of the study of the human prenatal organism have already been noted, and indeed, the continuing advance of technology may make some of these moot. The research evidence that has emerged has bolstered some of Lake's contentions regarding intra-uterine life.

For instance, the field of psychoneuroendocrinology is providing evidence regarding the extent to which "umbilical affect exchange" can and does affect the immediate and long-term morphology and psychology of behavior. Dorner's previously mentioned second rule of ontogenetic organization (Dorner 1988, 429) clearly delineates the effect that extra-uterine events can have on the embryo/fetus and how these effects can cause long-term changes. Likewise, Dorner's proposal of a "functional teratology" or a "teratopsychophysiology" to complement the widely accepted "structural teratology" or teratomorphology" would certainly be consonant with Lake's M-FDS.

The emergence of psychoneuroendocrinology and psychoneuroimmunology lays the groundwork for the discussion of an issue elicited by Lake's M-FDS, that of "prenatal psychology." Referring to the research done in these fields, Fedor-Freybergh and Vogel write:

> Psychoneuroendocrinologists have already elicited useful data from the preliminary theoretical research in recording fetal response to and retention of outside environmental stimuli (touch, sound, and light stimuli for the most part). Various highly specific biochemical structures (hormones, neurotransmitters and other polypeptide structures) are needed, in direct connection with input phenomena, for the transformation and storage of both sensorial and sensible types of information. Crucial to the formation of the primary central nervous system on the hypothalamic-pituitary-adrenal level, some of these functions are detectable in the very beginning of development of the human being. Thus the embryo successively develops a high sensibility and competency for the potential ability for perception (Fedor-Freybergh & Vogel, 1988, xix-xx).

To speak of a prenatal psychology is to emphasize the developmental continuity between the prenatal, neonatal and post-natal human organism. It is also to emphasize that there is "no possible separation between the physical and psychological development of the unborn" (Fedor-Freybergh & Vogel, 1988, xviii). Indeed, contrary to standard thinking, which assumes function following from structure in the embryo and fetus, research (Fedor-Freybergh, 1983) is finding just the opposite. Fedor-Freybergh and Vogel describe these results:

> It is the morphological structure which develops as a result of the inborn primal functional urge. An organ would not develop if there were no func-

tional urge compelling it to do so. In the same way, the psychological capacity of the human is not posterior to the completed morphological structure of the human body, not to its subsequent introduction into and experiencing of a particular sociocultural environment after birth. The unborn has its psychological processes functioning long before birth (Fedor-Freybergh & Vogel, 1988, xx).

As described earlier, the neglect of or denial of the significance of the prenatal period follows a certain pattern. Previous to this, the peri-natal, neonatal and post-natal stages were also considered, for the most part, as psychologically devoid of meaning. This attitude illustrates the propensity that exists to divide up human experience into "life periods" over against the continuous unity of development. Life-span developmental psychology seeks to study the continuity of development and as such, must include the prenatal period. Wucherer-Huldenfeld writes:

> In indisputable favour of prenatal psychology . . . [is] its ability to follow the specific human far back. The unity of the prenatal development as well as the total development that comes after birth, becomes more distinct in this way. And so appears a personage that exists and must not be separated in the stages that succeed each other, since they form a unity (Wucherer-Huldenfeld in Schindler, 1988, 33).

Certainly any prenatal or fetal psychology must at this time be somewhat limited due to the nature of its subjects. Much research remains to be done. Relatively sophisticated psychological concepts such as self-awareness, self-concept, self-consciousness, and personality remain beyond the pale of any present prenatal psychological constructions. Yet, researchers in other sub-fields within psychology, especially developmental, abnormal and clinical, would do well to investigate the prenatal factor.

Related to the M-FDS, this is especially true for abnormal psychology. If, as Lake and others (Moss, 1990) have contended, there is a fetal and even embryological origin for even some of the psychopathologies that exist, then their verification would be quite a profound addition to the knowledge of psychopathology. Certainly, given the relative lack of definitive answers regarding the etiology of pathologies utilizing the present post-natal paradigms is a reason to continue the search for pre-natal causes.

If, based on Lake's formulations or anyone else's, a prenatal psychology does exist that is continuous with a post-natal one, this gives rise to numerous ethical considerations given present practices. Primary among them is abortion. For instance, in a letter written in response to comments made by Rev. Canon Beeson regarding abortion on the radio, Lake wrote:

> I must question your assumption that what you call "a world of difference" between early and late intra-uterine life is of such an order as to make abortion permissible in the first half of the pregnancy without fear of doing mortal damage to a sentient human being, such as you would admit would be done by the aborting of a baby in the last months of intra-uterine life (Lake, 1979b, 3-4).

Lake goes on to affirm that he has been compelled to recognize that "consciousness of individuality, . . . extends back into the first trimester of intrauterine life" (Lake, 1979b, 1). He states unequivocally that "to destroy the small one by aborting it is as much a murder as it is to destroy the mother by killing her" (Lake, 1982c, 72).

Writing in *With Respect*, Lake draws the parallels between the acceptance of a prenatal psychology or lack of it with attitudes towards abortion:

> Those who advocate abortion for reasons of personal or social inconvenience are usually insistent that the foetus has no human sensibility, no self-aware-ness or knowledge that it has a life which, by the abortifacient agent, is being brought to a violent end. They state that in no sense could the foetus be regarded as a person or a human being (Lake, 1982c, 50).

Other related ethical issues also inevitably arise. What of fetal tissue re-search and "fetal harvesting"? What of extra-uterine fertilization and implantation? What of maternal abuse of various drugs while pregnant? What of societal views of maternal stress and its causes? While all of these questions are beyond the scope of this book, all arise as implica-tions of Lake's M-FDS.

Lake, while believing that the M-FDS was an objective theory, certainly saw nothing wrong with his subjective identification and en-thusiasm for it. In a paper written relatively near the end of his life, he appealed to the scientific process for vindication:

> It is . . . an objective theory. It does not derive from my beliefs, biases, prior assumptions or emotional needs. . . . I have not become subjectively identified with the importance of this advance in etiological theorizing, with its implications

for preventing so many psychological, psychosomatic and social disorders. This looks like, and indeed is, a "passionate commitment" but only after years of cool appraisal. Even "passionate commitment" is commended [i.e. Kerlinger, 1973] . . . as an appropriate attitude even a necessary one, to research in the behavioral sciences. If this is true it matters immensely. If it is false, my evidence will not stand up to examination and my finding will not be replicated -- and that fizzle will be the end of the story" (Lake, 1977a, 5).

Bibliography

Ainslie, R., Solyom, A., & M. McManus. (1982). "On the Infant's Meaning for the Parent: A Study of Four Mother-Daughter Pairs." *Child Psychiatry and Human Development* 13: 97-110.

Aldrich, C. (1928). "A New Test for Hearing in the Newborn: The Conditioned Reflex." *American Journal of the Disabled Child* 35: 36.

Allik, J. & Valsiner, J. (1980). "Visual Development in Ontogenesis: Some Reevaluations." In *Advances in Child Development and Behavior*, vol. 15, eds. H. Reese & L. Lipsitt. NY: Academic Press.

Anand, K. & P. Hickey. (1987). "Pain and its Effects in the Human Neonate and Fetus." *New England Journal of Medicine* 317: 1321-1329.

Anastasi, A. (1958). "Heredity, Environment, and the Question 'How?'" *Psychological Review* 65: 197-208.

Aslin, R. (1981). "Development of Smooth Pursuit in Human Infants." In *Eye Movements: Cognition and Visual Perception*, eds. D. Fisher, R. Monty, & J. Senders. Hillsdale, NJ: Lawrence Erlbaum.

Atkinson, D. (1982). Review of *Tight Corners in Pastoral Counselling*, by Frank Lake. In *Third Way* (September).

Augustine, A. (1961). *Confessions*. Trans. by R.S. Pine-Coffin. N.Y.: Penguin.

Augustine, A. (1857). *Expositions on the Book of Psalms*, Vol. 6. Trans. by J. Parker. London: F. & J. Rivington.

Ball. W., & E. Tronick. (1971). "Infant Responses to Impending Collision: Optical and Real." *Science* 171: 818-820.

Barber, T. (1962). "Hypnotic Age Regression: A Critical Review." *Psychosomatic Medicine* 24: 286-299.

Barnett, E. (1979). "The Negative Birth Experience in Analytical Hypnotherapy." Paper presented at the 22nd annual meeting of the American Society of Clinical Hypnosis, San Francisco.

Bartoshuk, A. (1962). "Human Neonatal Cardiac Acceleration to Sound: Habituation and Dishabituation." *Perceptual and Motor Skills* 15: 15-27.

Batchelor, E., Jr., Dean, R., Gray, J., & S. Wenck. (1991). "Classification Rates and Relative Risk Factors for Perinatal Events Predicting Emotional/ Behavioral Disorders in Children." *Pre- and Peri-Natal Psychology Journal* 5: 327-341.

Bekoff, M. & M. Fox. (1972). "Postnatal Neural Ontology." *Developmental Psychobiology* 5: 323-341.

Bender, H. (1988). "Psychological Aspects of Prematurity and of Neonatal Intensive Care: A Working Report." In *Prenatal Psychology and Medicine*, eds. P. Fedor-Freybergh & M. Vogel, 235-248. Park Ridge NJ: Parthenon.

Bennett, H., Giannini, J., & M. Kline. (1979). "Consequences of Hearing During Anesthesia," Paper presented at the Annual Meeting of the APA.

Benson, P., Little, B., Talbert, D., & J. Dewhurst. (1987). "Foetal Heart Rate and Maternal Emotional State." *British Journal of Medical Psychology* 60: 151-154.

Berkhof, L. (1939). *Systematic Theology*. Grand Rapids: Eerdmans.

Bernard, J., & L. Sontag. (1947). "Fetal Reactivity to Tonal Stimulation: A Preliminary Report." *Journal of Genetic Psychology* 70: 205.

Birnholz, J. & B. Benacerraf. (1983). "The Development of Human Fetal Hearing." *Science* 222: 516-518.

Blau, A., Slaff, B., Easton, K., Welkowitz, J., Springham, J., & J. Cohen. (1963). "The Psychogenic Etiology of Premature Births." *Psychosomatic Medicine* 25: 201-211.

Bornstein, M. & M. Sigman. (1954). "The Onset and Early Development of Behavior." In *Manual of Child Psychology*, 2d ed., ed. L. Carmichael, 60-185. NY: J. Wiley.

Bowen, E. (1983). *Pre-Birth Bonding*. San Diego: Heartstart/Lovestart.

Bowen, E. (1988). "A Program to Facilitate Pre-birth Bonding." *In Prenatal Psychology and Medicine*, eds. P. Fedor-Freybergh & M. Vogel, 267-271. Park Ridge NJ: Parthenon.

Bower, T. (1974). *Development in Infancy*. San Francisco: W.H. Freeman.

Bower, T., Broughton, J., & M. Moore. (1970). "Infant Responses to Approaching Objects: An Indicator of Response to Distal Variables." *Perception & Psychophysics* 9.

Bower, T., Broughton, J., & M. Moore. (1970). "Demonstration of Intention in the Reaching Behavior of Neonate Humans." *Nature* 228: 5272.

Bowes, W., Brackbill, Y., Conway, E. & A. Steinschneider. (1970). "The Effects of Obstetrical Medication on Fetus and Infant." *Monographs of the Society for Research in Child Development* 35: 3-25.

Brackbill, Y., & M. Koltsova. (1967). "Conditioning and Learning." In *Infancy and Early Childhood*, ed. Y. Brackbill, 207-288. NY: Free Press.

Bradley, R. & L. Stern. (1967). "The Development of the Human Taste Bud During the Foetal Period." *Journal of Anatomy* 101: 743-752.

Brewer, W., & J. Treyens. (1981). "Role of Schemata in Memory for Places." *Cognitive Psychology* 13: 207-230.

Brody, L., Zelazo, P., & H. Chaika. (1984). "Habituation-Dishabituation to Speech in the Neonate." *Developmental Psychology* 20: 114-119.

Brown, J. (1972). "Instrumental Control of the Sucking Response in Human Newborns." *Journal of Experimental Child Psychology* 14: 66-80.

Brown, N., Shevell, S., & L. Rips. (1986). "Public Memories and Their Personal Context." In *Autobiographical Memory*, ed. D.C. Rubin. Cambridge: Cambridge Univ. Press.

Bunyan, J. (1856). *The Pilgrim's Progress*. Rochester: Alden & Beardsley.

Caldwell, T. (1961). *The Man Who Listens*. London: Collins.

Campbell, A. (1982). Review of *Tight Corners in Pastoral Counseling*, by Frank Lake. In *Contact* 74: 25-26.

Caplan, F. (1973). *The First Twelve Months of Life*. NY: Grosset & Dunlap.

Carlson, B., & R. La Barba. (1979). "Maternal Emotionality During Pregnancy and Reproductive Outcome." *International Journal of Behavior Development* 2: 342-376.

Cernoch, J., & R. Porter. (1985). "Recognition of Maternal Odours by Infants." *Child Development* 56: 1593-98.

Chamberlain, D. (1981). "Birth Recall in Hypnosis." *Birth Psychology Bulletin* 2: 14-18.

Chamberlain, D. (1983). *Consciousness at Birth: A Review of the Empirical Evidence*. San Diego: Chamberlain Communications.

Chamberlain, D. (1986). "Reliability of Birth Memories: Evidence from Mother and Child Pairs in Hypnosis." *Journal of the American Academy of Medical Hypnoanalysis* 1: 89-98.

Chamberlain, D. (1987a). "Consciousness at Birth: The Range of Empirical Evidence." In *Pre- and Peri-Natal Psychology: An Introduction*, ed. Thomas R. Verny, 69-90. NY: Human Sciences Press.

Chamberlain, D. (1987b). "The Cognitive Newborn: A Scientific Update." *British Journal of Psychotherapy* 4: 30-71.

Chamberlain, D. (1988a). *The Mind of a Newborn Baby: Unexpected Thoughts and Memories at Birth*. Los Angeles: J.P. Tarcher.

Chamberlain, D. (1988b). "The Mind of the Newborn: Increasing Evidence of Competence." In *Prenatal Psychology and Medicine*, eds. P. Fedor-Freybergh and M. Vogel, 5-22. Park Ridge NJ: Parthenon.

Cheek, D. (1959). "Unconscious Perceptions of Meaningful Sounds During Surgical Anesthesia as Revealed under Hypnosis." *American Journal of Clinical Hypnosis* 1: 103-113.

Cheek, D. (1974). "Sequential Head and Shoulder Movements appearing with Age Regression in Hypnosis to Birth." *American Journal of Clinical Hypnosis* 16: 261-266.

Cheek, D. (1975). "Maladjustment Patterns Apparently Related to Imprinting at Birth." *American Journal of Clinical Hypnosis* 18: 75-82.

Cheek, D. (1986). "Prenatal and Perinatal Imprints: Apparent Prenatal Consciousness as Revealed by Hypnosis." *Pre & Peri-Natal Psychology Journal* 1: 97-110.

Cheek, D. & L. Lecron. (1968). *Clinical Hypnotherapy*. NY: Grune/Stratton.

Clements, M. (1977). "Observations on Certain Aspects of Neonatal Behavior in Response to Auditory Stimuli," Paper presented at the 5th International Congress of Psychosomatic Obstetrics and Gynecology, Rome.

Cocchi, R., Felici, M., Tonni, L., & G. Venanzi. (1984). "Behavior Troubles in Nursery School Children and Their Possible Relationship to Pregnancy or Delivery Difficulties." *Acta Psychiatrica Belgica* 84: 173-179.

Cohen, G. (1989). *Memory in the Real World*. London: Lawrence Erlbaum.

Cohen, G., & D. Faulkner. (1986). "Memory for Proper Names: Age Differences in Retrieval." *British Journal of Developmental Psychology* 4: 187-197.

Cohen, G., & D. Faulkner. (1988). "Life Span Changes in Autobiographical Memory." In *Practical Aspects of Memory*, eds. M. Gruneberg, P. Morris, & R. Sykes. Chichester: John Wiley & Sons.

Cohen, G., & D. Faulkner. (1988). "The Effects of Aging on Perceived and Generated Memories." In *Cognition in Adulthood and Later Life*, eds. L. Poon, D. Rubin, & B. Wilson. Cambridge: Cambridge Univ. Press.

Cohen, L. (1979). "Our Developing Knowledge of Infant Perception and Cognition." *American Psychologist* 34: 894-899.

Comparetti, A. (1981). "The Neurophysiological and Clinical Implications of Studies on Fetal Motor Behavior." *Seminars in Perinatology* 5: 2.

Comparetti, A. (1986). "Fetal and Neonatal Origins of Being a Person and Belonging to the World." *Maturation and Learning* : Supplement 5.

Comparetti, A. & E. Gidoni. (1967). "Pattern Analysis of Motor Development and its Disorders." *Developmental Medical and Child Neurology* 9: 5.

Comparetti, A. & E. Gidoni. (1976). "Dalla Parte del Neonatol Proposte per una Competenza Prognostica." *Neuropsichiatria Infantile* 3: 175.

Condon, J. (1985). "The Parental-Foetal Relationship: A Comparison of Male and Female Expectant Parents." *Journal of Psychosomatic Obstetrics and Gynaecology* 4: 271-284.

Condon, J. (1987). "Psychological and Physical Symptoms During Pregnancy: A Comparison of Male and Female Expectant Roles." *Journal of Reproductive and Infant Psychology* 5: 207-219.

Condon, W. (1977). "A Primary Phase in the Organization of Infant Responding." In *Studies in Mother-Infant Interaction*, ed. H. Schaffer, 153-176. NY: Academic Press.

Condon, W., & L. Sander. (1974). "Neonate Movement is Synchronized with Adult Speech: Interactional Participation and Language Acquisition." *Science* 183: 99-101.

Copher, D., & C. Huber. (1967). "Heart Rate Response of the Human Fetus to Induced Maternal Hypoxia." *American Journal of Obstetrics and Gynecology* 98: 320-335.

Crandon, A. (1979). "Maternal Anxiety and Obstetric Complications." *Journal of Psychosomatic Research* 23: 109-11.

D'Arcy, M. (1951). "Preface." In *Poems of St. John of the Cross*, trans. Roy Campbell. NY: Pantheon Books.

Davids, A., Holden, R., & G. Gray. (1963). "Maternal Anxiety During Pregnancy and Adequacy of Mother and Child Adjustment Eight Months Following Childbirth." *Child Development* 34: 993-1002.

Davies, G. (1973). "Revolutions and Cyclical Rhythms in Prenatal Life: Fetal Respiratory Movements Rediscovered." *Pediatrics* 51: 965.

Dayton, G., Jones, M., Aiu, P., Rawson, P., Steele, B., & M. Rose. (1964). "Developmental Study of Coordinated Eye Movements in the Human Infant: Visual Acuity in the Newborn Human." *Archives of Opthamology* 71: 865-870.

Dayton, G., Jones, M., Steel, B., & M. Rose. (1964). "Developmental Study of Coordinated Eye Movements in the Human Infant: An Electro-oculographic Study of the Fixation Reflex in the Newborn." *Archives of Opthamology* 71: 871-875.

Dean, R., & J. Gray. (1985). *Maternal Perinatal Scale*. Muncie, Ind.: Ball State University.

DeCasper, A., & W. Fefer. (1980). "Of Human Bonding: Newborn's Prefer their Mother's Voices." *Science* 208: 1174-1176.

DeCasper, A., & P. Prescott. (1984). "Human Newborn's Perception of Male Voices: Preference, Discrimination and Reinforcing Value." *Developmental Psychobiology* 17: 481-491.

DeCasper, A., & M. Spence. (1978). "Prenatal Maternal Speech Influences Newborn's Perception of Speech Sound." *Infant Behavior and Development* 1: 36-48.

de Caussade, J.P. (1971). *Self-Abandonment to Divine Providence*, trans. Algar Thorold. London: Collins.

DeMause, L. (1982). *Foundations of Psychohistory*. NY: Creative Roots, Inc.

DeMause, L. (1987) "The Fetal Origins of History." *In Pre- and Peri-Natal Psychology: An Introduction*, ed. Thomas R. Verny, 243-259. NY: Human Sciences Press.

De Muylder, X. (1986). "Attitudes Maternelles en cas de Travail Prémature," In *Memoire de License on Sexologie*. Louvain: Université de Louvain.

De Muylder, X., & S. Wesel. (1988). "Maternal Attitudes and Preterm Labor." In *Prenatal and Perinatal Psychology and Medicine*, eds. P. Fedor-Freybergh & M. Vogel, 87-92. Park Ridge, NJ: Parthenon.

Denenberg, V. (1964). "Critical Periods, Stimulus Input and Emotional Reactivity: A Theory of Infantile Stimulation." *Psychological Review*: 335-351.

De Rocha, A. (1911). *Les Vies Successives: Documents pour l'Etude de Cette Question*. Paris: Chacornac Freres.

De Snoo, K. (1937). "Das Trinkende Kind im Uterus." *Monatsschrift Geburtsh Gynaekologie* 5: 105.

De Sousa, A. (1974). "Causes of Behavior Problems in Children." *Child Psychiatry Quarterly* 7: 308.

Dobson, V. (1976). "Spectral Sensitivity of the 2-Month Infant as Measured by the Visually Evoked Cortical Potential." *Vision Research* 16: 367-374.

Dorner, G. (1967). "Tierexperimentelle Untersuchungen zur Frage einer hormonellen Pathogenese der Homosexualitat." *Acta Biologicus Medicus Germanica* 19: 569-584.

Dorner, G. (1968). "Hormone Induction and Prevention of Female Homo-sexuality" *Journal of Endocrinology* 42: 163-164.

Dorner, G. (1969). "Die Bedeutung der sexualhormonabhangigen Hypothala-musdifferenzierung für die Gonadenfunktion und das Sexualverhalten." *Acta Biologicus Medicus Germanica* 23: 709-712.

Dorner, G. (1970). "The Influence of Sex Hormones during the Hypothalamic Differentiation and Maturation Phases on Gonadal Function and Sexual Behavior during the Hypothalamic Functional Phase." *Endokrinologie* 56: 280-291.

Dorner, G. (1973). "Die mogliche Bedeutung der pra- und/oder perinatalen Ernahrung für die Pathogenese der Obesitas." *Acta Biologicus Medicus Germanica* 30: K19-K22.

Dorner, G. (1976). "Further Evidence of Permanent Behavioral Changes in Rats Treated Neonatally with Neurodrugs." *Endokrinologie* 68: 345-348.

Dorner, G. (1978). "Über den Einfluss der früpostnatalen Ernahrung auf die Korpergrosse im Adoleszentenalter." *Acta Biologicus Medicus Germanica* 37: 1149-1151.

Dorner, G. (1988). "Significance of Hormone-dependent Brain Development and Pre-and Early Postnatal Psychophysiology for Preventative Medicine." In *Prenatal Psychology and Medicine*, eds. P. Fedor-Freybergh and M. Vogel, 419-430. Park Ridge NJ: Parthenon.

Dorner, G., Bluth, R., & R. Tonjes. (1982) "Acetylcholine Concentrations in the Developing Brain Appear to Affect Emotionality and Mental Capacity in Later Life." *Acta Biologicus Medicus Germanica* 41: 721-723.

Dorner, G., Docke, F., & G. Hinz. (1968). "Entwicklung und Rückbildung neuroendokrin bedingter mannlicher Homosexualitat." *Act Biologicus Medicus Germanica* 21: 577-580.

Dorner, G., Docke, F., & G. Hinz. (1969). "Homo-and Hypersexuality in Rats with Hypothalamic Lesions." *Neuroendocrinology* 4: 20-24.

Dorner, G., Docke, F., & G. Hinz. (1971). "Paradoxical Effects of Estrogen on Brain Differentiation." *Neuroendocrinology* 7: 146-155.

Dorner, G., Docke, F., & S. Moustafa. (1968a). "Homosexuality in Female Rats Following Testosterone Implantation in the Anterior Hypothalamus." *Journal of Reproductive Fertility* 17: 173-175.

Dorner, G., Docke, F., & S. Moustafa. (1968b). "Differential Localization of a Male and a Female Hypothalamic Mating Center." *Journal of Reproductive Fertility* 17: 583-586.

Dorner, G., & J. Fatschel. (1970). "Wirkungen neonatal verabreichter Androgene und Antiandrogene auf Sexualverhalten und Fertilitat von Rattenweibchen," *Endokrinologie* 56: 29-48.

Dorner, G., Geier, T., Ahrens, L., Krell, L., Munx, G., Sieler, H., Kittner, E., & H. Muller. (1980). "Prenatal Stress as Possible Aetiogenetic Factor of Homosexuality in Human Males." *Endokrinologie* 75: 365-368

Dorner, G., & H. Grychtolik. (1978). "Long-Lasting Ill-effects of Neonatal Qualitative and/or Quantitative Dysnutrition in the Human." *Endokrinologie* 71: 81-88.

Dorner, G., Grychtolik, H., & M. Julitz. (1977). "Überernahrung in den ersten drei Lebensmonaten als entscheidender Riskofaktor für die Entwicklung von Fettsucht unter ihrer Folgeerkrankungen." *Deutsch Gesundheit Wesen* 32: 6-9.

Dorner, G., Hagen, N., & W. Witthuhn. (1976). "Die frühpostnatale Überernahrung als atiopathogenetischer Faktor der Erwachsenenfettsucht." *Acta Biologicus Medicus Germanica* 35: 799-803.

Dorner, G., Haller, H., & W. Leonhardt. (1973). "Zur moglichen Bedeutung der pra- und/oder frühpostnatalen Ernahrung für die Pathogenese der Arteriosklerose." *Acta Biologicus Medicus Germanica* 31: K31-K35.

Dorner, G., Hecht, K., & G. Hinz. (1976). "Teratopsychogenetic Effects Apparently Produced by Nonphysiological Neurotransmitter Concentrations during Brain Differentiation." *Endokrinologie* 68: 1-5.

Dorner, G., & G. Hinz. (1968). "Induction and Prevention of Male Homosexuality by Androgen." *Journal of Endocrinology* 40: 387-388.

Dorner, G., & G. Hinz. (1971). "Mannlicher Hypogonadismus mit sekundarer Hyposexualitat nach hochdosierten Gaben von Ostrogenen wahrend der hypothalamischen Differenzierungsphase." *Endokrinologie* 58: 227-33.

Dorner, G., & G. Hinz. (1978). "Apparent Effects of Neurotransmitters on Sexual Differentiation of the Brain without Mediation of Sex Hormones." *Endokrinologie* 71: 104-108.

Dorner, G., & A. Mohnike. (1973). "Zur moglichen Bedeutung der pra und/oder frühposnatalen Ernahrung für die Pathogenese des Diabetes mellitus." *Acta Biologicus Medicus Germanica* 31: K7-K10.

Dorner, G., & A. Mohnike. (1976). "Further Evidence for a Predominantly Maternal Transmission of Maturity-onset Diabetes." *Endokrinologie* 68: 121-124.

Dorner, G., & A. Mohnike. (1977). "Zur Bedeutung der perinatalen Überernahrung für die Pathogenese der Fettsucht under des Diabetes mellitus." *Deutsch Gesundheit Wesen* 32: 2325-2328.

Dorner, G., Mohnike, A., Honigmann, D., Singer, P., & H. Padelt. (1973). "Zur moglichen Bedeutung eines pranatalen Hyperinsulinismus für die postnatale Entwicklung Diabetes mellitus." *Endokrinologie* 61: 430-432.

Dorner, G., Mohnike, A., & E. Steindel. (1975). "On Possible Genetic and Epigenetic Modes of Diabetes Transmission." *Endokrinologie* 66: 225-227.

Dorner, G., Mohnike, A., & H. Thoelke. (1984). "Further Evidence for the Dependence of Diabetes Prevalence on Nutrition during Perinatal Life." *Experimental Clinical Endocrinology* 84: 129-133.

Dorner, G., Rohde, W., Stahl, F., Krell, L., & W.G. Masius. (1975). "A Neuroendocrine Predisposition for Homosexuality in Men." *Archives of Sexual Behavior* 4: 1-8.

Dorner, G., Schenk, B., Schmiedel, B., & L. Ahrens. (1983). "Stressful Events in Prenatal Life of Bi- and Homosexual Men." *Experimental Clinical Endocrinology* 81: 83-87.

Dorner, G., & J. Staudt. (1968). "Structural Changes in the Preoptic Anterior Hypothalamic Area of the Male Rat, Following Neonatal Castration and Androgen Treatment." *Neuroendocrinology* 3: 136-140.

Dorner, G., & J. Staudt. (1969). "Structural Changes in the Hypothalamic Ventromedial Nucleus of the Male Rat, Following Neonatal Castration and Androgen Treatment." *Neuroendocrinology* 4: 278-281.

Dryden, R. (1978). *Before Birth*. London: Heinemann.

Dubowtiz, L., Dubowtiz, V., Morante, A., & M. Verghote. (1980). "Visual Function in the Preterm and Fullterm Newborn Infant.*" Developmental Medicine and Child Neurology* 22: 465-75.

Ducasse, C. (1961). *A Critical Examination in the Belief in a Life after Death*. Springfield, Ill.: Charles Thomas.

Dudycha, G., & M. Dudycha. (1941). "Childhood Memories: A Review of the Literature," *Psychological Bulletin* 4: 668-682.

Dustman, R., & D. Callner. (1979). "Cortical Evoked Response and Response Decrement in Non-Retarded and Down's Syndrome Individuals," *American Journal of Mental Deficiency* 83: 391-397.

Eggersten, S., & T.J. Benedetti. (1984). "Fetal Well-Being Assessed by Maternal Daily Fetal-Movement Counting," *Journal of Family Practice* 18: 771-781.

Eisenberg, R. (1965). "Auditory Behavior in the Human Neonate: Methodologic problems and the Logical Design of Research Procedures." *Journal of Auditory Research* 5: 159-177.

Eisenberg, R. (1969). "Auditory Behavior in the Human Neonate: Functional Properties of Sound and Their Ontogenetic Implications." *International Audiology* 8: 34-45.

Eisenberg, R. & A. Marmarou. (1981).Behavioral Reactions of newborns to Speech-like Sounds and Their Implications for Developmental Studies." *Infant Mental Health Journal* 2: 129-138.

Emde, R. (1980). "Towards a Psychoanalytic Theory of Affect." in *The Course of Life*. Washington DC: US Dept. of Health and Human Services, 63-112.

Engen T. & L. Lipsitt. (1965). "Decrement and Recovery of Responses to Olfactory Stimuli in the Human Neonate." *Journal of Comparative & Physiological Psychology* 59: 312-316.

Engen, T., Lipsitt, L., & H. Kaye. (1963). "Olfactory Responses and Adaptation in the Human Neonate." *Journal of Comparative & Physiological Psychology* 56: 73.

Eskes, T. (1985). "Verloskundige consequenties van niet vermerke rouw over een perinataal gestorven kind." *Nederlands Tijdschrift voor Geneeskunde* 129: 433-436.

Evans, F., & J. Kihlstrom. (1975). "Contextual and Temporal Disorganization During Posthypnotic Amnesia." Paper presented at the Meeting of the American Psychological Association, Chicago.

Fairbairn, W. (1952a). *An Object Relations Theory of Personality*. NY: Basic.

Fairbairn, W. (1952b). *Psychoanalytic Studies of the Personality*. NY: Basic.

Fantz, R. (1961). "The Origin of Form Perception." *Scientific American* 204: 66-72.

Fantz, R. (1963). "Pattern Vision in Newborn Infants." *Science* 140: 296-297.

Fantz, R. (1964). "Visual Experience in Infants: Decreased Attention to Familiar Patterns Relative to Normal Ones." *Science* 146: 668-670.

Fantz, R. (1965). "Visual Perception from Birth as Shown by Pattern Selectivity." *Annals of the New York Academy of Sciences* 118: 793-814.

Farber, E., Vaughn, B., & B. Egeland. (1981). "The Relationship of Prenatal Maternal Anxiety to Infant Behavior and Mother-Infant Interactions during the First 6 Months of Life." *Early Human Development* 5: 267-277.

Fedor-Freybergh, P. (1983). "Psychophysische Gegebenheiten der Perinatalzeit als Umwelt des Kindes," In *Okologie der Perinatalzeit*, eds. S. Schindler & H. Zimprich. Stuttgart: Hippokrates Verlag.

Fedor-Freybergh, P. & M. Vogel. (1988). "Encounter With the Unborn: Philosophical Impetus Behind Prenatal and Perinatal Psychology and Medicine." In *Prenatal Psychology and Medicine*, eds. P. Fedor-Freybergh & M. Vogel, xviii-xxxii. Park Ridge, NJ: Parthenon.

Feher, L. (1980). *The Psychology of Birth*. London: Souvenir Press.

Feijoo, J. (1975). "Ut Conscientia Noscatue." *Cahier de Sophrologie* 13: 14-20.

Feijoo, J. (1981). "Le Foetus Pierre et le Loup: Ou Une Approache Originale de l'Audition Prénatale Humaine." In *L'Aube des Sens*, eds. H. Herbinet & M. Busnel. Paris: Stock.

Ferreira, A. (1960). "The Pregnant Woman's Emotional Attitude and its Reflection on the Newborn." *American Journal of Orthopsychiatry* 30: 553-561.

Ferreira, A. (1965). "Emotional Factors in Prenatal Environment." *The Journal of Nervous and Mental Disease* 141: 108-118.

Field, D. (1981). "Retrospective Reports by Healthy Intelligent Elderly People of Personal Events of their Adult Lives." *International Journal of Behavioral Development* 4: 77-97.

Field, T. (1985). "Stroking Dramatically Speeds up Preemies' Growth." *Brain/Mind Bulletin.* (December 9).

Field, T., Woodson, R., Greenberg, R., & D. Cohen. (1982). "Discrimination and Imitation of Facial Expressions by Neonates." *Science* 218: 179-181.

Finnegan, J. & B. Quarrington. (1979). "Pre-, Peri- and Neonatal Factors and Infantile Autism." *Journal of Child Psychology and Psychiatry* 20: 119-28.

Fodor, N. (1949a). *The Search for the Beloved: A Clinical Investigation of the Trauma of Birth and Pre-Natal Conditioning.* New York: Hermitage Press.

Fodor, N. (1949b). "The Trauma of Bearing." *Psychology Quarterly* 23: 59-70.

Fodor, N. (1971). *Freud, Jung and Occultism.* New York: University Books.

Forsyth, P.T. (1957). "The Taste of Death and the Life of Grace." In *God the Holy Father.* London: Independent Press.

Foulatier, F. (1987). "L'Enfant Autiste et la Metacommunication." *Evolution Psychiatrique* 52: 471-481.

Frankova, S. (1970). "Behavioral Responses of Rats to Early Overnutrition." *Nutritional Metabolism* 12: 228-239.

Freud, S. (1932). "Lecture #32," *in New Introductory Lectures on Psychoanalysis.* NY: W.W. Norton.

Freud, S. (1936). *Inhibitions, Symptoms and Anxiety.* London: Hogarth Press.

Freud, S. (1951). *Psychopathology of Everyday Life.* NY: Mentor Books.

Friedman, S., Nagy, A., & G. Carpenter. (1970). "Newborn Attention: Differential Response Decrement to Visual Stimuli." *Journal of Experimental Child Psychology* 10: 44-51.

Friedman, S., Zahn-Waxler, C., & M. Radke-Yarrow. (1982). "Perceptions of Cries of Full-term and Preterm Infants." *Infant Behavior and Development* 5: 161-173.

Gaffney, K. (1986). "Maternal-Fetal Attachment in Relation to Self-Concept and Anxiety." *Maternal Child Nursing Journal* 15: 91-101.

Gesell, A. (1945). *The Embryology of Behavior.* NY: Harper and Brothers.

Gidoni, E., Casonato, M., & N. Landi. (1988). "A Further Contribution to a Functional Interpretation of Fetal Movements." In *Prenatal and Perinatal Psychology and Medicine*, eds. P. Fedor-Freybergh & M. Vogel, 347-353. Park Ridge, NJ: Parthenon.

Gillberg, C. & C. Gillberg. (1983). "Infantile Autism: A Total Population Study of Reduced Optimality in the Pre-, Peri-, and Neonatal Period." *Journal of Autism and Developmental Disorders* 13: 153-166.

Glavin, G. (1984). "Prenatal Maternal Stress: Differential Effects upon Male and Female Offspring Responses to Restraint Stress as an Adult." *Pavlovian Journal of Biological Science* 19: 157-159.

Golanska, Z. & A. Bacz. (1988). "The Psychological Effects of Maternal Attitudes in Cases of Repeated Unfavorable Pregnancy Outcome." In *Prenatal and Perinatal Psychology and Medicine.* eds. P.Fedor-Freybergh & M. Vogel, 93-97. Park Ridge, NJ: Parthenon.

Goodlin, R. (1979). *Care of the Fetus.* NY: Masson Publishing Co.

Goodlin, R., & E. Lowe. (1974). "Multiphasic Foetal Monitoring: A Preliminary Evaluation." *American Journal of Obstetrics and Gynecology* 119: 341-357.

Goodman, W., Appleby, S., Scott, J., & P. Ireland. (1974). "Audiometry in Newborn Children by Electroencephalography." *Laryngoscope* 74: 1316-1328.

Goshen-Gottstein, E. (1969). *Marriage and First Pregnancy.* London: Tavistock.

Gotz, F., & G. Dorner. (1980). "Homosexual Behavior in Prenatally Stressed Male Rats after Castration and Estrogen Treatment in Adulthood." *Endokrinologie* 76: 115-117.

Graber, G. (1924). *Die Ambivalenz des Kindes.* Vienna: International Psychoanalytic Books.

Grace, J. (1989). "Development of Maternal-Fetal Attachment During Pregnancy." *Nursing Research* 38: 228-232.

Granier-Deferre, C., Lecanuet, J., Cohen, H., & M. Busnel. (1985). "Feasibility of a Prenatal Hearing Test." *Acta Oto Laryngologica*, Supplement 421: 93-101.

Grassi, L., & S. Caracciolo. (1983). "Rischio psicobiologico in gravidanza e parto." *Medicina Psicosomatica* 28: 301-320.

Gravelle, J. (1990). "Clinical Theology." In *Dictionary of Pastoral Care*, ed. A. Campbell, 38. NY: Crossroads Books.

Greenacre, P. (1945). "The Biological Economy of Birth." *Psychoanalytic Study of the Child* 1.

Greenacre, P. (1952). *Trauma, Growth, and Personality.* NY: International Universities Press.

Greenberg, M., Vuorenkoski, V., Partanen, T., & J. Lind. (1967). "Behavior and Cry Patterns in the First Two Hours of Life in Early and Late Clamped Newborns." *Finnish Annals of Pediatrics* 13.

Gregg, V. (1986). *Introduction to Human Memory.* London: Routledge.

Grof, S. (1975). *Realms of the Human Unconscious: Observations from LSD Research.* NY: Viking Press.

Grof, S., & J. Halifax. (1977). *The Human Encounter With Death.* NY: E.P. Dutton.

Gruzelier, J., & P. Venebles. (1972). "Skin Conductance Orienting Activity in a Heterogeneous Sample of Schizophrenics." *Journal of Nervous and Mental Disorders* 155: 277-287.

Gunter, L. (1963). "Psychopathology and Stress in the Life Experience of Mothers of Premature Infants: A Comparative Study." *American Journal of Obstetrics and Gynecology* 86: 333-340.

Guntrip, H. (1952). "A Study of Fairbairn's Theory of Schizoid Reactions." *British Journal of Medical Psychology* 25:2&3: 86-103.

Guntrip, H. (1957). *Psychotherapy and Religion.* NY: Harper Books.

Guntrip, H. (1961). *Personality Structure and Human Interaction.* NY: International Universities Press.

Guntrip, H. (1968). *Schizoid Phenomena, Object Relations and the Self.* London: Hogarth Press.

Hecht, K., Poppei, M., Schlegel, T., Hinz, G., Tonjes, R., Gotz, R., & G. Dorner. (1978). "Long-term Behavioral Effects of Psychotropic Drugs Administered during Brain Development in Rats." In *Hormones and Brain Development*, vol. 3, eds. G. Dorner & M. Kawakami, 277-283. Amsterdam: Elsevier/North Holland Biomedical Press.

Heidrich, S., & M. Cranley. (1989). "The Effect of Fetal Movement, Ultrasound Scans and Amniocentesis on Maternal-Fetal Attachment." *Nursing Research* 38: 81-84.

Hepper, P. (1988). "Foetal 'Soap' Addiction." *Lancet* 1: 1347-1348.

Hepper, P. (1989). "Foetal Learning: Implications for Psychiatry?" *British Journal of Psychiatry* 155: 289-293.

Hick, J. (1966). *Evil and the God of Love.* London: Macmillan.

Hick, J. (1981). "An Irenaean Theodicy." In *Encountering Evil*, ed. S. Davis. Atlanta: John Knox.

Hilgard, E. (1977). *Divided Consciousness: Multiple Controls in Human Thought and Action.* NY: John Wiley.

Hilgard, E. (1980). "Consciousness in Contemporary Psychology." *Annual Review of Psychology* 31: 1-26.

Hinde, R. (1970). *Behavioral Habituation.* NY: Cambridge University Press.

Hinz, G., Docke, F., & G. Dorner. (1978). "Long-term Changes of Sexual Functions in Rats Treated Neonatally with Psychotropic Drugs." *Hormones and Brain Development*, vol. 3, eds. G. Dorner & M. Kawakami, 121-127. Amsterdam: Elsevier/North Holland Biomedical Press.

Hinz, G., Hecht, K., Rhode, W., & G. Dorner. (1983). "Long-term Effects of Early Postnatal Nutrition on Subsequent Body Weight Gain, Emotionality and Learning Behavior in Male Rats." *Experimental Clinical Endocrinology* 82: 73-77.

Holding, D., Noonan, T., Pfau, H., & C. Holding. (1986). "Date Attribution, Age, and the Distribution of Lifetime Memories" *Journal of Gerontology* 41: 481-485.

Hooker, D. (1952). *The Prenatal Origin of Behavior*. Lawrence, Kansas: University of Kansas Press.

Humphrey, T. (1978). "Function of the Newborn Systems During Prenatal Life." In *Physiology of the Perinatal Period*, vol. 2, ed. U. Stave, 751-796. NY: Plenum Medical Books.

Hutchinson, P. (1977). "Response to 'The Work of Christ in the Healing of Primal Pain." *Theological Renewal* 71 (Oct/Nov).

Hutt, S., & C. Hutt. (1964). "Hyperactivity in a Group of Epileptic (and some non-Epileptic) Brain Damaged Children." *Epilepsia* 5: 334-351.

Huttunen, M., & P. Niskanen. (1978). "Prenatal Loss of Father and Psychiatric Disorders." *Archives of General Psychiatry* 4: 429-431.

Iannuruberto, A., & E. Tajani. (1981). "Ultrasonographic Study of Fetal Movements." *Seminars in Perinatology* 5: 175-181.

Iatrakis, G., Sakellaropoulos, G., Kourkoubas, A., & S. Kabounia. (1988). "Vomiting and Nausea in the First 12 Weeks of Pregnancy.*" Psychotherapy and Psychosomatics* 49: 22-24.

Isbister, J. (1977). "Response to 'The Work of Christ in the Healing of Primal Pain.'" *Theological Renewal* 71 (Oct/Nov).

Ishikawa, A., & E. Minamide. (1984). "Correlation Between Fetal Activity and Neonatal Behavioral Assessment Scale." *Early Child Development and Care* 17: 155-165.

Istvan, J. (1986). "Stress, Anxiety, and Birth Outcome: A Critical Review of the Evidence." *Psychological Bulletin* 100: 331-348.

Izard, C. & P. Read. (1986). *Measuring Emotions In Infants and Children*, vol. 2. NY: Cambridge Univ. Press.

Janov, A. (1970). *The Primal Scream*. NY: G.P. Putnam's Sons.

Janov, A. (1971). *The Anatomy of Mental Illness: The Scientific Basis of Primal Therapy*. NY: G.P. Putnam's Sons.

Janov, A. (1972). *The Primal Revolution*. NY: Simon & Schuster.

Janov, A. (1983). *Imprints: The Life-long Effects of the Birth Experience*. NY: Coward-McCann.

Jensen, O., & G. Flottorp. (1982). "A Method for Controlled Sound Stimulation of the Human Fetus." *Scandinavian Audiology* 11: 145-150.

Jernerg, M. (1988). "Promoting Prenatal and Perinatal Mother-Child Bonding: A Psychotherapeutic Assessment of Parental Attitudes." In *Prenatal Psychology and Medicine*, eds. P. Fedor-Freybergh & M. Vogel, 253-266. Park Ridge NJ: Parthenon.

John of the Cross. (1949). *The Complete Works of St. John of the Cross,* ed. & trans. E. Peers. Westminster, Maryland: The Newman Press.

John of the Cross. (1968). *The Poems of St. John of the Cross*, trans. W. Barnstone. NY: New Directions Books.

John of the Cross. (1979). *The Poems of St. John of the Cross*, 3d ed., trans. J. Nims. Chicago: University of Chicago Press.

John of the Cross. (1987). *Selected Writings*, ed. & trans. K. Kavanaugh. NY: Paulist Press.

Johnson, W., Emde, R., Pannabecker, B., Stenborg, C., & M. Davis. (1982). "Maternal Perception of Infant Emotion From Birth to 18 months." *Infant Behavior & Development* 5: 313-322.

Juntunen, K., Sirvio, P., & K. Michelsson. (1978). "Cry Analysis of Infants with Severe Malnutrition." *European Journal of Pediatrics* 128: 241-246.

Kagan, J. (1978). "On Emotion and its Development: A Working Paper." In *The Development of Affect*, eds. M. Lewis & L. Rosenblum, 37. NY: Plenum Press.

Kelsey, D. (1953). "Phantasies of Birth and Prenatal Experience Recovered from Patients Undergoing Hypnoanalysis." *Journal of Mental Science* 99: 216-223.

Kennell, J., & M. Klaus. (1983). "Early Events: Later Effects on the Infant." In *Frontiers of Infant Psychiatry*, eds. J. Call, E. Galenson & R. Tyson, 7-16. NY: Basic Books.

Kerlinger, F. (1973). *Foundations of Behavioral Research*. London: Holt, Reinhart & Winston.

Kessen, W., Haith, M., & P. Salapatek. (1970). "Human Infancy: A Bibliography and Guide." In *Carmichael's Manual of Child Development*, ed. P. Mussen, 287-444. NY: Wiley.

Kierkegaard, S. (1938). *The Journals*, trans. and ed. Alexander Dru. London: Oxford University Press.

Kierkegaard, S. (1941). *The Concept of Dread*, trans. Walter Lowrie. Princeton: Princeton University Press.

Kierkegaard, S. (1946). *Fear and Trembling and The Sickness Unto Death*, trans. Walter Lowrie. Princeton: Princeton University Press.

Kitamori, K. (1958). *Theology of the Pain of God*. Richmond, Virginia: John Knox Press.

Klein, M. (1975a). *Love, Guilt and Reparation and Other Works* (vol. 3). NY: Delacourt Press.

Klein, M. (1975b). *Envy and Gratitude and Other Works* (vol. 4). NY: Delacourt Press.

Kobre, K., & L. Lipsitt. (1972). "A Negative Contrast Effect in Newborns." *Journal of Experimental Child Psychology* 14: 81-91.

Kolata, G. (1984). "Studying Learning in the Womb." *Science* 225: 302-303.

Koyama, K. (1974). *Waterbuffalo Theology*. Maryknoll, NY: Orbis Books.

Koyama, K. (1977). *No Handle on the Cross: An Asian Meditation on the Crucified Mind*. Maryknoll, NY: Orbis Books.

Kramer, L., & M. Pierpoint. (1976). "Rocking Waterbeds and Auditory Stimuli to Enhance Growth of Preterm Infants." *Journal of Pediatrics* 88: 297-299.

Kruse, F. (1978). "Nos Souvenirs du Corps Maternal." *Psychologie Heute* (June): 56.

Laibow, R. (1986). "Birth Recall: A Clinical Report." *Pre- and Peri-Natal Psychology Journal* 1: 78-81.

Laibow, R. (1988). "Prenatal and Perinatal Experience and Developmental Impairment." In *Prenatal Psychology and Medicine*, eds. P. Fedor-Freybergh & M. Vogel, 295-308. Park Ridge NJ: Parthenon.

Lagercrantz, H., & T. Slotkin. (1986). "The 'Stress' of Being Born." *Scientific American* 254: 100-107.

Laing, R.D. (1978). *The Facts of Life*. NY: Pantheon Books.

Laing, R.D. (1982). *The Voice of Experience*. NY: Pantheon Books.

Lake, F. (1964). *Clinical Theology*. London: Darton, Longman & Todd.

Lake, F. (1967). "The Bearing of Our Knowledge of the Unconscious on the Theology of Evangelism and Pastoral Care," transcript of speech made at New College Theological Society, Nottingham: CTA.

Lake, F. (1973), to L. Eliason, 4 September. Nottingham: CTA.

Lake, F. (1975a). "I Don't Want to Feel Angry But I Do." *Renewal* 59 (Oct/Nov).

Lake, F. (1975b). "Power to Throw Away," *Renewal* 60 (Dec/Jan).

Lake, F. (1976a). "Perinatal Events and Origins of Religious Symbols, of Symptoms and Character Problems: The Possibility of Reliving Birth and its Effects." Nottingham: CTA.

Lake, F. (1976b). "The Significance of Birth and Prenatal Events in Individual, Family and Social Life." Nottingham: CTA.

Lake, F. (1977a). "The Internal Consistency of the Maternal-Fetal Distress Syndrome," Nottingham: CTA.

Lake, F. (1977b). "The Maternal-Fetal Distress Syndrome/Negative Umbilical Affect: Defenses Against Invasive Pain by Symbolic Displacement and Containment." Nottingham: CTA.

Lake, F. (1978a). "Report from the Research Department #1." Nottingham: CTA.

Lake, F. (1978b). "The Significance of Perinatal Experience," *Self & Society* 6: 35-45.

Lake, F. (1978c) "Theological Issues in Mental Health in India," Nottingham: CTA.

Lake, F. (1978d). "Transactional Analysis", *Contact* 58: 14-20.

Lake, F. (1978e). "Treating Psychosomatic Disorders Relating to Birth Trauma." *Journal of Psychosomatic Research* 22: 227-238.

Lake, F. (1979a). "Research and Pre-natal Reconciling," Appendix A, Letter from Frank Lake to CTA Members. Nottingham: CTA.

Lake, F. (1979b), to C. Beeson, 1 October. Nottingham: CTA.

Lake, F. (1980a). "Conception-to-Womb Talkdown," Nottingham: CTA.

Lake, F. (1980b). "Report from the Research Department #2." Nottingham: CTA.

Lake, F. (1980c). "The Theology of Pastoral Counselling," *Contact* 68: 1-48.

Lake, F. (1981a). *Clinical Theology Newsletter* #38. Nottingham: CTA.

Lake, F. (1981b). "Post Green Speech," transcript of a speech given at the Post Green Community, Dorset, UK. Nottingham: CTA.

Lake, F. (1981c). "Research into the Pre-natal Aetiology of Mental Illness, Personality, and Psychosomatic Disorders." Nottingham: CTA.

Lake, F. (1981d). "Studies in Constricted Confusion: Exploration of a Pre- and Peri-natal Paradigm." Nottingham: CTA.

Lake, F. (1981e). "Supplement to Newsletter No. 39," *Clinical Theology Newsletter* #39. Nottingham: CTA, December.

Lake, F. (1981f). "Theology and Personality," *Epworth Review* 8: 61-68.

Lake, F. (1981g). *Tight Corners in Pastoral Counselling*. London: Darton, Longman & Todd.

Lake, F. (1982a). "Letter to the Editor," *Contact* 75: 28-29.

Lake, F. (1982b). "Mutual Caring." Oxford: CTA.

Lake, F. (1982c). *With Respect: A Doctor's Response to a Healing Pope*. London: Darton, Longman & Todd.

Lake, F. (1986). "The Dynamic Cycle: An Introduction to the Model." *Lingdale Papers* #2. Oxford: CTA.

Lake, F. (1987). "Primal Integration Work," *Self & Society* 15: 167-173.

Lake, F. (1989). "The Work of Christ in the Healing of Primal Pain," Appendix A, in J. Peters, *Frank Lake: The Man and His Work*. 223-242. London: Darton, Longman & Todd.

Langeworthy, U. (1933). "Development of Behavior Patterns and Myelinization of the Nervous System in the Human Fetus and Infant." *Contributions to Embryology*. Washington, D.C.: The Carnegie Institute XXIV, No. 139.

Larouche, J. (1962). "Quelques Aspects Anatomiques du Development Cerebral." *Biologie Neonatal* 2: 126-153.

Laukaran, V. & B. Van den Berg. (1980). "The Relationship of Maternal Attitude to Pregnancy Outcomes and Obstetrical Complications. A Cohort Study of Unwanted Pregnancy." *American Journal of Obstetrics and Gynecology* 136: 374-379.

Leader, L., Baille, P., & B. Martin. (1982a). "Foetal Habituation in High-Risk Pregnancies." *British Journal of Obstetrics and Gynaecology* 89: 441-446.

Leader, L., Baille, P., & B. Martin. (1982b). "The Assessment and Significance of Habituation to a Repeated Stimulus by the Human Foetus." *Early Human Development* 7: 211-219.

Leader, L., Baille, P., & B. Martin. (1984). "Foetal Responses to Vibrotactile Stimulation: A Possible Predictor of Foetal and Neonatal Outcome." *Australian and New Zealand Journal of Obstetrics and Gynaecology* 24: 251-256.

Leboyer, F. (1975). *Birth Without Violence*. NY: Knopf.

Lecanuet, J., Granier-Deferre, C., Cohen, H., & R. le Houezec. (1986). "Fetal Responses to Acoustic Stimulation Depend on Heart Variability Pattern, Stimulus Intensity and Repetition." *Early Human Development* 13: 269-283.

Lecron, L. (1954). "A Hypnotic Technique for Uncovering Unconscious Material." *International Journal of Clinical & Experimental Hypnosis* 2: 1-3.

Lecron, L. (1963). "Uncovering Early Memories by Ideomotor Responses to Questions." *International Journal of Clinical & Experimental Hypnosis* 11: 137-142.

Leith, E., & J. Upatnicks. (1965). "Photography by Laser." *Scientific American* 212: 24-35.

Lester, B. (1976). "Spectrum Analysis of the Cry Sounds of Well-Nourished and Malnourished Infants." *Child Development* 47: 237-241.

Lester, B., & C. Boukydis. (1985). *Infant Crying: Theoretical and Research Perspectives*. NY: Plenum.

Liley, A. (1991). "The Fetus as Personality" *Pre- and Peri-Natal Psychology Journal* 5: 191-202.

Linton, M. (1982). "Transformations of Memory in Everyday Life." In *Memory Observed: Remembering in Natural Contexts*, ed. U. Neisser. San Francisco: W.H. Freeman.

Lipsitt, L. (1969). "Learning Capacities of the Human Infant." *In Brain and Early Behavior Development in the Fetus and Infant*, ed. R. Robinson, 227-249. London: Academic Press.

Lipsitt, L., & H. Kaye. (1977). "The Study of Sensory and Learning Processes of the Newborn." *Clinics in Perinatology* 4 : 163-186.

Lipsitt, L., & J. Werner. (1981)."The Infancy of Human Learning Processes." In *Developmental Plasticity*, ed. E. Gollin, 101-133. NY: Academic Press.

List, J. (1986). "Age and Schematic Differences in the Reliability of Eyewitness Testimony." *Developmental Psychology* 22: 50-57.

Loftus, E. (1975). "Leading Questions and the Eyewitness Report." *Cognitive Psychology* 7: 560-572.

Loftus, E. (1979a). *Eyewitness Testimony*. Cambridge: Harvard Univ. Press.

Loftus, E. (1979b). "Reactions to Blatantly Contradictory Information." *Memory and Cognition* 7: 368-374.

Loftus, E. (1980). *Memory*. Reading, Mass.: Addison-Wesley.

Loftus, E., & G. Greene. (1980). "Warning: Even Memory for Faces may be Contagious." *Law and Human Behavior* 4: 323-334.

Loftus, E., & G. Loftus. (1980)."On the Permanence of Stored Information in the Human Brain." *American Psychologist* 35: 409-420.

Loftus, E., Miller, D., & H. Burns. (1978). "Semantic Integration of Verbal Information into a Visual Memory." *Journal of Experimental Psychology, Human Learning and Memory* 4: 19-31.

Loftus, E., & W. Marburger. (1983). "Since the Eruption of Mount St. Helens Has Anyone Beat You Up? Improving the Accuracy of Retrospective Reports with Landmark Events." *Memory and Cognition* 11: 114-120.

Loftus, E., & J. Palmer. (1974). "Reconstruction of Automobile Destruction: An Example of the Interaction Between Language and Memory." *Journal of Verbal Learning and Verbal Behavior* 13: 585-589.

Logan, B. (1987). "Teaching the Unborn: Precept and Practice." *Pre-and Peri-Natal Psychology Journal* 2: 14-17.

Logan, B. (1988). "The Ultimate Preventive: Prenatal Stimulation." In *Prenatal and Perinatal Psychology and Medicine*, eds. P. Fedor-Freybergh & M. Vogel, 559-562. Park Ridge, NJ: Parthenon.

Logan, B. (1991). "Infant Outcomes of a Prenatal Stimulation Pilot Study." *Pre-and Peri-Natal Psychology Journal* 6: 7-31.

Lukesch, M. (1975). "Psychologie Faktoren der Schwangerschaft." Ph.D. diss., University of Salzburg.

Lundington-Hoe, S., & S. Galant. (1985). *How to Have A Smarter Baby*. NY: Collier-Macmillan.

Luther, M. (1892). "Operationes in Psalmos." *Luthers Werke*, vol. 5. Weimar: Herman Bohlau.

Luther, M. (1962). "The Heidelberg Disputation." In *Luther's Early Theological Works*, ed. and trans. J. Atkinson. London: SCM Press.

Macfarlane, A. (1975). "Olfaction in the Development of Social Preferences in the Human Neonate." *Parent-Child Interaction*, CIBA Symposium 33.

MacInnes, D. (1977). "Response to 'The Work of Christ in the Healing of Primal Pain'." *Theological Renewal* 71 (Oct/Nov).

MacNutt, F. (1974). *Healing*. Notre Dame, Indiana: Ave Maria Press.

Madison, L. (1986). "Fetal Response Decrement: True Habituation?" *Journal of Developmental and Behavioral Pediatrics* 7: 14-20.

Madison, L., Adubato, S., & J. Madison. (1986). "Foetal Response Decrement: True Habituation." *Developmental and Behavioral Pediatrics* 7: 14-20.

Madison, L., Madison, J., & S. Adubato. "Infant Behavior and Development in Relation to Fetal Movement and Habituation." *Child Development* 57: 1475-1482.

Mantel, N. (1963). "Chi-square Tests With One Degree of Freedom: Extensions of the Mantel-Haenszel Procedure." *Journal of American Statistics* 58: 690-700.

Martin, G. (1981). "Newborns Pacified by Tapes of Their Own Crying." *Brain/Mind Bulletin* October 5: 2.

Mason-Brothers, A., Ritvo, E. & B. Guze. (1987). "Pre-, Peri- and Postnatal Factors in 181 Autistic Patients from Single and Multiple Incidence Families." *Journal of the American Academy of Child and Adolescent Psychiatry* 26: 39-42.

McClosky, M., & M. Zaragoza. (1985). "Misleading Postevent Information and Memory for Events: Arguments and Evidence Against Memory Impairment Hypotheses." *Journal of Experimental Psychology: General* 114: 1-16.

McDonald, R. (1968). "The Role of Emotional Factors in Obstetric Complications." *Psychosomatic Medicine* 30: 222-237.

McLellan, D. (1989). *Simone Weil: Utopian Pessimist.* London: Macmillan.

Means, B., Mingay, D., Nigam, A., & M. Zarrow. (1988). "A Cognitive Approach to Enhancing Health Survey Reports of Medical Visits." In *Practical Aspects of Memory: Current Research and Issues*, eds. M. Gruneberg, P. Morris, & R. Sykes. Chichester: John Wiley & Sons.

Medick, S., Machon, R., & M. Huttunen. (1988). "Adult Schizophrenia Following Prenatal Exposure to an Influenza Epidemic." *Archives of General Psychiatry* 45: 189-192.

Melinsky, M. (1970). "Clinical Theology: A Survey." In *Religion and Medicine.* London: SCM Press.

Meltzogg, A., & Borton, R. (1979). "Intermodal Matching by Human Neonates." *Nature* 282:403-404.

Meltzoff, A., & M. Moore. (1977). "Imitation of Facial and Manual Gestures by Human Neonates." *Science* 195: 75-78.

Meltzoff, A., & M. Moore. (1983). "The Origins of Imitation in Infancy: Paradigm, Phenomena, and Theories." In *Advances in Infancy Research*, vol. 2, eds. L. Lipsitt & C. Rovee-Collier, 265-301. Norwood, NJ: Ablex.

Mercer, R., Ferketich, S., May, K., & J. DeJoseph. (1988). "Further Exploration of Maternal and Paternal Fetal Attachment." *Research in Nursing and Health* 11: 83-95.

Michel, C. & H. Fritz-Niggli. (1978). "Induction of Developmental Anomalies in Mice by Maternal Stress." *Experientia* 34: 105-106.

Miller, G., Galanter, E., & K. Pribram. (1960). *Plans and the Structure of Behavior.* NY: Holt, Rinehart & Winston.

Mistretta, C., & R. Bradley. (1977). "Taste in Utero: Theoretical Considerations." In *Taste and Development: The Genesis of Sweet Preference*, ed. J. Weiffenbach, 51-69. Washington DC: US Government Printing Office.

Molliver, M., Kostovic, I. & H. Van der Loos. (1973). "The Development of Synapses in the Cerebral Cortex of the Human Fetus." *Brain Research* 50: 403-407.

Moltmann, J. (1972). *Der gekreuzigte Gott: Das Kreuz Christi als Grund und Kritik chrislicher Theologie.* München: Chr. Kaiser Verlag.

Montagu, A. (1962). *Prenatal Influences.* Springfield, Ill.: Charles Thomas.

Moss, R. (1983a) "Primal Integration, A First Report from the Workshops" *CTA Occasional Paper #1* May.

Moss, R. (1983b). "Frank Lake's Maternal-Fetal Distress Syndrome and Primal Integration Workshops" *CTA Occasional Paper #2* December.

Moss, R. (1984). "Review of Research: Frank Lake's Primal Integration Workshops." Oxford: CTA March 25.

Moss, R. (1986). "Frank Lake's Maternal-Fetal Distress Syndrome and Primal Integration Workshops," *Pre- and Peri-Natal Psychology Journal* 1: 52-63.

Moss, R. (1987). "Frank Lake's Maternal-Fetal Distress Syndrome: Clinical and Theoretical Considerations." In *Pre- and Peri-Natal Psychology: An Introduction*, ed. Thomas R. Verny, 201-208. New York: Human Sciences Press.

Moss, R. (1990). "In the Beginning: A Handbook on Primal Integration." Exeter, U.K.

Mott, F. (1964). *The Universal Design of Creation*. Edenbridge, U.K.: Mark Beech Publishers.

Moyer, J., Herrenkohl, L., & D. Jacobowitz. (1978). "Stress During pregnancy: Effect on Catecholamines in Discrete Regions of Offspring as Adults." *Brain Research* 144: 173-178.

Mulders, L., Muijsers, G., Jongsma, H., & J. Nijhuis. (1986). "The Umbilical Artery Blood Flow Velocity Waveform in Relation to Fetal Breathing Movements, Fetal Heart Rate and Fetal Behavior States in Normal Pregnancy at 37 to 39 Weeks." *Early Human Development* 14: 283-293.

Murray, M. (1981). "The Jagged Edge: A Biographical Essay on Simone Weil." In *Simone Weil: Interpretations of a Life*, ed. G. White. Amherst, Mass.: The University of Massachusetts Press.

Mustaph, M. (1988). "The Importance of Early Skin Contact in Emotional Care." In *Prenatal Psychology and Medicine*, eds. P. Fedor-Freybergh & M. Vogel, 249-252. Park Ridge NJ: Parthenon.

Neighbour, R. (1980). "Antenatal Memories and Psychopathology." *The Journal of the Royal College of General Practitioners*.

Norcia, A., & C. Tyler. (1985). "Spacial Frequency Weep VEP: Visual Acuity During the First Year of Life." *Vision Research* 25: 1399-1408.

Ockleford, E., Vince, M., & C. Layton. (1988). "Responses of Neonates to Parent's and Other's Voices." *Early Human Development* 18: 27-36.

Olds, C. (1986). "A Sound Start in Life." *Pre- and Peri-Natal Psychology Journal* 1: 82-85.

Orne, M. (1962). "Hypnotically Induced Hallucinations." In *Hallucinations*, ed. L. West. NY: Grune & Stratton.

Orne, M. (1979). "The Use and Misuse of Hypnosis in Court." *International Journal of Clinical and Experimental Hypnosis* 27: 311-341.

Orr, L., & S. Ray. (1977). *Rebirthing in the New Age*. Berkeley, Ca.: Celestial.

Papousek, H. (1967). "Experimental Studies of Appetitional Behavior in Human Newborns and Infants." In *Early Behavior: Comparative and Developmental Approaches*, eds. H. Stevenson, E. Hess, & H. Rheingold, 249-277. NY: John Wiley.

Papousek, H. (1969). "Individual Variability in Learned Responses in Human Infants." In *Brain and Early Behavior*, ed. R. Robinson. London: Academic Press.

Papousek, H., & M. Papousek. (1977). "Mothering and the Cognitive Head-Start: Psychobiological Considerations." *In Studies in Mother-Infant Interaction*, ed. H. Schaffer, ch. 4. London: Academic Press.

Papousek, H., & M. Papousek. (1982). "Integration into the Social World: Survey of Research." In *Psychobiology of the Human Newborn*, ed. P. Stratton, 367-390. NY: John Wiley.

Papousek, H., & M. Papousek. (1987). "Intuitive Parenting: A Didactic Counterpart to the Infant's Precocity in Integrative Capacities." *Handbook of Infant Development*, 2d ed., ed. J. Osofsky. NY: John Wiley.

Papousek, H., Papousek, M., & B. Harris. (1986). "The Emergence of Play in Parent-Infant Interactions." In *Curiosity, Imagination, & Play: On the Development of Spontaneous Cognitive and Motivational Processes*, eds. D. Gorlitz & J. Wohlwill, 214-246. NY: Erlbaum Associates.

Pavlov, I. (1928), *Lectures on Conditioned Reflexes*, vols. 1 and 2, trans. W. Gantt. NY: International Publishers.

Pavlov, I. (1957). *Experimental Psychology and Other Essays*. NY: Philosophical Library.

Pavlov, I. (1960*). Conditioned Reflexes: An Investigation of the Physiological Activity of the Cerebral Cortex*, ed. and trans. G. Anrep. NY: Dover.

Peek, H., & M. Hertz. (1973). *Habituation*, vols. 1 & 2. NY: Academic Press.

Peerbolte, M. (1951)."Psychotherapeutic Evaluations of Birth-Trauma Analysis." *Psychiatric Quarterly* 25: 596-600.

Peerbolte, M. (1954). *Psychic Energy in Prenatal Dynamics*. Amsterdam: Wassener.

Peiper, A. (1925). "Sinnesemp findungen des Kindes vor seiner geburt." *Monatsschirft fur Kinderheilkunde* 29: 237-241.

Peiper, A. (1963). *Cerebral Function in Infancy and Childhood*. NY: Consultants Bureau.

Peterfreund, E. (1971). *Information, Systems and Psychoanalysis*. NY: International Universities Press.

Peters, D. (1988). "Effects of Maternal Stress During Different Gestational Periods on the Serotonergic System in Adult Rat Offspring." *Pharmacology, Biochemistry and Behavior* 31: 839-843.

Peters, J (1989). *Frank Lake: The Man and His Work*. London: Darton, Longman & Todd.

Petersen, P., Stewart, W., Greer, C., & G. Shepherd. (1983). "Evidence for Olfactory Function in Utero." *Science* 221: 478-480.

Peterson, G., Mehl, L., & J. McRae. (1988). "Relationship of Psychiatric Diagnoses, Anxiety and Stress with Birth Complications." In *Prenatal and Perinatal Psychology and Medicine*, eds. P. Fedor-Freybergh & M. Vogel, 399-416. Park Ridge, NJ: Parthenon.

Plantinga, A. (1974). *God, Freedom and Evil*. Grand Rapids: Eerdmans.

Ployé, P. (1973). "Does Prenatal Mental Life Exist?" *International Journal of Psycho-Analysis* 54: 241-246.

Ployé, P. (1976). "Existe-t-il un Psychisme Pré-natal?" *L'Evolution Psychiatrique* 41: 663-674.

Polikanina, R. (1961). "The Relation Between Autonomic and Somatic Components in the Development of the Conditioned Reflex in Premature Infants." *Pavlov Journal of Higher Nervous Activity* 11: 51.

Porter, F., Miller, R. & R. Marshall. (1986). "Neonatal Pain Cries: Effect of Circumcision on Acoustic Features of Perceived Urgency." *Child Development* 57: 790-802.

Prechtl, H., & J. Nijhuis. (1983). "Eye Movements in the Human Fetus and Newborn." *Behavioral Brain Research* 10: 119-124.

Preyer, R. (1885). *Spezielle Physiologic des Embryo*. Leipzig.

Pribram, K. (1969). "The Four R's of Remembering." In *On the Biology of Learning*, ed. K. Pribram, 191-225. NY: Harcourt, Brace.

Pribram, K. *Languages of the Brain: Experimental Paradoxes and Principles in Neuropsychology*. Englewood Cliffs, NJ: Prentice-Hall.

Pribram, K., & D. Broadbent. (1970). *Biology of Memory*. NY: Academic Press.

Purpura, D. (1975). "Dendrite Differentiation in Human Cerebral Cortex." *Advances in Neurology* 12: 91-116.

Purpura, D. (1979). "Consciousness." *Behavior Today* 27: 437-448.

Putnam, W. (1979). "Hypnosis and Distortions in Eyewitness Testimony." *International Journal of Clinical and Experimental Hypnosis* 27: 437-448.

Raikov, V. (1980). "Age Regression to Infancy by Adult Subjects in Deep Hypnosis." *American Journal of Clinical Hypnosis* 22: 156-163.

Raikov, V. (1982). "Hypnotic Age-Regression to the Neonatal Period: Comparisons With Role Playing." *International Journal of Clinical & Experimental Hypnosis* 30: 108-116.

Rank, O. (1952). *The Trauma of Birth*. NY: Robert Brunner.

Rau, H. (1982). "Frühe Kindheit." In *Entwicklungpsychologie*, eds. R. Oerter & L. Montada. München: Urban & Schwarzenberg.

Rau, H. (1983). "Frühkindliche Entwicklung." In *Entwinklungspsychologie*, eds. R. Silberseisen & L. Montada, 83. München: Urban & Schwarzenberg.

Ravelli, G. (1976). "Obesity in Young Men after Famine Exposure in utero and Early Infancy." *The New England Journal of Medicine* 228: 349-353.

Ray, E., & H. Martinez. (1984). *Rational Handling of the Premature Child*. NY: UNICEF.

Ray, W. (1932). "A Preliminary Report on the Study of Foetal Conditioning." *Child Development* 3: 175-177.

Reading, A. (1983). "The Influence of Maternal Anxiety on the Course and Outcome of Pregnancy: A Review." *Health Psychology* 2: 187-202.

Reading, A., Cox, D., Sledmere, C., & S. Campbell. (1984). "Psychological Changes Over the Course of Pregnancy: A Study in Attitudes Toward the Fetus/Neonate." *Health Psychology* 3: 211-221.

Reich, W. (1972). *Character Analysis*, 3rd ed., trans. V. Carfagno. NY: Farrer, Straus & Giroux.

Reppert, S., Henshaw, D., Schwartz, W., & D. Weaver. (1987). "The Circadian-gated Timing of Birth in Rats: Disruption by Maternal SCN Lesions or by Removal of the Fetal Brain." *Brain Research* 403: 398-402.

Reppert, S., & W. Schwartz. (1983). "Maternal Coordination of Fetal Biological Clock 'in utero.'" *Science* 220: 969-971.

Reppert, S., Weaver, D., & S. Rivkees. (1988). "Maternal Communication of Circadian Phase to the Developing Mammal." *Psychoneuroendocrinology* 13: 63-78.

Rhodes, J. (1991). "Report on Research Project: Interviews with 2 1/2 to 3 1/2 Year Old Children Regarding Their Memories of Birth and the Pre-Natal Period." *Pre- and Peri-Natal Psychology Journal* 6: 97-103.

Rice, R. (1977). "Neurophysiological Development in Premature Infants Following Stimulation." *Developmental Psychology* 13: 69-76.

Richmond, J. & J. Herzog. (1979). "From Conception to Delivery," In *Basic Handbook of Child Psychiatry*, vol. 1, ed. J. Noshpitz. NY: Basic Books.

Rider, R., Rosenthal, D., Wender, P. & H. Blumenthal. (1975). "The Offspring of Schizophrenics: Fetal and Neonatal Deaths." *Archives of General Psychiatry* 32: 200-211.

Ridgeway, R. (1987). *The Unborn Child*. London: Wildwood House.

Rieser, J., Yonas, A., & K. Wikner. (1976). "Radial Localization of Odors by Human Newborns." *Child Development* 47: 856-859.

Riley, C. (1988). "Teaching Mother/Fetus Communication: A Workshop on how to Teach Pregnant Mothers to Communicate with their Unborn Children." *Pre- and Peri-Natal Psychology Journal* 3: 77-86.

Ringler, N., Trause, M., Klaus, M., & J. Kennell. (1978). "The Effects of Extra Post-partum Contact and Maternal Speech Patterns on Children's IQ's, Speech, and Language Comprehension at Five." *Child Development* 49: 862-865.

Ritzman, T. (1989). "Schizophrenia, It's Cause and Cure." *Medical Hypno-analysis Journal* 4: 27-37.

Roberts, A., Griffin, D., Mooney, R., & D. Cooper. (1980). "Fetal Activity in 100 Normal Third Trimester Pregnancies." *British Journal of Obstetrics and Gynecology* 87: 480-484.

Roberts, F. (1972). "Clinical Theology: An Assessment." *Theological Students Fellowship Bulletin* Autumn: 21-25.

Rodgers, B. (1978). "Feeding in Infancy and Later Ability and Attainment: A Longitudinal Study." *Developmental Medical Child Neurology* 20: 421-426.

Roffwarg, H., Muzio, J., & W. Dement. (1966). "Ontogenetic Development of the Human Dream Cycle." *Science* 152: 604-619.

Rose, S., & I. Wallace. (1985). "Visual Recognition Memory: A Predictor of Later Cognitive Functioning in Preterms." *Child Development* 56: 843-852.

Rossi, N. (1987). "La ricerca psicologica di fronte alla vita fetale. Prospettive e metodi di indagine." *Eta-evolutiva* 26: 65-70.

Rossi, N., Avveduti, P., Rizzo, N., & R. Lorusso. (1989). "Maternal Stress and Fetal Motor Behavior: A Preliminary Report." *Pre- and Peri-Natal Psychology Journal* 3: 311-318.

Rottman, G. (1974). "Untersuchungen über Einstellung zur Schwanger schaft und zür fotalen Entwicklung." In *Pranatale Psychologie*, ed. H. Graber. Munchen: Kindler Verlag.

Rovee-Collier, C. (1985). "Baby's Memory." *APA Monitor* October: 25.

Rubin, D., & M. Kozin. (1984). "Vivid Memories." *Cognition* 16: 81-95.

Rubin, D., Wetzler, S., & R. Nebes. (1986). "Autobiographical Memory Across the Life Span." In *Autobiographical Memory*, ed. D. Rubin. Cambridge: Cambridge University Press.

Rutt, C., & D. Offord. (1971). "Prenatal and Perinatal Complications in Childhood Schizophrenics and Their Siblings." *Journal of Nervous and Mental Disorders* 152: 324-331.

Ryan, V. (1977). "Effect of Prenatal and Postnatal Nutrition on Development, Behavior, and Physiology of the Rat." Ph.D. diss., Wayne State University.

Ryder, G. (1943). "Vagitus Uterinus." *American Journal of Obstetrics and Gynecology* 46: 867-872.

Sadger, J. (1941). "Preliminary Study of the Psychic Life of the Fetus and the Primary Germ," *The Psychoanalytic Review* 28.

Sagi, A., & M. Hoffman. (1976). "Empathetic Distress in the Newborn. " *Developmental Psychology* 12: 175-176.

Salk, L. (1970). "The Critical Nature of the Postpartum Period in the Human for the Establishment of the Mother-Infant Bond: A Controlled Study." *Diseases of the Nervous System* 31: 110-116.

Salk, L. (1973). "The Role of the Heartbeat in the Relations Between the Mother and Infant." *Scientific American* May: 24-29.

Sameroff, A. (1972). "Learning and Adaptation in Infancy: A Comparison of Models." *Advances in Child Development* 7: 170-214.

Sander, L. (1980). "New Knowledge About the Infant From Current Research: Implications for Psychoanalysis." *Journal of the American Psychoanalytic Association* 28: 181-198.

Sanford, A. (1966). *Healing Gifts of the Spirit.* Winchester, Va.: Arthur James Publishing.

Sarbin, T. (1950). "Contributions to Role-taking Theory: Hypnotic Behavior. *Psychological Review* 57: 255-270.

Scanlan, M. (1974). *Inner Healing.* NY: Paulist Press.

Scarr-Salapatek, S. & M. Williams. (1973). "The Effects of an Early Stimulation Program for Low Birth Weight Infants." *Child Development* 44: 94-100.

Schaal, B. (1988). "Olfaction in Infants and Children: Developmental and Functional Perspectives." *Chemical Senses* 13: 145-190.

Schindler, S. (1988). "A New View of the Unborn: Toward a Developmental Psychology of the Prenatal Period." In *Prenatal and Perinatal Psychology and Medicine*, eds. P. Fedor-Freybergh & M. Vogel, 23-33. Park Ridge, NJ: Parthenon.

Simkin, P. (1986). "Stress, Pain and Catecholamines in Labor: I. A Review." *Birth Issues in Perinatal Care and Education* 13: 227-233.

Simner, M. (1971). "Newborns' Response to the Cry of Another Infant." *Developmental Psychology* 5: 136-150.

Siqueland, E., & L. Lipsitt. (1966). "Conditioned Head-turning in Human Newborns." *Journal of Experimental Child Psychology* 3: 356-376.

Sjogren, B., & N. Uddenberg. (1988). "Prenatal Diagnosis and Maternal Attachment to the Child-to-Be: A Prospective Study of 211 Women Undergoing Prenatal Diagnosis with Amniocentesis or Chronic Villi Biopsy." *Journal of Psychosomatic Obstetrics and Gynaecology* 9: 73-87.

Slater, A., Morison, V., & D. Rose. (1982). "Visual Imagery at Birth." *British Journal of Psychology* 73: 519-525.

Smotherman, W. (1982). "Odor Aversion Learning by the Rat Fetus." *Physiology and Behavior* 29: 769-771.

Smythe, C. (1965). "Experimental Methods for Testing the Integrity of the Foetus and Neonate." *Journal of Obstetrics and Gynecology of the British Commonwealth* 72: 920.

Sontag, L. (1944). "War and the Maternal-Fetal Relationship." *Marriage and Family Living* 6: 1-5.

Sontag, L. (1966). "Implications of Fetal Behavior and Environment for Adult Personalities." *Annals of the New York Academy of Sciences* 134: 782-786.

Sontag, L., & R. Wallace. (1934). "Preliminary Report of the Fels Fund: Study of Foetal Reactivity." *American Journal of Diseases of Children* 48: 1050-1057.

Spelt, D. (1948). "The Conditioning of a Human Fetus 'in Utero.'" *Journal of Experimental Psychology* 38: 338-346.

Spielberger, C. & G. Jacobs. (1979). "Emotional Reactions to the Stress of Pregnancy and Obstetrics Complications." In *Emotion and Reproduction*, eds. L. Carenza & L. Zichella, 13. London: Academic Press.

Stahl, F., Gotz, F., Poppe, I., Amendt, P., & G. Dorner. "Pre- and Early Postnatal Testosterone Levels in Rat and Human." In *Hormones and Brain Development. Developments in Endocrinology*, vol. 3, eds. G. Dorner & M. Kawakami, 99-109. Amsterdam: Elsevier/North-Holland Biomedical Press.

Stainton, C. (1985). "The Fetus: A Growing Member of the Family." *Family Relations Journal of Applied Family and Child Studies* 34: 321-326.

Star, R. (1986). *The Healing Power of Birth*. Austin, Tx.: Star Publishing.

Steiner, J. (1977). "Facial Expressions of the Neonate Infant Indicating Hedonics of Food-Related Chemical Stimuli." *In Tastes and Development: The Genesis of Sweet Preference*, ed. J. Weiffenbach. Washington DC: US Government Printing Office.

Steiner, J. (1979). "Human Facial Expressions in Response to Taste and Smell Stimulation." *Advances in Child Development and Behavior* 13: 257-295.

Stone, L., Smith, H., & L. Murphy. (1973). "The Competence of Infants." In *The Competent Infant: Research and Commentary*, eds. L. Stone, H. Smith & L. Murphy. NY: Basic Books.

Stott, D. (1973). "Follow-up Study from Birth of the Effects of Prenatal Stresses." *Developmental Medicine and Child Neurology* 15: 770-787.

Stott, D. (1977). "Children in the Womb: The Effects of Stress." *New Society* May: 329-331.

Stott, D. & S. Latchford. (1976). "Prenatal Antecedents of Child Health, Development, and Behavior: An Epidemiological Report of Incidence and Association." *Journal of the American Academy of Child Psychiatry* 15: 161-191.

Taft, J. (1958). *Otto Rank: A Biographical Study Based on Notebooks, Letters, Collected Writings, Therapeutic Achievements and Personal Associations.* NY: Julian Press.

Thiery, M., Le Sian Yo, A., Vrijens, M. & D. Janssens. (1973). "Vagitus Uterinus." *Journal of Obstetrics and Gynaecology of the British Commonwealth* 80: 183-185.

Thompson, R., & W. Spenser. (1966). "Habituation: A Model for the Study of Neuronal Substrates of Behavior." *Psychological Review* 73: 16-43.

Thurman, L. (1988). "Parental Singing During Pregnancy and Infancy can Assist in Cultivating Bonding and Later Development." *In Prenatal Psychology and Medicine*, eds. P. Fedor-Freybergh & M. Vogel, 273-282. Park Ridge NJ: Parthenon.

Tomatis, A. (1987). "Ontogenesis of the Faculty of Hearing." *In Pre- and Peri-Natal Psychology: An Introduction*, ed. T. Verny, 23-35. NY: Human Sciences Press.

Torry, E., Hersh, S., & K. McCabe. (1975). "Early Childhood Psychosis and Bleeding During Pregnancy: A Prospective Study of Gravid Women and Their Offspring." *Journal of Autism and Childhood Schizophrenia* 5: 289-297.

Trowell, J. (1982). "Effects of Obstetric Management on the Mother-Child Relationship." In *The Place of Attachment in Human Behavior*, eds. C. Parks & J. Stevenson-Hinde, 79-94. NY: Basic Books.

Truby, H. (1975). "Prenatal and Neonatal Speech, Pre-Speech, and an Infantile Speech Lexicon." *Child Language/Word* 27: Parts 1-3.

Truby, H., & J. Lind. (1965). "Cry Sounds of the Newborn Infant." In *Newborn Infant Cry*, ed. J. Lind. *Acta Paediatrica Scandinavica* 163.

Tulving, E. (1972). "Episodic and Semantic Memory." *In Organization of Memory*, eds. E. Tulving & W. Donaldson. London: Wiley.

Tulving, E. (1983). *Elements of Episodic Memory*. Oxford: Oxford University Press.

Tulving, E. (1985). "How Many Memory Systems are There?" *American Psychologist* 40: 385-398.

Turner, E. (1956). "The Syndrome in the Infant Resulting from Maternal Emotional Tension During Pregnancy." *The Medical Journal of Australia* 4: 221-222.

Turner, J. (1988). "Birth, Life and More Life: Reactive Patterning Based on Prebirth Events." In *Prenatal Psychology and Medicine*, eds. P. Fedor-Freybergh & M. Vogel, 309-316. Park Ridge NJ: Parthenon.

Ungerer, J., Brody, L., & P. Zelazo. (1978). "Long-term Memory for Speech in 2-4 Week-old Infants." *Infant Behavior & Development* 1: 177-186.

Valentin, L. & K. Marsal. (1986). "Fetal Movement in the Third Trimester of Normal Pregnancy." *Early Human Development* 14: 295-306.

van de Carr, K., & M. Lehrer. (1986). "Enhancing Early Speech, Parental Bonding, and Infant Physical Development Using Prenatal Intervention in Standard Obstetrical Practice." *Pre-and Per-Natal Psychology Journal* 1: 20-30.

van de Carr, K., van de Carr, R., & M. Lehrer. (1988). "Effects of a Prenatal Intervention Program." In *Prenatal and Perinatal Psychology and Medicine*, eds. P. Fedor-Freybergh & M. Vogel, 489-496. Park Ridge, NJ: Parthenon.

van de Carr, R., & M. Lehrer. (1988). "Prenatal University: Commitment to Fetal-Family Bonding and the Strengthening of the Family Unit as an Educational Institution." *Pre- and Peri-Natal Psychology Journal* 3: 87-102.

van de Kasteele, P. (1984). "A New Shape for Ministry." *CTA Occasional Paper #3* Oxford: CTA.

Van den Bergh, B. (1983). "Der Psychische Toestand van de zwangere en de Prenatale Ontwikkeling: Literatuurstudie en schets van een heuristische Model." *Tijdschrift vor Orthopedagogie, Kinderpsychiatrie en Kliinische Kinderpsychologie* 8: 18-37.

Van den Bergh, B. (1988). "The Relationship Between Maternal Emotionality During Pregnancy and the Behavioral Development of the Fetus and Neonatus." In *Prenatal Psychology and Medicine*, eds. P. Fedor-Freybergh & M. Vogel, 131-142. Park Ridge NJ: Parthenon.

Van den Bergh, B. (1990). "The Influence of Maternal Emotions During Pregnancy on Fetal and Neonatal Behavior." *Pre- and Peri-Natal Psychology Journal* 5: 119-130.

Van den Bergh, B., Mulder, E., Visser, G., & G. Poelmann-Wessjes. (1989). "The Effect of (induced) Maternal Emotions on Fetal Behavior: A Controlled Study." *Early Human Development* 19: 9-19.

Van Dongen, L., & E. Goudie. (1980). "Fetal Movements in the First Trimester of Pregnancy." *British Journal of Obstetrics and Gynecology* 87: 191-193.

Van Woerden, E., Van Geijn, H., Caron, F., & J. Swartjes. (1989). "Automated Assignment of Behavioral States in the Human Near Term Fetus." *Early Human Development* 19: 137-146.

Varley, C. (1984). "Attention Deficit Disorder (the hyperactivity syndrome): A Review of Selected Issues." *Journal of Developmental and Behavioral Pediatrics* 5: 254-258.

Vaughn, H. (1975). "Electrophysiological Analysis of Regional Cortical Maturation." *Biological Psychiatry* 10: 513-526.

Vaughn, B., Bradley, C., Joffe, L., Seifer, R., & C. Barglow. (1987). "Maternal Characteristics Measured Prenatally are Predictive of Ratings of Temperament 'Difficulty' on the Caret Temperament Questionnaire." *Developmental Psychology* 23: 152-161.

Verny, T. (1981). *The Secret Life of the Unborn Child.* NY: Summit Books.

Vitz, P. (1972). "Preference for Tones as a Function of Frequency (hertz) and Intensity (decibels)." *Perception and Psychophysics* 11: 84-88.

von Hofsten, C. (1983). "Foundations of Perceptual Development." In *Advances in Infancy Research*, vol. 2, eds. L. Lipsitt & C. Rovee-Collier, 241-264. Norwood, NJ: Ablex Books.

Vuorenkoski, V., Lind, J., Partanen, T., Lejeune, J., & O. Wasz-Hockert. (1966). "Spectrographic Analysis of Cries from Children with 'Maladie du Cri du Chat'." *Annales Paediatricias Fenniae* 12: 174-180.

Wagenaar, W. (1986). "My Memory: A Study of Autobiographical Memory Over Six Years." *Cognitive Psychology* 18: 225-252.

Wasz, O., Lind, J., Vuorenkoski, V., Partanen, T. & E. Valanne. (1968). *The Infant Cry: A Spectrographic & Auditory Analysis.* London: Spestics International Medical Publications/William Heinnemann Medical Books.

Wasz-Hockert, O., Koivisto, M., Vuorenkoski, M., Partanen, T., & J. Lind. (1971). "Spectrographic Analysis of the Pain Cry in Hyperbilirubinemia." *Biology of the Neonate* 17: 260-271.

Weaver, D., & S. Reppert. (1989). "Direct in utero Perception of Light by the Mammalian Fetus." *Developmental Brain Research* 47: 151-155.

Wedenberg, E. & B. Johansson. (1970). "When the Fetus Isn't Listening." *Medical World News* April 1970: 28-29.

Weil, S. (1951). *Waiting for God.* NY: G.P. Putnam & Sons.

Weil, S. (1952). *Gravity and Grace.* London: Routledge & Kegan Paul.

Weitzman, E., Fishbein, W., & L. Graziani. (1965). "Auditory Evoked Responses Obtained From the Scalp Electroencephalogram of the Full Term Neonate During Sleep." *Pediatrics* 35: 458-462.

Werner, J., & L. Lipsitt. (1981). "The Infancy of Human Sensory Systems." In *Developmental Plasticity*, ed. E. Gollin, 35-38. NY: Academic Press.

Werner, J., & E. Siqueland. (1978). "Visual Recognition Memory in the Preterm Infant." *Infant Behavior and Development* 1: 79-94.

Wertheimer, M. (1961). "Psychomotor Coordination of Auditory and Visual Space at Birth." *Science* 134: 1692.

Williams, R. (1979). *Christian Spirituality*. Atlanta: John Knox Press.

Windle, W. (1971). *Physiology of the Fetus*. Springfield, Ill.: Charles C. Thomas.

Winnicott, D.W. (1957). *Mother and Child: A Primer of First Relationships*. NY: Basic Books.

Winnicott, D.W. (1958). *Collected Papers: Through Pediatrics to Psycho-Analysis*. NY: Basic Books.

Winnicott, D.W. (1972). *The Maturational Processes and the Facilitating Environment*. London: Hogarth Press.

Wojtyla, K. (1979a). *Easter Vigil and Other Poems*, trans. J. Peterkiewicz. London: Hutchinson.

Wojtyla, K. (1979b). *Sign of Contradiction*. London: Hodder and Stoughton.

Wojtyla, K. (1980). *Dives in Misericordia*. Rome: Catholic Truth Society.

Wolff, P. (1978). "The Natural History of Crying and Other Vocalizations in Early Infancy." *Determinants of Infant Behavior*, vol. 4, ed. B. Foss. London: Methuen.

Wolff, P., & L. White. (1965). "Visual Pursuit and Attention in Young Infants." *Journal of the American Academy of Child Psychiatry* 4: 437-484.

Wolkind, S. (1981). "Pre-natal Emotional Stress-- Effects on the Fetus." In *Pregnancy: A Psychological and Social Study,* ed. S. Wolkind, 177-194. London: Academic Press.

Wu, J., & M. Eichmann. (1988). "Fetal Sex Identification and Prenatal Bonding." *Psychological Reports* 63: 199-202.

Wucherer-Huldenfeld, A. (1973). "Ursprung und Anfang des menschlichen lebens." In *Vorgeburtliches Seelenleben*, eds. G. Graber & F. Kruse. München: Goldman.

Zeskind P., & B. Lester. (1978). "Acoustic Features and Auditory Perceptions of the Cries of Newborns With Prenatal and Perinatal Complications." *Child Development* 49: 580-589.

Index